THE FOREIGN POLICY PROCESS

LINCOLN P. BLOOMFIELD

M.I.T.

THE FOREIGN POLICY PROCESS

a modern primer

Prentice-Hall, Inc.
Englewood Cliffs, New Jersey 07632

Library of Congress Cataloging in Publication Data

BLOOMFIELD, LINCOLN PALMER, (date)
The foreign policy process.

Bibliography.
Includes index.
1. United States—Foreign relations. 2. International relations. I. Title.
JX1417.B559 353.0089 81-15319
ISBN 0-13-326504-8 AACR2

For author's acknowledgments of permission to adapt material, please see page 237.

Editorial production/supervision and interior design: Jeanne Hoeting
Cover design: Jorge Hernandez
Manufacturing Buyer: Edmund W. Leone

Printed in the United States of America

10 9 8 7 6 5 4 3 2 1

Prentice-Hall International, Inc., *London*
Prentice-Hall of Australia Pty. Limited, *Sydney*
Prentice-Hall of Canada, Ltd., *Toronto*
Prentice-Hall of India Private Limited, *New Delhi*
Prentice-Hall of Japan, Inc., *Tokyo*
Prentice-Hall of Southeast Asia Pte. Ltd., *Singapore*
Whitehall Books Limited, *Wellington, New Zealand*

To colleagues in the two worlds I have inhabited—the conscientious bureaucrats and dedicated scholars, on whose broad shoulders I have stood to tell this story.

To colleagues in the two worlds I have inhabited—the conscientious bureaucrats and dedicated scholars, on whose broad shoulders I have stood to tell this story.

CONTENTS

PREFACE

PRIMERS

This is a primer about the making of foreign policy, U.S. foreign policy in particular.

It is written for busy students (which does not necessarily mean only people formally enrolled in educational instructions).

It is a primer because busy students cannot spend the time and energy to become experts. It is also a primer because most books on public policy are (a) too long, (b) too wordy, (c) too detailed, (d) too full of jargon.

Its goal is to make the foreign policy process interesting, intelligible, and simple to understand. But it would be misleading to pretend that the *subject* is simple. On the contrary, making foreign policy is a complex and sophisticated topic. I want to sort out, and briefly explain, that complexity. My goal is to try to do so, as the great mathematician Albert Einstein urged, in a way that is "as simple as possible but not one bit simpler." We will concentrate on the heart of the process, meaning the President, Congress, White House Staff, State Department, interdependence, and diplomacy, and not get into the details of military, intelligence and other agencies. We will try to stick to the *process*, and not get too diverted by the *content* of foreign policy (fascinating as that is) except for purposes of illustration. You can read the "What?" of foreign policy in your daily papers—Middle East wars, NATO allies, energy crises, Soviet and Chinese behavior, and Central American revolutions. Here we probe the mysteries of the "How?" and to a degree the "Why?" But remember that all the government machinery and personalities involved are supposed to be working to make a safer, and maybe even better, world for this country to live in. You can judge for yourself the extent to which they succeed or fail.

THE U.S.

This book is mainly about making foreign policy in the United States. But many of the things it says apply to foreign governments as well.

The U.S. policy process is important to the policies the process turns out. Those policies are important to many people in the world. The reason is that the U.S., whatever its virtues and faults, is still in many ways the leading country in the world.

One lead that happily survives times of troubles is the undeniable U.S. commitment at home to political freedom and restraints on government, as well as still unparalleled opportunity to succeed and prosper. The undiminished desire by people in many countries to emigrate to America testifies to the unique place the U.S. still holds.

A second, darker kind of lead is shared with the Soviet Union in the nuclear weapons capability to put much of civilization back into the Dark Ages. A third lead is that, *un*like the Soviet Union, the U.S. has enough widespread national wealth to justify a comment once made by Senator J. William Fulbright that the reason Americans around the world act as if they own the place is that they just about do. (Some Arab oil-producing states are gaining fast.)

A fourth kind of lead lies in U.S. technology—managerial and marketing skills, information processisng, and agricultural production —much of it still the envy of others, notably Communist states and developing countries.

However, a fifth kind of lead is something to *worry* rather than boast about. Americans have cars, houses, color TVs, outboards, discos, advertising, leisure time, political freedom, limited government—*and* widespread boredom, alienation, and a worrisome

So do some members of Congress. So does the president's assistant for national security affairs and on occasion his senior staff. Sometimes that wide range of deciders funtion smoothly. At other times it leaves foreigners bewildered as to how many American foreign policies there really are.

At least in these pages, no one is arguing for perfection in the policy process. In foreign policy, the issue is all too often a choice of evils, and it is usually unrealistic to expect to achieve a *first* best policy in a world which no one controls. (My own philosophy calls for ensuring that policy decisions represent at least the *second* best rather than the third or fourth best.) The job is never done: Foreign policy is never-ending. Thomas L. Hughes once likened it to Penelope's mythical loom, whose cloth was woven by day and unravelled by night.

Nevertheless, what follows often has a critical tone. That is one of the reasons America is a great country: We all can criticize the process of governance without being carted off to jail. One soberly recalls TV newsman Sander Vanocur's definition of a critic: "Someone who comes down from the mountain after the battle and shoots the wounded." I don't want to do that here. The main reason to try to explain—and to criticize—the foreign policy process was said best by the late President John F. Kennedy: "Domestic policy can only defeat us; foreign policy can kill us."[5]

A final prefatory note. For the reader who just wants a relatively straightforward introduction to the political world of foreign policy making, going through Chapters One through Seven should do the trick. These are written with a minimum of jargon and often use dialogue or drama to illustrate the point. The reader who wishes to go further in probing the more sophisticated aspects of policy making might want to read Chapters Eight on theories of foreign policy making and Nine on policy planning techniques and problems. These are somewhat in the advanced social science tradition and need not detain the general reader, but all might get something of value from reading and using the gaming technique found in the Appendix.

[5] As quoted in Arthur M. Schlesinger, Jr., in *A Thousand Days: John F. Kennedy in the White House* (Boston: Houghton Mifflin, 1975), p. 426.

chapter one

MAPPING THE FOREIGN POLICY PROCESS

THE COMPLEXITY FACTOR

It used to be that if people wanted to know how U.S. foreign policy was made, they looked at the organization chart of the U.S. government. Locate the White House, the Department of State, the Department of Defense, the Central Intelligence Agency (CIA), and the Congress. Throw in the Treasury, Commerce, and Agriculture Departments. You have now listed the parts of government that most people believe are involved in the process. But does that tell you how foreign policy is really made?

Certainly in U.S. history the State Department is the place where America deals with relations with the rest of the world. Logically, then, if we want to draw a picture of the foreign policy process, we would start with a chart consisting of little boxes showing the secretary of state and deputy secretary at the top, next the three deputy under secretaries, next the fifteen or so assistant secretaries with their various bureaus, and of course all the American embassies abroad. Isn't that enough for a start? Don't the embassies (and CIA) send in reports on what is going on in foreign countries? Don't the State Department country desks study those reports and then recommend to the secretary of state and his deputies what the U.S. response should be?

What is so complicated—or interesting, for that matter—about that process?

Well, for a start the U.S. Constitution, drafted in 1789, does not even *mention* the State Department or, for that matter, foreign policy. All it says is that the president is commander in chief of the army and navy (no air force then). The president can make treaties "by and with the Advice and Consent of the Senate." (Americans vividly recalled that rule during the 1977 battle—successful—over ratification of the Panama Canal Treaty and the 1979 battle—unsuccessful—over the SALT II Treaty.) Article II of the Constitution empowers the president to nominate and—again with the Senate's concurrence—appoint ambassadors. That is about all it says on the foreign policy powers of the executive branch.

The Constitution also gives some powerful handles to the Congress over foreign policy making, including the money to make foreign policy possible. (We look in Chapters 4 and 5 to the president and the Congress.) The point is: do not look to the Constitution for the *details*.

There is another catch in the older maps of the foreign policy process. Life today on our planet is fantastically complicated, compared with what was going on in 1787—or even 1947. The Constitution is a marvelous document. It passes the test Napoleon Bonaparte prescribed, in being "short and ambiguous." It is sufficiently flexible to have endured long enough to be the world's oldest existing written constitution. As the need arose, pieces of the governmental policy machine evolved around its general provisions.

Congress passed a statute in 1789 creating the State Department. A couple of hundred years later Congress (and the president) were still at it, creating agencies undreamed of two generations ago, for example, the National Aeronautics and Space Administration, the Nuclear Regulatory Commission, and the Department of Energy. Those agencies operate primarily *domestic* programs, but outer space, energy, and nuclear power are obviously also vital to *foreign* policy. (So are deep seabed manganese nodules, weather modification experiments, fertilizer-intensive miracle hybrid grains, coal to substitute for oil, currency fluctuations, and population-controlling contraception. We look at some of these *interdependence* issues in Chapter 2 in terms of where they fit in the process.)

Just as the U.S. Constitution made no mention of the State Department (or, for that matter, the Defense Department, the CIA, or the National Security Council) so the State Department's traditional organization does not provide an adequate priority for the technological, ecological, and planetary *global issues* that can vitally affect both national and international security.

The process of *diplomacy* should not be scorned, as some would do who focus on interdependence, or multinational corporations, or military power. International relations cannot happen without the network of transactions between sovereign states, and that has been true for four hundred years. There are other important actors on the stage beside states—multinational corporations, religious movements, cultural ties that bind closely and deeply. However, the diplomatic process handles the complex matrix of interactions at the core of international relations and is absolutely indispensable. Diplomacy is not just *bilateral,* between pairs of states, or among pairs of allies. In addition there is the UN, its 15 specialized agencies, and dozens of other *international organizations* to which many states belong and where *multilateral* diplomacy is the name of the process.

LOOKING AT THE WHOLE

So we really need a wide-angle lens to see the foreign policy process in its full perspective. We need to describe relationships that crisscross the globe like a giant web of connective tissue in a complex organism whose ganglia were classically described by political scientist Karl Deutsch in a book called *The Nerves of Government.*[1]

The wide-angle lens gives us the total picture, but to see the dynamics of that picture, we need a zoom lens. This lets us start looking very close up, focusing first on the detailed workings of the process; then we can zoom out to ever-larger pictures, until finally we have some sense of the whole.

What follows borrows that principle of the blow-up picture. We start with what we see under the policy microscope, so to speak. From there we expand the field of vision the way a cosmic observer might look at the foreign affairs system as a whole, perhaps the way astronauts look back from space at the planet Earth.

[1]Karl Deutsch, *The Nerves of Government: Models of Political Communication and Control* (New York: Free Press, 1963).

First a couple of words of caution. Don't be fooled by the apparent orderliness of the diagrams and maps that follow. Like the boxes and flow charts of any organization, whether the State Department, a university department, IBM, or the Communist Party of the Soviet Union, the realities of power and influence often flow not just up and down in formal lines but also invisibly *across* formal structures in diagonal or indirect lines.

And don't be fooled that even this complex picture of the system of foreign policy institutions and relationships does adequate justice to the complex realities of people, populations, territory, power, wealth, war and peace, welfare and misery. It does not.

OPERATION BLOW-UP

At its simplest, the foreign affairs machine is really an *input-output* system. This can be illustrated by a hypothetical policy crisis.

A foreign government—call it Ruritania—does or says something important to America. The U.S. embassy in Ruritania's capital city observes that event. Perhaps it receives a message from the Ruritanian Foreign Ministry. The American ambassador sends the information in the form of a cable to the State Department in Washington, D.C. The message could equally well be sent in the form of a diplomatic note to the U.S. Government from the Ruritanian embassy in Washington by means of a messenger to the State Department.

In either case, the message will go straight to the country desk in the State Department for *action*. What that means is that the country director for Ruritanian affairs in the State Department's Bureau of (let us say) European Affairs (EUR) is supposed to do something about it.

Figure 1.1 (p. 7) is a simplified diagram of what has just happened.

The Ruritanian Desk in EUR decides that this message is a diplomatic "hot potato" (maybe Ruritania has threatened to break relations with our friend Slobbovia if we do not do something Ruritania wants us to do). After some worried chatter at the desk level, accompanied by large amounts of coffee, the country officer crosses the hall to make sure that *her* superior (say, the director of the Office of Central European Affairs) agrees with her that the matter has to be raised at the EUR assistant secretary's 11 A.M. staff meeting.

decline in public and private morality. (So do many other countries, particularly in the rich, industrialized West.)

It is hard for many foreigners (and some Americans) to accept this continuing American role of world pathbreaker. Certainly, as Ralf Dahrendorf drily noted, "The power to destroy the earth does not imply the power to run the earth."[1] There is a "radical critique" of U.S. foreign policy which would doubtless disapprove the present book on the grounds that the U.S. policy machine automatically produces evil results.[2] I myself reject that "systemic" attack on U.S. bonafides, although there are real damages of arrogance and *machismo* to watch out for.[3] This nation is only now beginning to recover from a period in foreign policy and domestic life that got downright nasty. The late 1960s to early 1970s featured, among other things, the unprecedented driving from office of two Presidents—Lyndon Johnson and Richard Nixon. Some people in the 1980s still reject the idea of the U.S. as a model to follow; indeed, they blame the U.S. for all the world's ills.

Two "Laws" illustrate the point. One is the Scottish *Drunkard's Law:* When two men, one a known drunkard, have been drinking and a fight starts, the drunkard always gets the blame. Some people since Vietnam and Watergate automatically assign the "known drunkard's" role to the U.S.

However, things, as always, are changing. For example, look at the changing corollaries to *Murphy's Law.* Murphy's Law says: "If anything can go wrong, it will." In many parts of the world from 1945 to around 1965, the first corollary to Murphy's Law was "And the United States should fix it." The second corollary, from 1965 to around 1977 was "And it's the United States' fault." The third corollary is beginning to sound a bit like "Where's the United States, now that we need it again?"

In the following chapters the reader will discover a powerful, if sometimes muscle-bound, U.S. decision-making process that is being once again geared to a major U.S. world role.

[1]Ralf Dahrendorf, "International Power: A European Perspective." Reprinted by permission of *Foreign Affairs,* October 1977, p. 79. © by Council on foreign Relations, Inc.

[2]Representative samples of this line of criticism are Gabriel Kolko *The Roots of American Foreign Policy* (Boston: Beacon Press, 1969), and various works by Daniel Ellsberg and Noam Chomsky, to name only a few.

[3]My views are expressed in a book called *In Search of American Foreign Policy: The Humane Use of Power* (New York: Oxford University Press, 1974).

CRITICS

There will be many references in this book to *bureaucrats* and *politicians.* Neither of these is necessarily a dirty word.

Americans have been suspicious of government ever since the late eighteenth century when they designed a scheme for limiting it which is the very basis of the political and civil rights Americans cherish and proclaim. However, that virtue also bred contempt for politicians, as well as endless jokes about bureaucrats. Running a government (including the making of its foreign policy) is a *political* process. "Politician" is only a dirty word when venal or corrupt people are entrusted with power.

Similarly, "bureaucrat" is also a neutral word. Foreign service officers, civil servants, and other official experts on the legal, economic, and intelligence sectors of the foreign policy machine all have their faults. But the great majority tend to be well educated, intelligent, honest, decent people, just as in any other professional organization. At its best, "bureaucrat" should be not a pejorative but rather (if I can coin a much-needed word) a "mejorative." What makes for trouble, inefficiency, waste, delay, and frustration, and turns nice people into bad bureaucrats is the bureau*cracy.* Louis D. Brandeis wrote a book about giant U.S. business before he became one of the great U.S. Supreme Court justices. It was called *The Curse of Bigness,*[4] and should be updated to apply to giant *governments.*

Some people, by the way, say *policy makers* when they really mean *staff,* or *analysts,* or *working level.* Most people in the foreign affairs bureaucracy below the level of assistant secretary of state are not "chiefs" but "Indians," since they deal with a limited sector of foreign policy. In their work they discuss, analyze, give their expert recommendations, suggest initiatives, and carry out the decisions.

Only a handful are chiefs, that is, foreign policy *makers.* These are the president, the secretary of state, and on lesser problems that fit within agreed policy guidelines, the rest of the subcabinet officials appointed by the president—deputy secretary, under secretaries, assistant secretaries, sometimes deputy assistant secretaries. The secretaries of defense and treasury also sometimes act like foreign policy makers.

[4]Louis D. Brandeis, *The Curse of Bigness,* ed. Osmond K. Fraenkel (New York: Viking, 1935).

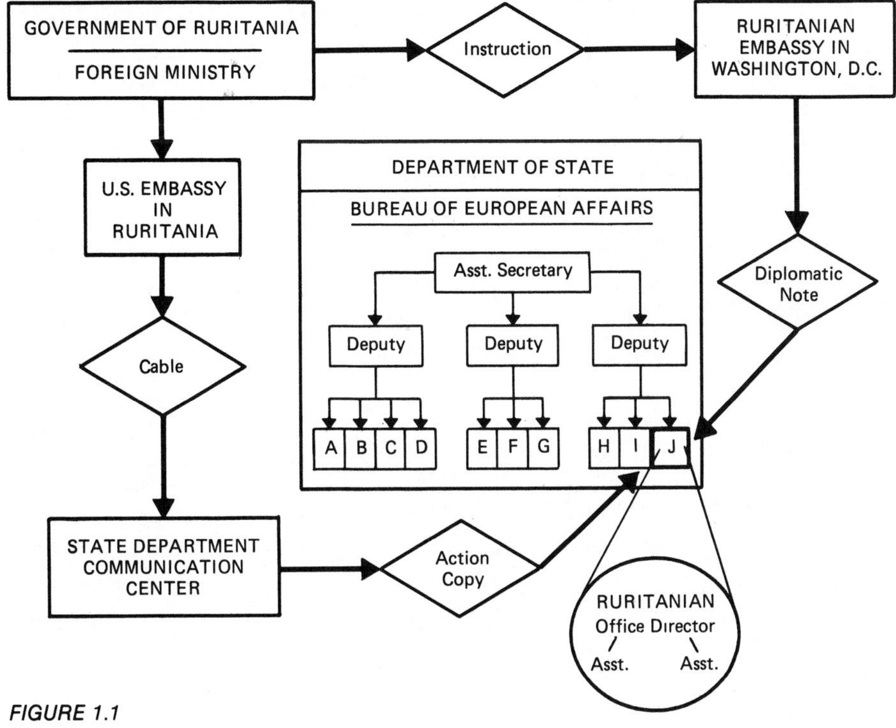

FIGURE 1.1

It could be that an agreed-upon reply emerges from that staff meeting. In that case, the assistant secretary for European affairs could sign the reply in the name of the secretary of state (all State Department cables are signed with the name of the secretary, although he sees few of them). Alternatively, he could take it upstairs to the seventh floor for approval by the under secretary for political affairs, the deputy secretary, or even the secretary.

Our map (Figure 1.2 p. 8) now gets larger.

Other parts of the government are also in the information circuit, and they might get involved in decisions if the matter is serious enough. The State Department Communications Center had of course distributed copies of the "AmEmbassy Ruritania" cable around State's rambling building in Washington's Foggy Bottom (so nicknamed because bullfrogs in the building's original swampy site inspired the earlier label "Froggy Bottom"). The same cable clattered out of the printer in the White House basement for the information of the National Security Council staff. The cable may also have been

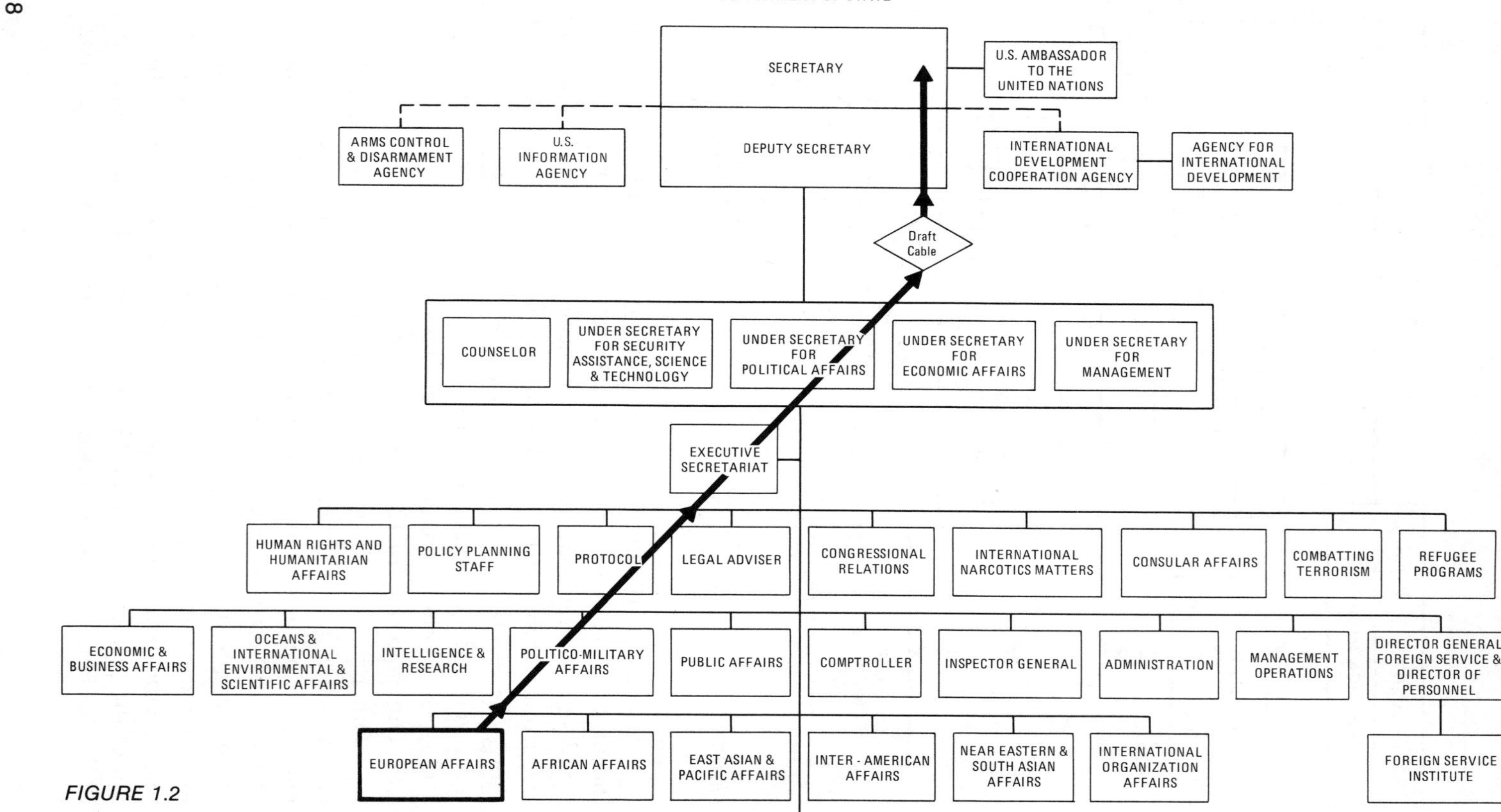
DEPARTMENT OF STATE
SECRETARY
DEPUTY SECRETARY
U.S. AMBASSADOR TO THE UNITED NATIONS
ARMS CONTROL & DISARMAMENT AGENCY
U.S. INFORMATION AGENCY
INTERNATIONAL DEVELOPMENT COOPERATION AGENCY
AGENCY FOR INTERNATIONAL DEVELOPMENT
Draft Cable
COUNSELOR
UNDER SECRETARY FOR SECURITY ASSISTANCE, SCIENCE & TECHNOLOGY
UNDER SECRETARY FOR POLITICAL AFFAIRS
UNDER SECRETARY FOR ECONOMIC AFFAIRS
UNDER SECRETARY FOR MANAGEMENT
EXECUTIVE SECRETARIAT
HUMAN RIGHTS AND HUMANITARIAN AFFAIRS
POLICY PLANNING STAFF
PROTOCOL
LEGAL ADVISER
CONGRESSIONAL RELATIONS
INTERNATIONAL NARCOTICS MATTERS
CONSULAR AFFAIRS
COMBATTING TERRORISM
REFUGEE PROGRAMS
ECONOMIC & BUSINESS AFFAIRS
OCEANS & INTERNATIONAL ENVIRONMENTAL & SCIENTIFIC AFFAIRS
INTELLIGENCE & RESEARCH
POLITICO-MILITARY AFFAIRS
PUBLIC AFFAIRS
COMPTROLLER
INSPECTOR GENERAL
ADMINISTRATION
MANAGEMENT OPERATIONS
DIRECTOR GENERAL FOREIGN SERVICE & DIRECTOR OF PERSONNEL
EUROPEAN AFFAIRS
AFRICAN AFFAIRS
EAST ASIAN & PACIFIC AFFAIRS
INTER - AMERICAN AFFAIRS
NEAR EASTERN & SOUTH ASIAN AFFAIRS
INTERNATIONAL ORGANIZATION AFFAIRS
FOREIGN SERVICE INSTITUTE

FIGURE 1.2

distributed by computer-based distribution procedures to the Pentagon and the CIA. The latter will doubtless check the data already received from intelligence gathering activities abroad. An estimate of the situation may well be produced by the National Intelligence Officer (NIO) for the region.

What if the Department of Defense (DOD) dislikes the reply State proposes to send? At this point, maybe a phone call from the assistant secretary of state to a lieutenant general on the Joint Staff in the Pentagon will bring about agreement between the two agencies. In that case, there does not have to be held one of the numerous interagency meetings where decisions get thrashed out between agencies. Or a complicated clearance process might be required *within* the Pentagon, rising from ISA—the Assistant Secretary of Defense for International Security Affairs—through the under secretary for policy, to the office of the secretary of defense (OSD).

What if the government is seriously divided as to what to do? Perhaps the matter is serious enough to be raised in a meeting of an interagency committee. If it is major enough, it could command the attention of the National Security Council itself. In any case, the staff of the NSC, under the president's assistant for national security affairs, will be aware of the problem and may play a part in the game (more on State-Defense-NSC coordination—and competition—in Chapter 3).

But let's keep it relatively simple, at least for preliminary mapping purposes. Let's postulate a harmonious (some would say utopian) Washington universe. Let us say that the country officer's phone call does the trick. State keeps the initiative and gets an easy "O.K." from DOD. But bureaucratic caution may still suggest that State forward the agreed reply to the White House for approval on the time-honored bureaucratic principle of "CYA" (Cover Your You-Know-What). Backing away further from our boxes so our perspective can broaden out, Figure 1.3 (p. 10) illustrates how that circuit looks.

So—back goes the answer (which probably says something like "The U.S. Government counsels moderation and urges the Ruritanian Government not to take any steps that would exacerbate the delicate situation," and so on). *Bilateral diplomacy,* practiced since the memory of man runneth not to the contrary, is what we are looking at.

Also notice that *heads of government*—presidents, prime ministers, sometimes kings, occasionally dictators—are more and more getting

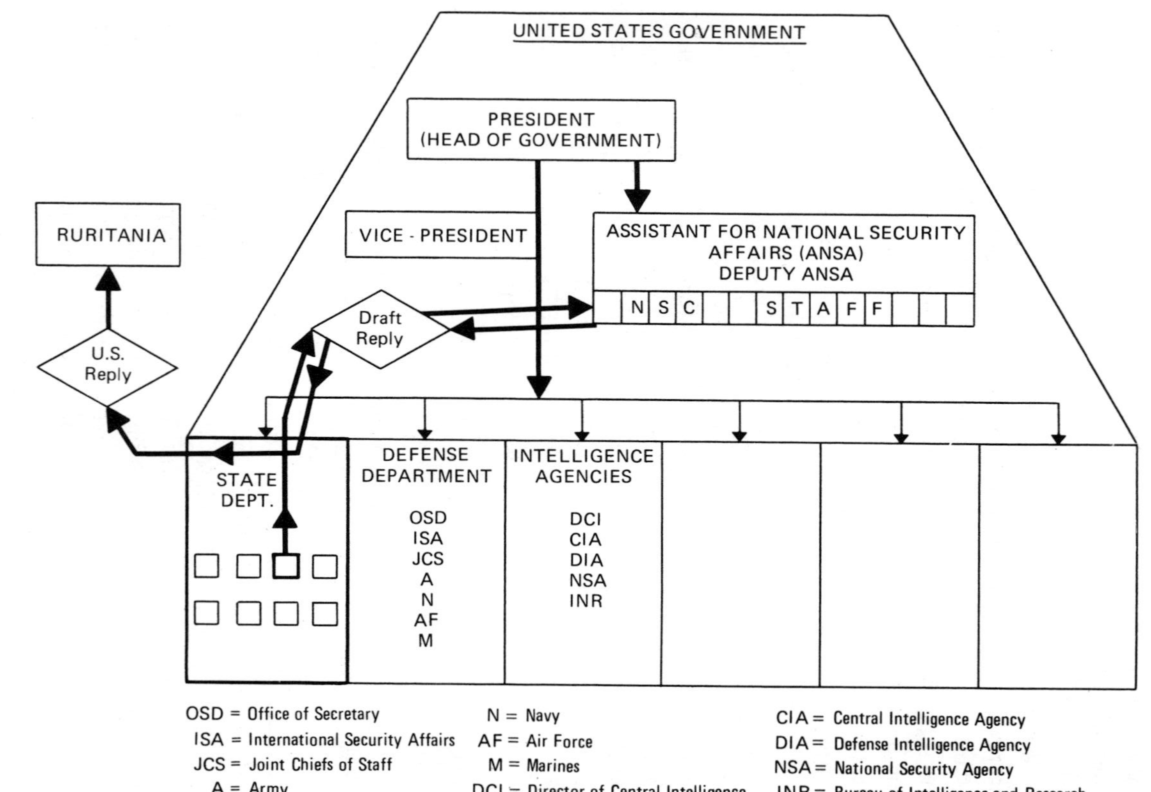
UNITED STATES GOVERNMENT
PRESIDENT
(HEAD OF GOVERNMENT)
VICE - PRESIDENT
ASSISTANT FOR NATIONAL SECURITY
AFFAIRS (ANSA)
DEPUTY ANSA
NSC STAFF
RURITANIA
Draft
Reply
U.S.
Reply
STATE
DEPT.
DEFENSE
DEPARTMENT
OSD
ISA
JCS
A
N
AF
M
INTELLIGENCE
AGENCIES
DCI
CIA
DIA
NSA
INR
OSD = Office of Secretary
ISA = International Security Affairs
JCS = Joint Chiefs of Staff
A = Army
N = Navy
AF = Air Force
M = Marines
DCI = Director of Central Intelligence
CIA = Central Intelligence Agency
DIA = Defense Intelligence Agency
NSA = National Security Agency
INR = Bureau of Intelligence and Research

FIGURE 1.3

into the diplomatic act.[2] Heads-of-government summits used to be rare and were big news. Nowadays it sometimes seems that the heads of government—the White House, Kremlin, Elysée Palace, whatever—perform an amazing share of the diplomatic duties that foreign ministries and State Departments are supposedly paid to do.

The empty boxes in the chart on page 10 (Figure 1.3) stand for other agencies and branches of the national government. They illustrate the reason our map of the action process would be out of date if it showed *only* State, Defense, CIA, and the White House. As pointed out at the beginning of this chapter, many seemingly domestic agencies of government have a finger and often a hand in international relations and foreign policy. We come to them in the next chapter.

We still do not have a complete picture. The U.S. Constitution calls for shared (would you believe: fought over?) powers. So the *Congress* deserves a prominent place on our foreign policy process map, in a variety of ways we look at in Chapter 5. What about the rest of American society? What about the nongovernmental sectors that we know play an increasingly active role in U.S. foreign affairs?

A WORD ABOUT NONGOVERNMENTS

Americans, more than most people, have always known that their national *government,* while obviously indispensable, is not the whole story. American political philosophy tells us that government exists to serve the people. (In numerous other societies the reverse seems to be the rule: The people exist to serve the government, or so their rulers believe.) As that amazingly insightful French observer Alexis de Tocqueville noted when he visited here in the 1830s, Americans are a nation of joiners—societies, clubs, unions, associations, you name it.[3] *Public opinion* includes 226 million active or potential voters, lobbyists, and members of groups that among them have an interest in virtually every foreign policy issue (we talk about that in Chapter 6).

With the help of this refinement of the U.S. map (Figure 1.5 p. 13), now let us look at the foreign *relations* map. (Figure 1.4.) Obviously

[2]The head of *state,* who in the American case is *also* the president, elsewhere would be the ceremonial chief who does *not* run the government, for example, the British queen, German president, and so on.

[3]See Alexis de Tocqueville, *Democracy in America* (New York: Knopf, 1960).

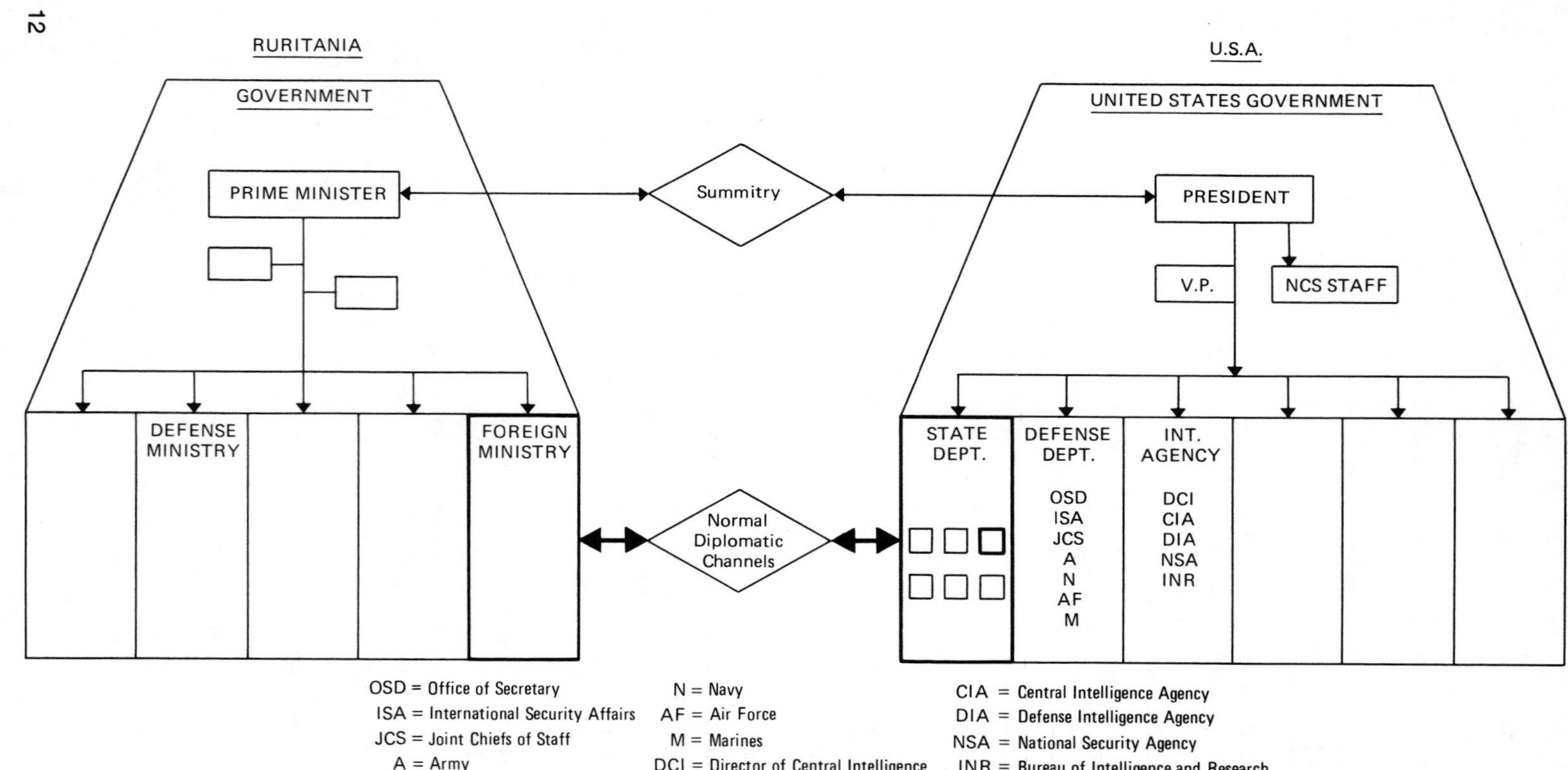

RURITANIA
GOVERNMENT
PRIME MINISTER
DEFENSE MINISTRY
FOREIGN MINISTRY
Summitry
Normal Diplomatic Channels
U.S.A.
UNITED STATES GOVERNMENT
PRESIDENT
V.P.
NCS STAFF
STATE DEPT.
DEFENSE DEPT.
OSD
ISA
JCS
A
N
AF
M
INT. AGENCY
DCI
CIA
DIA
NSA
INR
OSD = Office of Secretary
ISA = International Security Affairs
JCS = Joint Chiefs of Staff
A = Army
N = Navy
AF = Air Force
M = Marines
DCI = Director of Central Intelligence
CIA = Central Intelligence Agency
DIA = Defense Intelligence Agency
NSA = National Security Agency
INR = Bureau of Intelligence and Research

FIGURE 1.4

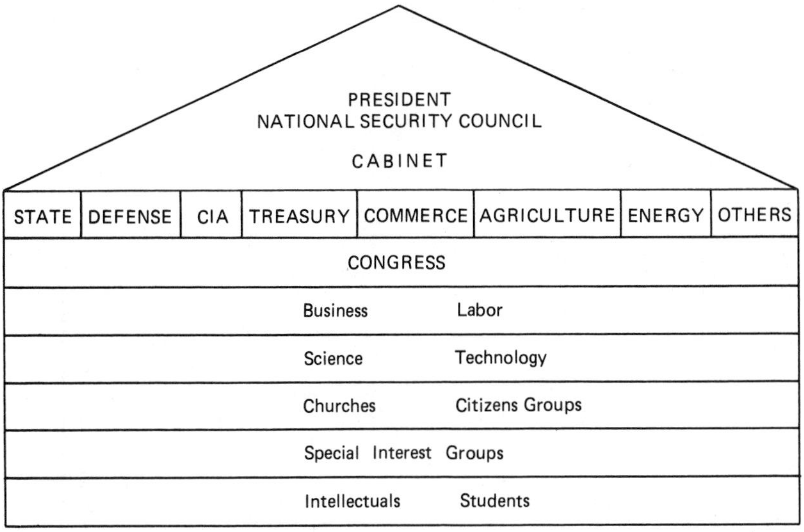

PRESIDENT
NATIONAL SECURITY COUNCIL

CABINET

STATE	DEFENSE	CIA	TREASURY	COMMERCE	AGRICULTURE	ENERGY	OTHERS

CONGRESS

Business Labor

Science Technology

Churches Citizens Groups

Special Interest Groups

Intellectuals Students

FIGURE 1.5

a nation's foreign policy does not exist in a vacuum. The U.S. and Ruritania both have friends and allies (not to mention enemies). They probably belong to *alliances* and to *regional organizations and groupings.* The U.S., for example, belongs to NATO, OAS, OECD, and other sets of initials standing for regional alliances and economic organizations. Ruritania may belong to the OAS, OAU, Baghdad Pact, Arab League (or, if Ruritania is Communist, it probably belongs to the Warsaw Pact and COM-ECON[4]).

There are around 160 countries in the world, give or take a few. The U.S. and Ruritania (plus about 155 other states) belong to the *United Nations.* The UN, with all its faults, is nevertheless the world's only universal (or close-to-universal) political and security organization. The UN family also includes many economic and social organs and agencies. Both the U.S. and Ruritania belong to most or all of the fifteen specialized agencies of the UN system (Figure 1.6 p. 14.)

We have been talking all along about states. As I said at the outset, states are still very much the official actors in the drama of foreign policy. The reader should be clear here that we are not necessarily talking about *nations.* Some people have fallen into the habit of calling all states *nation-states,* doubtless in memory of the sixteenth century when nations (which used to be tribes) began to acquire the

[4]North Atlantic Treaty Organization, Organization of American States, Organization for Economic Cooperation and Development, Organization for African Unity, Council for Mutual Economic Assistance.

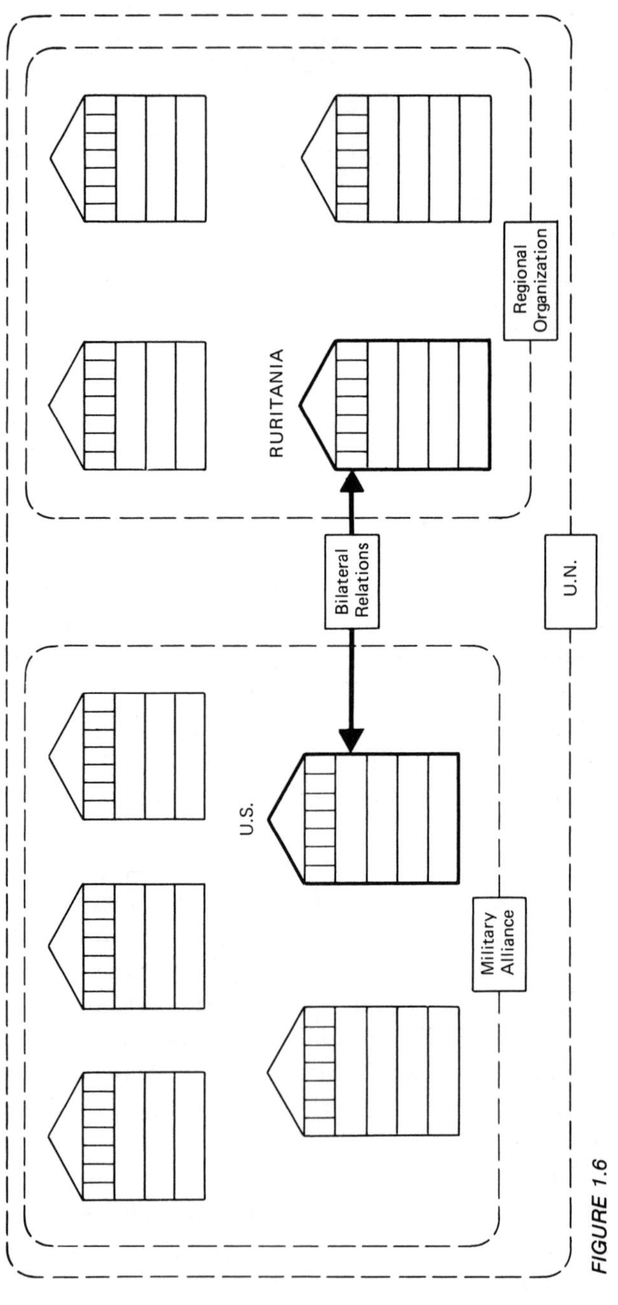
Regional Organization
RURITANIA
Bilateral Relations
U.N.
U.S.
Military Alliance
FIGURE 1.6

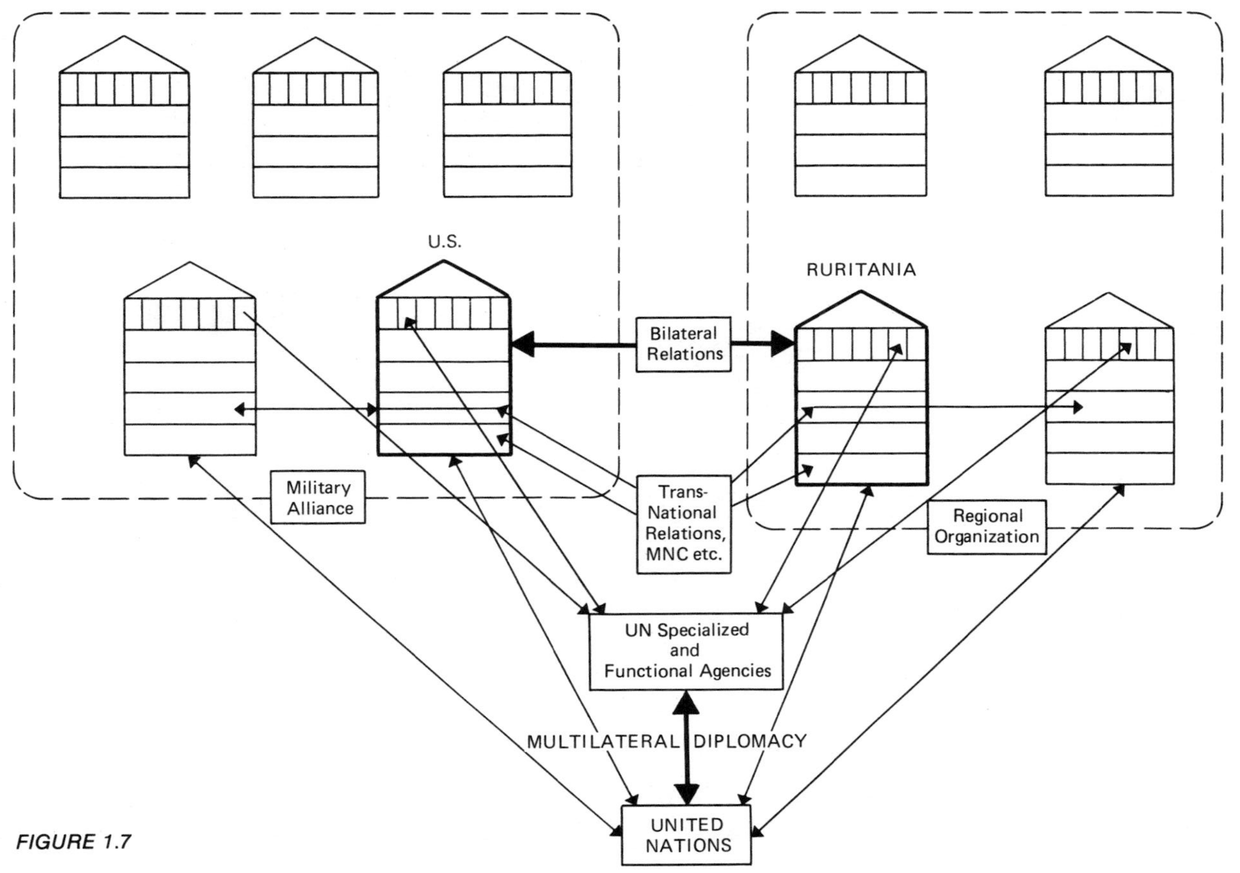
U.S.
RURITANIA
Bilateral
Relations
Military
Alliance
Trans-
National
Relations,
MNC etc.
Regional
Organization
UN Specialized
and
Functional Agencies
MULTILATERAL DIPLOMACY
UNITED
NATIONS

FIGURE 1.7

chapter two

INTERDEPENDENCE: THE EXPANDED FOREIGN POLICY AGENDA

In the first part of Chapter 1 we walked through a typical flap in the U.S. foreign policy arena. To recap what happened, a foreign government (Ruritania) did something that called for a U.S. reaction. The problem was acted on—whether successfully or not we do not know—by the government officials who traditionally make U.S. foreign policy. The problem was fairly straightforward. It was *political* in nature; the process was *diplomatic;* the relevant actors were officials of the *national security* community. They included the State Department, Defense Department, Central Intelligence Agency, National Security Council staff, and maybe the president (though we do not know if he actually took the time to okay that cable or instead delegated it to one of his immediate staff, probably his assistant for national security affairs).

The map we expanded as we went along the route got pretty complicated, but in fact what we looked at is only a part—though very important—of the foreign policy scene. In recent years something unprecedented has happened to the agenda of issues on which a president and his foreign policy advisers must focus.

What has happened is that *economic* problems, arising from trade, investment, and money, have become much more central to foreign policy. The reasons (which we can only sketch here) are the explosive expansion of health, science, management, information, knowledge, skills, communications, demands, possibilities—and frustrations. For the same general reasons a comparable upgrading has happened with social and technological problems of feeding people, pumping oil and gas from the ground (or making it from rocks, sand, coal ore), mining minerals from the deep seabed, migrations of workers looking for jobs (such as unemployed Mexicans slipping across the U.S. border by the millions), polluting one's own and other countries' air and water, and using nuclear energy to light cities (and make bombs).

We can call this the *Interdependence Agenda.* It has moved up from near the bottom of the list of concerns for the top diplomats and foreign policy makers, to somewhat a bit closer to the top. Some people think such interdependence or global issue questions belong at the very top of the *critical list* that should be given priority attention by presidents, secretaries of state, and National Security Councils (which should perhaps be renamed).

People may be aware of these new global agenda items, but they may see military defense and strategy as far more important to a country's security, and thus to its foreign policy. To be sure, when guns are firing or crises threatening, presidents and their decision machinery are going to give priority to short-term crisis management.

However, the interdependence problems have a strong claim to higher priorities. The environment, weather, food, population, energy, trade, and poverty are not going to wait. Probably no government in the world is yet properly organized and staffed to cope effectively (though there are about seventy national environment ministries today, compared with none before the UN Environment Conference in 1972). These agenda items represent a big piece of reality today, and they are getting bigger all the time.

The truth is that *both* types of problems—the traditional diplomatic-military-security concerns, and the interdependence, global issues—constitute the essential stuff of foreign policy today. This can be dramatically demonstrated.

THE DUAL REALITY: AN ILLUSTRATIVE SCENARIO

You are a visitor to Washington, but, unlike most tourists, you have a pass that entitles you to enter any building or meeting, or listen to any classified (that is, top secret, secret, or confidential) official conversation.

So you walk into the U.S. Department of State building in Washington's Foggy Bottom. Entering through the Diplomatic Entrance at 22nd and C Streets, NW, you stroll about the building, trying to see what is new.

As far as you can *see,* except for very modern paper reproduction and communications equipment, it does not look all that different from, say, fifty or sixty years ago. Officials still receive hundreds of cables and other dispatches from the country's emissaries abroad each day. As we saw in Chapter 1, they spend some time conferring about how to respond to something thrown at them by a foreign government. They draft cables to U.S. ambassadors accredited to other countries (or to the United Nations), instructing them what to say to another nation's foreign minister (or how to vote at an international conference).

At the U.S. Department of State today, it is still as true as it was before the modern "interdependence revolution" that the most prestigious operating units are the *geographic* bureaus, divided into individual *country desks.* We glimpsed in Chapter 1 how political problems involving U.S. relations with 150 or so other countries are often dealt with on a day-to-day basis.

In the State Department there are also so-called *functional areas*—economic affairs, international organization questions, intelligence and research, environment and science, and policy planning. Moreover, there are three times as many countries to deal with as fifty years ago. Still, regional bureaus have the greatest clout in terms of taking up the time of the secretary of state, and the president, too, because bilateral diplomacy is conducted with other governments on a country-by-country basis (and coordinated with other bureaus when it comes to taking positions in the UN and the thousand or so international conferences the U.S. takes part in each year).

We leave State and walk a few blocks northeast, past the White House to the massive buildings housing the Treasury, and, soon after, the Department of Agriculture. In the enormous headquarters of the Agriculture Department, we stumble into a meeting discussing how best to parcel out the predicted surplus of grains to be harvested by the highly productive American farmer later this year. The chief consideration in the minds of Agriculture Department officials is how to keep prices at a level American farmers—their constituency—will accept. This means selling wheat, corn, and soybeans to those who can pay the going world prices for them—including the Soviet Union. (It may mean less food available to give to needy countries and higher prices for U.S. consumers.)

Over at Treasury, the finishing touches are being put on a policy paper for discussion by the cabinet at one of its regular meetings. The paper argues that the traditional free market system has made America rich, productive, and the world's number one trader. Many poorer or less competitive countries want floor and ceiling prices, even quotas, put on some commodities in international commerce. Treasury officials argue persuasively that if the U.S. agreed to world controls on the prices of essential materials such as copper, tin, bauxite, manganese, and coffee, as demanded by the developing countries, it would be a disastrous step backward for the world economy. They argue that price floors would encourage inefficient producers while price ceilings are unenforceable. (The State Department has been arguing somewhat differently, because *its* constituency is the mass of foreign countries it deals with daily on behalf of the United States.)

That's not all that is happening on your day in Washington. On the same day, three countries that never did sign the 1968 Treaty on the Nonproliferation of Nuclear Weapons (NPT) are reported to be taking new and worrying steps to build their own uranium enrichment plants. They said they need an assured nuclear energy supply because the price of oil has gone out of sight, but those plants would also give them the option to produce nuclear weapons.

On the same day in Bonn, Zurich, and Paris, the U.S. dollar, despite optimistic U.S. presidential statements, spins downward in value, making imports more expensive and pushing inflation up further.

The United Press International (UPI) news ticker reports that a New York-Brussels-Tokyo-based company, Multinational Inc., has signed a new contract with a Persian Gulf oil-producing state. Under the reported terms, the multinational corporation (MNC) has guaranteed to market all of that Arab state's petroleum output, in exchange for training and supplying its still-primitive military gendarmie.

Finally, according to the Associated Press ticker (AP), there has been another major oil supertanker spill, this time threatening the Carolina beaches at the height of the tourist season.

The secretaries of State and Agriculture have an appointment to meet with the president at 2 P.M. to discuss their differences on U.S. food policy. The president, as a politician looking for consensus among American voting groups, is torn between Agriculture's position (which puts a priority on profits for America's farmers, one-third of whose arable land is planted for the export trade), and State's argument that the U.S. image abroad, particularly in the Third World of less-developed countries (LDCs), will suffer unless a significantly greater proportion of the US food surplus is channeled to food-deficit and famine areas in South Asia and Africa, on a *concessional* (that is, subsidized) basis. The president also has to decide between the AFL-CIO labor federation's complaint that U.S. grain sales help the Soviets cover up the weakness of their system, and the argument of other citizen groups on the need to improve U.S.-Soviet relations.

Present at the meeting is one key player in the Washington game who is often overlooked by students of foreign policy. The meeting involves two things he has great clout with on behalf of the president. One is interagency arguments about bureaucratic turf and the other is money. He is director of the Office of Management and Budget (OMB). At the more formal cabinet meeting on trade and investment that follows (including the head of OMB and the National Security Adviser) a portrait of Abraham Lincoln gazes down benignly on the argument that has predictably developed between State and Treasury. The secretary of state reports that a great majority of countries are demanding speedier action toward the New International Economic Order, including guaranteed prices for their raw commodities, forgiveness of their enormous debts to Western banks and governments, and the right to create new cartels like OPEC and nationalize foreign holdings without being bound to international rules regarding compensation. Most of all, they want U.S. consumer markets opened much more widely for *their* manufactured goods.

The president rejects the nationalization argument as extreme and unacceptable, but, he says, the United States must be more responsive to the poor countries. He agrees to new negotiations on guaranteed floor prices, plus a stepped-up world food stockpile program. However, he is uncomfortably aware that the whole ideology of a free market and an entrepreneurial economy is threatened by moves toward what looks like a socialist type of command international economic system. Moreover, it is clear to him that he will (in his own colorful words) "catch hell" from both U.S. labor and business if cheap foreign textiles, autos, steel, shoes, and Lord knows what else are allowed to flood the already depressed U.S. domestic market.

Unexpectedly an aide enters and hands the president a note. His frown deepens as he excuses himself. He walks down the hall and down the stairs to the basement floor of the White House West Wing. There he joins his assistant for national security affairs, the director of Central Intelligence, and several hastily gathered NSC staff members and members of the Joint Chiefs of Staff. Sitting around the small table in the completely secure Situation Room, they go over the *Flash* (meaning wake up NOW) cables that the duty officer summoned them to read. The secretaries of state and defense join them.

The immediate problem is the sinking of two U.S. fishing vessels that were trawling 150 miles off the coastline of an unfriendly Asian country that has claimed sovereignty two hundred miles out to sea. The sinkings were quickly followed by officially inspired fire bombings of the U.S. embassy of that capital and the severe wounding of the ambassador. A member of the NSC staff reminds the small tense group that the U.S. has consistently said it was willing to accept a twelve-mile limit to sovereign waters, plus a 200-mile *economic resources zone,* but only after the UN Law of the Sea Conference, now in its second decade, reaches final agreement on new rules. That has not yet happened.

The president says he has no choice but to rescue the captured seamen who were victims of unwarranted piracy, not to mention deliberately provocative behavior by a chronically unfriendly state. The permanent U.S. representative to the UN in New York could ask for an emergency meeting of the UN Security Council; but action there might be vetoed, and precious time would be lost. Under the U.S. Constitution, the president is still the commander in chief of the armed forces. Despite the limits placed on his freedom of action by the 1973 War Powers Act, he can still act to protect American citizens.

So he tells the secretary of defense to order the chairman of the Joint Chiefs of Staff (who has by now arrived from the Pentagon) to alert a nuclear naval task force in the area and to place some units of the Strategic Air Command on a modified alert, as a clear signal that the U.S. cannot be pushed around. The president then tells his press secretary (who is standing by the door) to explain why, when U.S. national interest is threatened, there is no choice but to respond in kind, at least toward that country. An hour later 85 million Americans are startled to see their favorite programs interrupted for a sober-faced presidential statement.

What is going on in this scenario (or rather, *pair of linked scenarios*)? Are we describing the traditional behavior a great power, able to control its fate by the usual bilateral adjustments and unilateral actions? Or has the world changed so drastically following the two world wars and a host of revolutions that national sovereignty is just a hollow pretense? In this age of interdependence is the belief that a country can still "go it alone" a myth that is clung to only by striped-pants diplomats and isolationist politicians?

The answer to each of these questions is yes—and no. It is obvious from our scenario that a powerful nation like the United States is in control of instruments of power with which, without consulting anyone else, it can hurt, even annihilate, people in another country. However, it is equally true that on some key socioeconomic issues, like food and trade, U.S. relations with dozens of nations are profoundly affected, and so are the jobs, the standard of living, even the survival of millions of human beings, including Americans.

So we are saying two things: (1) Unilateral military moves are still possible, and do in fact take place. (2) In the *non*military sectors of global life, we are using a different kind of world map than the old geostrategic one, one that plots an explosive quest for equity, justice, and new rules to govern the global economic game. That in turn affects conflict situations, superpower actions, and the strategies of the world's political actors.

The only sensible conclusion is that *both* sectors of foreign policy—economic and military—are deeply related to U.S. *security*. Of course, at root security has to do with physical protection from harm or even extinction of a given piece of territory and the people on it. However, the general well-being of people is far more affected today than before by world economic forces that generate inflation, unemployment, and threats to availability of resources and energy. Governments used to be able to shield their citizens from many of these threats to what the Preamble to the U.S. Constitution calls "the General Welfare." Today, unemployment in Detroit is directly tied to trade policies of the Japanese auto industry. The ability of other countries to preserve the savings of their citizens is linked to how much gasoline American drivers use on their summer vacations. (Bayliss Manning christened these combined international-domestic issues *Intermestic.*)[1]

---

[1]See Bayless Manning, *The Conduct of U.S. Foreign Policy in the Third Century* (Claremont, Calif: Claremont University Press, 1975).

We can—and frequently do—argue about which gets first prize for threatening the national security, military aggression or socioeconomic system breakdown. My own answer is both.

ORGANIZING FOR INTERDEPENDENCE

Considering these new facts of life, shouldn't governments reorganize their traditional structures and practices the better to handle these linked and complex problems? The answer is, of course, "Yes, they should."

Three kinds of arrangements have recently been tried.

Interagency coordinating

This is the method used in the process just described. The major departments of government, each representing a different constituency (farmers, business, foreign relations, oil, gas and coal producers, consumers, budget cutters, and so on), internally decide what U.S. policy should be, in their particular lights. If the problem is important enough, the heads of these agencies will try to negotiate a compromise between their conflicting preferences. If they cannot agree, they go before the president. Of all the actors on the policy stage, he is the only one whose role cuts across all the departments, interests, and constituencies, whether foreign or domestic, farm or factory, city or country. He and he alone acts the part of Mr. Interdependence.

Most problems do not go that far. *Interagency coordination* operates through committees or task forces in which representatives of the various agencies meet at lower levels to thrash out their arguments. (The interesting thing is that *all* agencies of government usually are convinced that *their* position is one that reflects the best interests of the United States and the American people. This is invariably true whether it is trade, or tariff, or law of the sea, or nuclear proliferation, or oil exploration, or whatever.)

It is curious but true that different agencies *do* have different interests to protect and defend, and that their personnel act to defend and perpetuate those interests. (The same thing is true in industry, banks, university departments, and other bureaucracies. In Chapter 8 we look at that notion.)

Many of the committees set up under the orderly President Eisenhower were abolished by the freewheeling President Kennedy when he came into office in 1961. President Lyndon B. Johnson, on succeeding Kennedy, set up a system of interagency coordinating committes known as the SIG-IRG system (for Senior Interdepartmental Group and Interdepartmental Regional Groups). His successors tinkered with the committee system in ways to be described in Chapter 3.

President Reagan broke the cabinet down into half a dozen "councils," and the State Department organized some foreign policy interagency committees that had previously been coordinated under the NSC. But earlier, President Kennedy did something else that constitutes a *second* type of arrangement for trying to put together widely differing and often incompatible views and interests that converge in the U.S. foreign policy process.

Integrating from the White House

This method might be called White House coordination. By pulling governmental power far more centrally into the Executive Office of the President, Kennedy created for the first time an operating organization, directly under the president, intended to help him get a direct handle on both domestic and international problems. The White House-based foreign and domestic policy staffs were supposed to bring into a coherent focus for presidential decision the multiplicity of facts, analyses, and opinions about policy which percolate up toward the president from the dozens of agencies of government.

In the next chapter we look at the NSC system of coordinating and managing the foreign policy process for the president, through his assistant for national security affairs (as well as through other special advisors, ambassadors-at-large, and so on).

But as we shall see in Chapter 9, while short-term integration has improved, longer term planning has suffered, particularly planning that *integrates* the pieces of what I have been calling the *Interdependence Agenda.*

The president and his chief foreign policy advisors—the secretaries of state, defense and treasury, and the NSC staff under the assistant for national security affairs—will, by the nature of things, deal with the most pressing problems first. There will always be crises, whether the Middle East, a new oil price, war in Asia or Africa, arms control negotiating impasses, or controversies in superpower relationships. The top officials' priorities will set the priorities for the bureaucracy as a whole. The State Department is the "lead agency" in foreign affairs. But the White House staff is the only part of the executive branch whose mandate cuts across issues and agencies. Logically, somewhere at the top of the policy pyramid one should find the perspective to evolve U.S. policies truly adapted to the complexity of the outside and inside world.

But is is difficult to find a council, group, or committee at the top of the U.S. government whose specific task is to range *across* issues, identify *clusters* that *mix* foreign and domestic, *look ahead,* in short, *integrate* the policy process and thus the policy. A genuine *planning* function does not really exist in the White House, or indeed anywhere in government.

Beefing up the State Department

A third approach is to reorganize the chief foreign policy agency—the Department of State—in a way that better reflects the multiple interdependencies of foreign policy problems and areas we have been discussing.

I suggested earlier that the State Department invariably gives political-diplomatic matters a favored place. To be sure, since World War II there has been an under secretary of state responsible for international economic policy. Under him and the assistant secretary for economic and business affairs are offices that monitor trade, investment, aid, commodities, resources, and questions arising in U.S. dealings with governments or with the UN and related multilateral organizations.

Since World War II there have also been officers assigned to handle State's "foreign" concerns with such interdependence questions as atomic energy, fisheries, and oil. In 1962 a bureau was set up on international scientific affairs (now the Bureau of Oceans and International Environment and Scientific Affairs). Since 1947 there has been a Policy Planning Staff attached to the Office of the Secretary of State.

But without knocking any of these functions or the people carrying them out, in almost all cases, regardless of the particular secretary's breadth of vision (or ambition), State Department officers watch over *State's* interest in trade, money, oil, fish, the spread of nuclear technology, rules for the seabed, pollution, the role of U.S.-based multinational corporations, and so on. And for sure, the diplomatic aspects of these issues are important. But the State Department's official concern has tended to stop at the water's edge.

It seems clear that two important things still need to be done. The first is to *manage the priceless time and energy* of both the president and the secretary of state so that they can, in fact rather than just theory, play the integrating role that cannot be delegated to subordinates. If a president is going to spend "hundreds of hours" (his words) as chief negotiator of the Egyptian-Israeli Treaty (as President Carter did in 1978), and if the secretary of state is going to shuttle for weeks at a time in airplanes acting as his own flying ambassador-at-large (as most have), neither will have the time, strength, or perspective to range thoughtfully over the total panorama of global affairs in which the U.S. has a vital concern. No one else can give direction to the vast bureaucracy, and it is not reasonable to expect subordinate units to stop looking at policy questions with a kind of institutional tunnel vision based on competing agency missions and short-range time frames.

The final integration of scattered executive branch functions can only be done by the White House. What is still missing is a formal *structure of government* that routinely provides for the integrating of traditional security concerns with the new global agenda, taking into account both foreign and domestic aspects. The foreign policy-making system should be structured to correct the tilting of rewards and incentives in favor of expertise on political-strategic concerns. One solution might be to convert the National Security Council into a National *Foreign Policy* Council (its *staff* today in fact deals with most major interdependence issues). The senior NSC membership should bring to bear at the presidential level the multiple vital interests of the U.S. in a way that enables the government more systematically to integrate into often fateful U.S. policy responses to events and forces in the outside world, the goals of stable trade and money, a habitable planet, manageable social change, adequate defense, and raw material access.

chapter three

POLITICAL–SECURITY DECISION MAKING

SECURITY VS. INTERDEPENDENCE?

The reader may wonder why this subject, traditionally given pride of place, follows our glimpse into the "Interdependence Complex." The reason is that political-military affairs represent only part of the foreign policy universe. Even in periods of crisis many people still believe that their security, *broadly defined,* rests less on diplomacy and military power than on the economy that houses and feeds them, the environment in which they breathe and drink, and the resource interdependencies that knit our planet into a global village, regardless of who shoots whom.

But this is one of those cases in life where two important things can both be true, even if you are only interested in one of them. We can still be incinerated in an all-out nuclear exchange. A nonnuclear war like Korea or Vietnam can kill or maim a lot of people. Events show again and again that a conflict in the Middle East, the Caribbean, Africa, or Southwest Asia may involve both the nuclear superpowers in a direct confrontation, and in any event profoundly affect America's relations in the region.

In the preparation of this chapter, the research assistance of Kathleen Troia is gratefully acknowledged.

So, however we may want to concentrate on other problems, Soviet policy and U.S. (and Chinese) responses can still decide what kind of future everyone will have. The U.S., Western European, and Canadian allies are not only important trading partners, but also fellow members of the North Atlantic Treaty Organization (NATO) that stands, more than three decades after its creation, face to face with Moscow's organization of the states of Eastern Europe in their own military grouping, the Warsaw Pact. Japan and China are of obvious political, strategic, and economic importance to this country.

Apart from allies and adversaries, most of the world's peoples live in that amazingly diverse group of over 100 countries known as the Third World, some fantastically rich with oil money, some developing, some dropping behind the process, and some just plain grindingly poor. The U.S. has ties with virtually all of them, whether in day-to-day diplomatic relations, in confrontations at the UN on economic and social issues, in temporary coalitions in which they lined up with us to denounce the 1979 seizure of the U.S. embassy in Teheran and the Soviet invasion of Afghanistan, or in the fastest growing sector of all in U.S. foreign trade.

So whether the American people *feel* isolationist or interventionist, whether the Cold War is on or off, and whatever political party is in office, the United States is deeply involved in the world (as we demonstrated in the last chapter). Like other countries it tries to protect its interests and those of its allies (as we will demonstrate in this one). To carry out its inescapably major role, the U.S. maintains diplomatic relations with 133 countries, negotiates with many of them in scores of international organizations such as the UN, is affected in one way or another by quarrels between them, and from time to time gets militarily involved, even to the point of war.

What we look at here are the parts of the U.S. government that deal with national security issues. Under the presidency of Richard Nixon, *national security* got a bad name because he sometimes used it as a cloak for illegal domestic intelligence operations. But national security is an absolutely indispensable concept for all nations, including ours. It certainly relates to trade, investment, and resources, but more importantly, it concerns survival, defense, protection, power, strategy, vital interests, and the diplomatic, economic, and military means to carry out those interests. At worst, a national security crisis can put at risk the entire nation (and much of the rest of the world as well).

Mercifully, there has been only one such extreme case so far—the Cuban Missile Crisis of 1962. One participant—the late Robert F. Kennedy, then attorney general and confidant of his brother, President John F. Kennedy—described with authority the incredible pressures on the top political, diplomatic, and military leaders of the nation when they looked down into the nuclear abyss.[1]

Much of the time the U.S. national security machinery operates at a considerably less apocalyptic level. Like the airline pilot's description of his job (hours of boredom punctuated by moments of terror), the crisis manager spends his days with a burdensome agenda of often tedious or mundane matters—but may be awakened at 3 A.M. with a "FLASH" message that spells big trouble.

Below the top level of government, most people in the foreign policy-making machine deal with matters of routine "political" diplomacy. Indeed, one reason it is a mistake to look at the Cuban Missile Crisis as a case study of how the government performs is that things were so grave in 1962 the president and a handful of his advisers simply cut themselves off from the main machinery of government so they could devote full time to the crisis, even to the point of Secretary of State Rusk personally typing out some of the group's working papers.

STATE DEPARTMENT—THE "SENIOR AGENCY"[2]

We looked at the State Department in the first two chapters as the natural center for American foreign policy activity. And so it is. But in recent years it got into a protracted fight about who ran things.

For most of the nation's almost 200-year history the Department of State had a monopoly on the handling of U.S. overseas relationships. Our first true Secretary of State, Thomas Jefferson, had when he opened shop in 1789 four clerks, one part-time translator, and one messenger. His budget in 1791 was $57,619. There were two U.S.

---

[1]Robert F. Kennedy, *Thirteen Days: A Memoir of the Cuban Missile Crisis* (New York: W.W. Norton & Co., Inc., 1969).

[2]I use this label as a kind of tongue-in-cheek comparison with the "Senior Service" of the British military—the navy. The secretary of state traditionally sits on the president's right at meetings, but that is because his department was the first created by Congress. In fact, neither State nor Navy is automatically granted precedence by their fellow agencies.

diplomatic missions abroad (called *legations*). For generations, international diplomacy was conducted at a leisurely pace. There was ample time to digest information, then decide if anything needed to be done. A dispatch from U.S. Minister Ben Franklin in Paris would take weeks to arrive on a boat to Philadelphia or New York. The turn-around time to reach Washington and then get word back to Europe was not hours, as now, but months. How *could* one be in a hurry?

Moreover, the U.S. wasn't all that involved in the world's doings. Increasing business and financial interests, yes. Freedom of the seas required a navy, of course. And U.S. consuls provided help to drunken sailors and impoverished tourists who lost their passports or went to jail. However, the convulsive expansion of U.S. rule at the turn of the twentieth century to the Philippines and Puerto Rico—an "empire acquired in a fit of absentmindedness"—was basically a deviation from the historic sense of isolation and detachment from the unedifying quarrels of foreigners. So, for that matter, was the belated U.S. entry into World War I. Until the beginning of Warld War II (1941 for the U.S.), global involvement was something Americans regarded as optional, and they usually opted not to be involved. All that changed in 1941–1945, when U.S. thinking caught up with the changing facts.

Today the United States maintains diplomatic missions in 133 foreign capitals, complete with ambassadors, deputy chiefs of mission, political, economic, and public affairs counselors, diplomatic secretaries, defense attachés, CIA agents, and usually attachés from dozens of other federal departments. In addition, the U.S. has 100 consular posts. (See Chapter 7 on Diplomacy.)

Up to 50,000 Americans fill overseas jobs—and most of them do *not* come from the State Department. (The State Department itself has 5800 employees abroad in addition to the 8500 at home.)

In 1790—and even in 1890—the State Department might have handled a dozen pieces of official correspondence in a week. As we shall see in Chapter 7, today 1,000 official telegrams flow out of State every day.

These "gee whiz" statistics are impressive, but they still don't tell us much about how *influential* the State Department actually is in the American foreign policy-making system. They only show how burdened the system is by personnel and paper flow.

The sad fact is that, on all the evidence, the State Department has been gradually losing influence at about the same rate as it has been growing in size. The downgrading process started with U.S. entry into World War II. If, as Clemenceau said, war is too important to leave to the generals, President Roosevelt felt wartime diplomacy was too important to leave to the diplomats. The president and Congress created a host of new agencies for information, propaganda, intelligence, and wartime aid to allies. Roosevelt also began the now-entrenched White House custom of setting up his own diplomatic agents, *and* his own communication channels, both outside the normal ambassadorial and departmental structures. Averell Harriman was put in London, bypassing Ambassador John Winant; Harry Hopkins shuttled to Moscow, bypassing the American embassy there (as Henry Kissinger did thirty years later); Under Secretary of State Sumner Welles became the president's chief diplomat, bypassing Secretary of State Cordell Hull.

By the time the war ended, the Office of Strategic Services (OSS) was undertaking intelligence gathering and covert political operations behind enemy lines, with a staff large enough to man a small army division. OSS was broken up after the war, but its core formed what eventually became the Central Intelligence Agency (CIA), and only some research functions went to the State Department.

The big postwar economic programs, like the Marshall Plan for Europe, were administered not by the State Department but by quasi-independent aid agencies, like today's Agency for International Development (AID). When disarmament became a serious foreign policy issue in the early 1960s, a new office was set up in the White House, followed by creation of the U.S. Arms Control and Disarmament Agency (ACDA). Like the U.S. Information Agency (renamed the U.S. International Communication Agency—USICA) it is able to report directly to the White House. Even the Peace Corps, so important to the U.S. image in many developing countries, is independent of State.

As we saw in the last chapter, the Department of Agriculture handles world food matters (it also administers the Food for Peace Program); Commerce was given the lead by President Carter over all official commercial overseas activities; Energy supervises U.S. participation in the International Energy Agency; the president's trade representative negotiates international trade agreements.

Paradoxically, the heart of U.S. diplomacy—the Foreign Service—had meantime become a true professional career service for the practice of diplomacy, thanks to the Rogers Act of 1924, the

Hoover Commission Report of 1955, and the 1954 Wriston Committee report. But in reality, power was in fact hemorrhaging from the constantly-expanding building in Foggy Bottom, flowing ever more swiftly in the direction of the Pentagon, the CIA, and, above all, the White House.

THE STATE DEPARTMENT AS WHIPPING BOY

One of the most extraordinary transformations in the U.S. government machinery in recent years was the creation by presidents of what amounted to their own personal foreign affairs and national security establishments *within* the White House itself.

There is nothing illegal about this shift in real power. The Constitution makes the president, not the State Department, the nation's chief foreign policy maker, with the secretary of state his chief adviser, by statute. Nuclear-era diplomacy obviously needs centralized top-level direction and control. And it might as well be admitted that, by contrast with intractable domestic problems like energy and inflation, red-carpet state visits and diplomatic negotiations are far more fun. Sometimes—but only sometimes—they also represent a president's highest duty.

So it isn't surprising that recent presidents have tried, with a good deal of success, to take control of the foreign policy-making process. President Reagan early in his administration seemed to move much of the action back to General Haig's State Department. Only time will tell if the system can run successfully the way it was intended. During a twenty-year period, from 1961 to 1981, the State Department got bigger than ever, with more and more responsibilities, and continued to sail along majestically in diplomatic matters like a stately galleon under full sail—but only made about five knots in the water, while the speedy little presidential staff raced around it in ever-fancier circles.

The reason usually given was that presidents didn't really trust the formal U.S. diplomatic machine to do their bidding how, when, and where they wanted it to. Former Secretary of State Dean Acheson, famed for his candor, once said

> All Presidents I have known have had uneasy doubts about the State Department. . . . (The doubts) are strongest at the begin-

> ning of presidential terms, when the incumbent . . . believes(s) that foreign affairs are simpler than they in fact are. . . . Foreign Service officers seem to them cynical, unimaginative, and negative.[3]

Almost a hundred years earlier, that keen observer Henry Adams noted a similar erosion of State Department authority. He described a Washington which featured a second "Department of Foreign Relations over which Senator Sumner ruled with a high hand at the Capitol; and . . . a third Foreign Office in the War Department, with President Grant himself for chief."[4]

Presidential complaints began in earnest in the modern era with wartime President Franklin D. Roosevelt. To him, the State Department's worry about political problems smacked of foot-dragging. It is also reported by some that Roosevelt once said "dealing with the State Department is like watching an elephant become pregnant; everything's done on a very high level, there's a lot of commotion, and it takes twenty-two months for anything to happen."

As it happened, Roosevelt's successors, Harry Truman and Dwight Eisenhower, were genuinely respectful of their secretaries of state, Dean Acheson, George Marshall, and John Foster Dulles. The latter three were all potent figures in their own right, both in Washington and in the country at large.

But in 1961 the young activist President John F. Kennedy lost no time in becoming impatient with the State Department "for whom the risks have always outweighed the opportunities," and which (according to Kennedy's biographer Arthur M. Schlesinger, Jr.) suffered from "intellectual exhaustion."[5] Longtime Foreign Service Soviet expert Charles ("Chip") Bohlen recalls in his memoirs Kennedy one day exploding: "Chip, what is wrong with that God-dammed department of yours?" Bohlen, who had watched Kennedy bypassing the Depart-

---

[3]Dean Acheson, *Present at the Creation: My Years in The State Department* (New York: W.W. Norton & Co., Inc., 1969), p. 250.

[4]Henry Adams, *The Education of Henry Adams: An Autobiography* (New York: Modern Library, 1931) p. 274. Reprinted courtesy of Random House, Inc. Not to be missed by anyone interested in American roots—or in good writing.

[5]Arthur M. Schlesinger, Jr., *A Thousand Days: John F. Kennedy in the White House* (Boston: Houghton Mifflin, 1965), pp. 414, 416.

ment's chain of command in his aggressive quest for immediate action, bravely replied, "You are."[6]

President Richard Nixon, like all other modern American presidents, certainly had no love for the United States State Department. Journalist Henry Brandon wrote that Nixon regarded the State Department bureaucracy as "an incorrigibly lethargic snail protected by a thick shell of tradition, incapable of creative ideas or firm action."[7]

We can readily notice that what bothered recent presidents was that when they wanted innovative ideas, the State Department was unimaginative; when they wanted quick action, the State Department seemed lethargic; when they wanted certain kinds of information, they were likely to prefer sources that were personally rather than institutionally loyal.

Certainly, typical State Department slowness or unimaginativeness is a legitimate reason for presidential impatience, but sometimes the State Department's unexciting responses are the result of steady erosion of the State Department's original mission by congressional and presidential action setting up competing centers of foreign policy action.

There is a deeper reason for this chronic tension between White House demands and State Department shortfalls. It is at a more philosophical level, and each reader can judge whether it is a good or bad reason. In general, diplomacy's basic purpose is to *slow things down, cool things off, avoid confrontations,* and, at its best, *preserve peace.* To an activist or confrontational temperament, this probably looks like intolerable slothfulness. And at some moments in history when large ideas or quick initiatives are needed it might be inexcusable. To another perspective, the defect is really a virtue. To the traditional diplomat slowness, deliberateness, and even procrastination, can be indispensable antidotes to hotheaded political leaders or White House hotshots whose posturing, or passion for action, might lead the nation into a disastrous quagmire. The point can of course be argued both ways!

One shrewd observer compared the relatively passive role of the State Department ("mainly to observe, to report, to negotiate, to ad-

---

[6]Charles E. Bohlen, *Witness to History, 1929–1969* (New York: W.W, Norton & Co., Inc., 1973), p. 490.

[7]Henry Brandon, *The Retreat of American Power* (Garden City, N.Y.: Doubleday, 1973), p. 24.

vise, to assist, and to propagandize . . . to find ways to avoid or postpone action . . .") with the role of the U.S. Defense Department, whose function is to act ("for Defense, action is the object; for State it is the danger to be avoided.")[8]

It is a fair point. At worst, the State Department consists of people who by temperament, as once was said of British Prime Minister Lloyd George, have been sitting on the fence so long that the iron has entered their souls.[9] At its foot-dragging, cautious, cover-your-rear, don't-rock-the-boat worst, the State Department could easily be the source of Bloomfield's Law that "nothing ever happens in Washington until it has to."

But at its best that prudential attitude might have saved us from some classic historic blunders, whether the 1961 Bay of Pigs, the 1965 Dominican invasion, or the stubborn presidential refusal to see until too late the blind alley in Vietnam. In a hair-trigger nuclear world full of temptations to take hasty action in situations that may be ambiguous or premature, a good case can be made for foot-dragging at times when the U.S. risks the danger of going off half-cocked. Of course, there are times when the U.S. should act fast and decisively. But experience suggests that there are also times when it is in the highest interest of the United States *not* to take a hasty or ill-considered initiative. Those are the times when the best advice that can be given a White House whose glands (or sensitivity to domestic pressures) are in overdrive is to switch around a common saying and recommend: "Don't just do something—stand there!" A career bureaucracy can get that message across, if only by inaction.[10]

To the extent the differences between State and White House staff are unintended, the problem probably lies not with the people but with the *institution.* Above all, the State Department is a victim of its size, its rigidity, and its resistance to change. At their best the professional State Department staff constitutes an uncommonly intelligent and experienced corps of specialists and generalists, many of whom are outstanding authorities on various parts of the world or

[8]Adam Yarmolinsky, "Bureaucratic Structures and Political Outcomes," *Journal of International Affairs,* 23 (1969), 229.

[9]Another quote I owe to the inventive Thomas L. Hughes.

[10]So can the White House staff. Nixon top aide H. R. Haldeman was quoted as saying that it is a staff officer's duty to ignore any clearly inappropriate demand, even if the president had insisted on it. Bob Woodward and Carl Bernstein, *The Final Days* (New York: Simon & Schuster, 1976), p. 265.

problem areas and who represent the United States abroad in a manner that would make any American proud—including the president.

THE RISE OF WHITE HOUSE CONTROL

Until 1947, presidents solved the problem of frustration caused by a slow-moving and unimaginative bureaucracy through the device of personal advisers—what in Andrew Jackson's day was called the *kitchen cabinet.* Colonel Edward M. House was President Woodrow Wilson's loyal, trustworthy, and always-available aide in the making of both war and peace. New York social worker Harry Hopkins did the same for Franklin Roosevelt.[11]

In 1947 Congress passed the landmark National Security Act, which set up the National Security Council. From that day to this, the basic framework has been in place for a massive expansion of the White House staff dealing, in the name of the president, with political, diplomatic, and military questions that are at the same time the statutory responsibility of the line departments of government, chiefly State and Defense. The president has benefited greatly from a strengthened ability to do his job of direction and coordination, but a big new question was created as to just how the government was to function.

The main problem the Act sought to solve was coordination between the political and military agencies. By 1947, two years after World War II ended, the U.S. government included a kaleidescope of fragmentary bits and pieces of military and intelligence operations left over from World War II. Wartime coordination between the hitherto autonomous uniformed chiefs of the armed services (army, navy, and eventually air force) had been forced by the urgency of the times and the demands of the president as commander in chief. However, after victory in 1945 the services fell to squabbling once again over their share of the pie of congressional appropriations. Wartime liaison with the diplomatic branch was continued in a fitful way through a relatively powerless State-War-Navy-Coordinating Committee (SWNCC). Something was needed to introduce the Pentagon to the State Department.

[11]See the superb biography by playwright Robert E. Sherwood, *Roosevelt and Hopkins: An Intimate History* (New York: Harper & Bros., 1948).

In that Act of 1947, Congress established the National Security Council as a formal means of coordinating U.S. security policy, and advising the president on "matters involving the national security." The original idea was that this would be done not through a staff but in the British fashion of bringing top operational executives together in one committee. The statutory members were the president, vice-president (added in 1949), secretaries of state and defense, and the director of the Office of Emergency Planning (whose title changed several times and who was finally omitted). Statutory advisers are the chairman of the Joint Chiefs of Staff and the director of Central Intelligence.

The council was to recommend to the president action involving U.S. national security and the use of military power, and assign follow-up actions to the agencies concerned with national security. The aim was to eliminate poorly defined assignments, unclear delegation of responsibility, and duplication of effort—all valuable and badly needed reforms.

We have been talking about the council itself. But the real controversy has built up over the NSC *staff*. It started out as a modest secretariat to the council, coordinating the latter's meetings and projects behind the scenes. It turned out that use of the council itself by a succession of presidents was uneven and spotty, accompanied, however, by a steady growth in function and responsibility of the NSC staff. So it has been the staff, rather than the formal council, that has increasingly taken on the duty of advancing and protecting the president's interests against what sometimes seemed the president's natural "enemies" in the military and diplomatic bureaucracies. (The preceding is said as a pleasantry; under Richard Nixon's presidency, it became an ugly actuality.) The NSC staff, starting out as a neutral switching point helping make information and decision papers flow up and down the hierarchy more efficiently, began to assume a far more independent role. The real crunch came when it began, in the 1960s and 1970s, to *offer policy advice on its own* along with coordinating the recommendations of the agencies. In place of cooperative relations there began to be growing tension and resentments in relationships between White House staff and State and Defense. This seemed to change somewhat in the '80s. But how the problem evolved is instructive and may help us make predictions about the future of top-level decision making in Washington.

From 1947–1950 the National Security Council itself did in fact meet regularly and offer advice to President Truman in the form of written memoranda. (Neither then nor in the future were verbatim transcripts ever made of NSC meetings, presumably not to inhibit free interplay of discussion.) President Truman himself rarely attended NSC meetings. When he did, he did not participate in the debate, in order to emphasize that the NSC was purely advisory and that he was not bound by its advice. Sidney Souers, the Council's first executive secretary (and predecessor of later National Security Advisers) described his role as that of an "anonymous servant of the Council" and "broker of ideas in criss-crossing proposals among a team of responsible officials."[12] Certainly that does not describe a policy *advocate*—the role which was later to be so controversial. It does describe what Alexander George has labelled a "Custodian-Manager."

In the spring of 1949, after the beginning of Truman's second term, the NSC staff took on the job of preparing periodic general reviews of policy. These papers would discuss the available policy alternatives but without making specific recommendations. The main problems facing the council from 1947–1950 were atomic energy, internal security, defense mobilization, and military strategy. Some major U.S. policy documents such as the famous "NSC-68" paper were proposed for NSC decision. But until the Korean War broke out in 1950 the NSC itself did not play a central role in national security policy making.

A few days after the North Korean attack on the South in June 1950, Truman decided to tighten up his decision-making process. He issued a memorandum ordering that all national security issues should be brought to him by means of the NSC mechanism, directed the NSC to meet every Thursday, and began to regularly attend NSC meetings himself.

In July 1950 the National Security Council staff was reshuffled: the permanent executive secretary remained, but the previous arrangement of relying on so-called consultants from the departments was replaced by a senior staff served by staff assistants. The senior

[12]Sidney M. Souers, "Policy Formulation for National Security," *American Political Science Review,* June 1949, p. 537.

staff, which included representatives of State, Department of Defense (DOD), Joint Chiefs of Staff (JCS), Treasury, and CIA, was headed by the executive secretary. The senior staff met twice weekly to prepare papers for the council. By the end of his administration, Truman treated the NSC as his major foreign policy advisory body.

President Eisenhower, steeped in orderly and well-staffed military organization forms, restructured the NSC to serve as the mechanism by which national security policies were defined and brought before the president for decision. To facilitate this, he created a new position of *special assistant for national security affairs* to head a reorganized National Security Council staff. Eisenhower also formalized the National Security Council committee system.

Council activities were divided into policy planning and operations implementation. The senior staff was upgraded to a Planning Board and charged with developing and defining the issues to be placed before the council for debate. The Planning Board, spearheaded by State Department Policy Planning Chief Robert Bowie, met twice a week to thrash out interagency policy differences, with the special assistant acting as neutral chairman. If the Planning Board was unable to come to agreement, the issues and options were set out for discussion by the council, aimed at presidential decision. An Operations Coordinating Board (OCB), chaired by the under secretary of state, was also established to coordinate the carrying out of presidential decisions by the various departments. (One of the chronic presidential complaints about the bureaucracy was that orders were issued by the White House, but sometimes nothing seemed to happen—see Chapter 4.)

The NSC staff was enlarged and strengthened in other ways, including the capacity to make its own independent analyses (but not policy recommendations). It remained in concept a career staff operating on the assumption that most of its members would stay on from administration to administration. (Eisenhower had three special assistants during his two administrations—Robert Cutler, a Boston investment banker; Houston lawyer and writer Dillon Anderson; and Gordon Gray, who had been Truman's secretary of the army and later was president of the University of North Carolina.)

An influential Senate subcommittee chaired by Senator Henry M. ("Scoop") Jackson saw the NSC as analogous to the Joint Chiefs of Staff:

> a corporate body, composed of individuals advising the President in their own right rather than as representatives of their respective departments and agencies. Their function should be to seek, with their background of experience, the most statesmanlike solution to the problem of national security, rather than to reach solutions which represent merely a compromise of departmental positions.[13]

However, some critics felt the National Security Council had instead become a huge committee—with all the weaknesses of committees, including the parochial interests of agencies and departments. Former Secretary of State Dean Acheson sometimes characterized NSC advice as "agreement by exhaustion."

John F. Kennedy, who brought a freewheeling and personalized style to the Oval Office, downgraded the National Security Council system in favor of an inner core of trusted advisers including his own new special assistant for national security affairs, Dean McGeorge Bundy of Harvard. Under Kennedy the special assistant, along with a few other key staff aides, began the process of becoming in effect the president's personal State Department.

Senator Jackson's subcommittee had recommended that the NSC be made into a more intimate forum to help the president by exposing him to searching discussion of a limited number of critical problems. Kennedy followed that advice and proceeded to dismantle the elaborate Eisenhower system of interdepartmental committees, many of them in the NSC framework. He substituted a loose, pragmatic set of procedures for decision making and implementation, in the process also abolishing the OCB. NSC meetings were held only occasionally. The fateful Cuban Missile Crisis decisions in 1962 were made by an informal grouping of top NSC members and Kennedy advisers, the group christened NSC "Excom," for Executive Committee. Kennedy's closest personal aide argued that the NSC itself only made minor decisions, or pretended to make important ones that had already been decided.[14]

Like virtually all presidents during the period of growing NSC staff activism, President Kennedy in principle wanted primary re-

---

[13]U.S. Congress, Senate, Committee on Government Operations, Subcommittee on National Policy Machinery, *Organizing for National Security*, 87th Congress, 1st Session, Vol. 2 (Washington, D.C.: Government Printing Office, 1961), p. 129.

[14]Theodore Sorensen, *Kennedy* (New York: Harper and Row Pub., 1965), p. 284.

sponsibility to be taken by the departments and agencies. In the words of his Special Assistant Bundy:

> The President has made it very clear that he does not want a large separate organization . . . between him and his Secretary of State. Neither does he wish any question to arise as to the clear authority and responsibility of the Secretary of State, not only in his own Department, and not only in such large-scale related areas as foreign aid and information policy, but also as the agent of coordination in all of our major policies toward other nations.[15]

The dismantling of the elaborate NSC structure did result in some increased reliance on the Department of State (despite Kennedy's impatience with what he privately called that "bowl of jelly"). McGeorge Bundy maintained a fairly low profile himself. But his assistants were heard to complain that while they *wanted* the State Department to do its job the NSC staff was having to become a center of advice and power because of State's failure to carry the ball.

Despite the best intentions of the president, the complexity and urgency of events, plus the activism of this youthful president, in fact created the conditions for a major role by an immediately available, bright, unencumbered, and responsive presidential staff.

Thus the special assistant and his staff inevitably acquired an unprecedentedly powerful status. Moreover, when Kennedy turned to a small group of intimates for foreign policy advice, Bundy was almost always included, which increased his influence and, through him, the impact of the NSC staff. The result was a major evolution in their role to serve not so much the NSC but the president directly, as an in-house staff for foreign and defense policy. An unintended consequence was to transform the special assistant position from a neutral custodian of the machinery to what eventually amounted to a one-man NSC. From the special assistant and his staff came many of the draft action recommendations that were eventually issued as presidential directives for action—the so-called NSAMs (National Security Action Memorandum).

Paradoxically, the size of the NSC staff shrank to around 10 to 15 professionals—a bright group of operators identified with the

---

[15]Letter of September 4, 1961, in *Organizing for National Security,* Vol. 1, pp. 1337–1338.

Kennedy administration and fiercely loyal to the president. They were prone not to wait for papers to arrive from Foggy Bottom or the Pentagon but rather to seek out issues and challenge departmental opinions, to look for policy options which had been buried by the bureaucracy, and to see to the implementation of the president's desires.

The precedent was established that virtually every memorandum to the president from the Department of State reached him only after preparation of a cover memorandum from the NSC staff, typically briefer and tighter than State's paper. (This may seem like a petty difference, but to an overburdened president it becomes crucial.)

If advice is a vehicle of influence, access to information—being in the know—is a vital source of power in Washington. A major innovation of the Kennedy NSC apparatus was to establish a White House communications center.

The Situation Room in the White House basement was equipped with machinery and procedures so that the White House could, for the first time, automatically receive all priority messages from military, diplomatic, and intelligence centers around the world simultaneously with their receipt at State, Defense, and the CIA. This was a major change from the White House's previous dependency on the agencies to select and forward such communications. Immediate access to cable traffic made it possible for Bundy and his staff to deal with the bureaucracy on an equally informed basis, as well as being the president's primary source of government-wide information. (Flagging of such messages for the White House later reverted to the hands of the agencies, probably because of the overwhelming volume, but the process had by then become sufficiently automated that any omission of White House distribution required a positive—and suspicion-inducing—act.)

The NSC staff was now clearly playing an expanded role in developing, coordinating, and sometimes pressing for a broad, government-wide presidential view encompassing diplomatic, military, and increasingly, economic elements in foreign policy. This trend was carried over, in modified form, under President Lyndon B. Johnson.

Johnson followed a pragmatic policy-making approach similar to Kennedy's. In place of the National Security Council, his Tuesday lunch group gradually developed into an authoritative, if somewhat crude, policy tool. The secretaries of state and defense plus the special assistant met with the president. The group was later broadened to include the press secretary, the CIA director, and the chairman of the Joint Chiefs of Staff.

Johnson's preference was to concentrate on a few key issues—which he dominated—and to lean on the secretaries of state and defense for other advice. After Bundy left in early 1966, the power of the special assistant and his staff was somewhat reduced. Yet former M.I.T. economics professor Walt Rostow (who had been Bundy's deputy before heading State's Policy Planning Staff) as special assistant ended up performing essentially the same functions as had Bundy. He and his staff coordinated the flow of information and intelligence, as well as managing the flow of decision papers to the president. In addition, the NSC staff monitored government operations to promote coordination and responsiveness to the president's interests, and communicated presidential decisions and instructions to departments and agencies. Rostow also acted as the president's liaison with cabinet officers and other high foreign policy officials. While Rostow and the NSC staff continued to serve Johnson as personal advisers and the source of staff analysis, they tended to work more in concert with the State Department than had Bundy, perhaps because Johnson relied increasingly on Secretary of State Dean Rusk for advice, particularly on the Vietnam War.

One innovation (suggested by ex-Chairman of the Joint Chiefs of Staff Maxwell Taylor) was creation of a Senior Interdepartmental Group (SIG) headed by the under secretary of state (later called deputy secretary) and including representatives from DOD, Treasury, CIA, and others, backed up by Interdepartmental Regional Groups (IRGs), each chaired by an assistant secretary of state. This arrangement worked only moderately well. (The SIG which replaced the NSC Planning Board disappeared for a while but the IRGs, converted to IGs, continues to function when needed.) While the Johnson administration groped for institutional substitutes for the National Security Council, it had not found effective new answers before his term of office ended in 1968.

During his 1968 presidential campaign, Richard Nixon had promised to restore the National Security Council to its preeminent role in national security planning. In fact he came in with a determination to gather as much power as possible into his White House. Once in office he reestablished with a vengeance an Eisenhower-style NSC committee structure, topped by the council as the principal forum for consideration of national security policy issues. In his first year the NSC met almost every week. The immediate result was a spectacular retightening of the policy lines back into the White House in a network of top-level NSC committees, virtually all chaired by Assistant to the President, Harvard Professor Henry A. Kissinger.

That the lead clearly came from Nixon was underscored in Kissinger's memoirs. When Nixon offered him the job, "The President-elect repeated . . . his view of the incompetence of the CIA and the untrustworthiness of the State Department. The position of security adviser was therefore crucial to him and to his plan to run foreign policy from the White House."[16] Nixon's devious nature was nicely illustrated by the contrast between this private act and his public statement on naming Kissinger, that the latter would not be involved in day-to-day policy issues.

By 1973, the NSC itself became one of many victims of Nixon's distrustful and closed habits and lapsed into unprecedented disuse. Advice to the president came by and through Dr. Kissinger and his staff. The machinery of interdepartmental committees and paperwork had been made much more elaborate. But Kissinger himself was made the custodian of NSC interagency machinery.

The Nixon NSC system operated through a network of such committees: the Senior Review Group, Defense Programs Review Committee (DPRC), Vietnam Special Studies Committee, Verification Panel (on SALT negotiations), Washington Special Actions Group (WSAG), the "40 Committee" which supervised covert intelligence, and the Under Secretaries Committee. All but the last were chaired by the ubiquitous Dr. Kissinger (a member of his staff chaired the Vietnam Committee). Below the Senior Review Group were the six interdepartmental IGs[17] charged with formulating policy options and analyzing the pros and cons of various courses of action.

With the DPRC, the White House sought (not very successfully) to get a handhold on defense planning and budgeting while it was still tentative. WSAG was in effect a top-level operations center created in

[16]Henry A. Kissinger, *White House Years,* (Boston: Little, Brown, 1979), p. 15.

[17]One each on Europe, the Far East, Middle East, Africa, Latin America, and Political-Military Affairs.

April 1969, after Nixon's surprise and embarrassment when North Korea shot down an American EC-121 aircraft.

When he took office Nixon, through Kissinger, "tasked" (meaning charged) the NSC system with preparing an overall review of American foreign policy. This was done by issuing a series of interdepartmental study assignments called National Security Study Memoranda (NSSMs) which were responded to by the various NSC subgroups, principally the IGs, with contributions from the departments and agencies. These NSSMs formulated policy options and analyzed pros and cons of actions to deal with an issue. Presidential decisions that resulted took the form of NSDMs (National Security Decision Memorandum).

Some 85 NSSMs were prepared during Nixon's first year on a wide range of policy alternatives concerning Vietnam, the Middle East, basic military strategy and military programs, foreign aid, NATO, China policy, U.S.-Soviet relations, as well as a host of lesser subjects. Some disgruntled "Indians" in the bureaucracy suspected, not wholly without reason, that the NSSM program was designed to tie up the agencies with a mountain of papers and meetings while Kissinger and his staff took control of the policy process. (Observers also noted that Kissinger rather slyly sent NSSMs to the Defense Department for evaluation of problems normally in the State Department's bailiwick, and vice versa.)

As for the council itself, it suited the Nixon style to make clear that the NSC was an advisory, not a decision-making body. According to Kissinger's later account, President Nixon would normally announce his own decision, not during NSC meetings but afterwards, usually in writing or through intermediaries. This avoided two things he disliked: face-to-face disputation and challenges to his orders.[18]

Attempted White House "oversight" of the Pentagon's budget process was only one element of friction between Kissinger and the secretary of defense, but the latter had more clout than state and often won the battle. A far clearer result of the Nixon NSC system was to sharply undercut the position of the secretary of state, in this case former Eisenhower-era Attorney General William Rogers. Although a longtime personal friend of Nixon with a reputation as a capable administrator, Rogers was completely unschooled in foreign affairs.

---

[18]See Henry A. Kissinger, *White House Years,* p. 491.

The effect of the new structure was that Rogers was in no position to compete with Kissinger, and was frequently humiliated by being not only excluded, but sometimes not even informed of important foreign policy actions.

Rogers' failure to challenge Kissinger also tended to demoralize the assistant secretaries of state, who were in an invidious situation: The regional IGs which they chaired sent papers to the Senior Review Group, chaired by Kissinger. Thus the assistant secretaries were in the awkward position of reporting directly to Kissinger, while formally responsible to the secretary of state.

Another far-reaching change was the direct relationship established by the White House with foreign embassies in Washington, which normally worked through the State Department. According to Tad Szulc, on Inauguration Day personal letters to fifteen heads of governments from Nixon were,

> unbeknownst to Secretary Rogers . . . delivered by NSC aides to Washington embassies of these countries for transmission home. They were the first Nixon-Kissinger secret. Although these letters simply expressed Nixon's desire to improve relations between the United States and the recipient country, an NSC official described them as "the beginning of the effort to establish channels directly from the White House. . . . It was one of the early incidents of bypassing the State Department."[19]

Key ambassadors in Washington soon realized where influence lay. The long black limousines began to show up regularly at the White House West Wing (where the president and Dr. Kissinger worked.) The State Department's downgrading was complete. The "back-channel" to foreign governments caused more than one glitch in the foreign policy process. But there is little doubt it proved to be positively helpful to the negotiation of the first SALT agreement with the Soviets in 1972.

Kissinger's NSC staff of foreign policy experts consisted of between 45 and 55 professionals, with 50 to 60 supporting personnel. The staff's principal task was to monitor the executive branch agencies to ensure the success of central control. The staff collected data from the agencies, managed interagency working groups, analyzed

[19] Tad Szulc, *The Illusion of Peace: Foreign Policy in the Nixon Years* (New York: Viking, 1978), p. 13.

the results of NSSMs, and wrote covering memoranda on incoming policy papers from the agencies with recommendations to Kissinger and, through him, to the president. They also prepared briefing papers for Kissinger's and the president's use in negotiations, generally submitting the longer State briefing papers as back-up material. Drawing on materials ground out in State, Defense, CIA and other sources, the staff, through Kissinger, kept the president informed of developments overseas, briefed him on current issues, and drafted answers to presidential correspondence. The press officer on the NSC staff served as the coordinator for State, Defense, and White House foreign policy responses at press briefings.

Kissinger himself took charge of a number of policy initiatives for the president *outside* the NSC system, notably the U.S. opening to China, U.S.-Soviet relations, the SALT I negotiations, and the Vietnam peace talks. By 1971 Kissinger had become the president's personal, confidential envoy.

Until the secret 1971 trip to China, however, Kissinger remained relatively anonymous as a public figure, leaving the credit to Nixon. Thereafter he increasingly became the government's foreign policy spokesman, particularly on matters for which he was responsible (which after 1973 included the Middle East peace negotiations). As Nixon became more and more consumed by Watergate in the later years of his administration, Kissinger stepped into the limelight as both secretary of state and foreign policy chief, as well as public spokesman and star briefer of the press. (However, Kissinger did not testify before Congress, since Nixon claimed executive privilege. Kissinger would meet with senators privately to brief them on developments while he was national security adviser.)

Kissinger's superstar role and his working style, combined with Nixon's secretive nature, had the effect of limiting direct access of Kissinger's subordinates to the president, and even to Kissinger himself. Usually staff members would submit written memoranda to Kissinger or speak with him by telephone to keep him informed of developments or to request guidance. Kissinger saw his staff regularly only at weekly NSC staff meetings.[20]

[20]See Henry A. Kissinger, *White House Years,* for details. A somewhat lurid account by a former Kissinger staffer of wheelings and dealings between Nixon, Kissinger, the staff, and the bureaucracies is found in Roger Morris, *Uncertain Greatness: Henry Kissinger and American Foreign Policy* (New York: Harper & Row, Pub., 1977).

The authority of the White House in general and of Kissinger in particular, was enhanced by a seemingly minor technological renovation of the White House Situation Room. The installation of secure Long Distance Xerox (LDX) communications equipment gave the NSC staff the additional ability to step up its control over important communications flow, including a capability to provide speedy NSC clearance of important outgoing cables before State sent them to the field. White House communication facilities made it no longer necessary for the White House, when it wanted a private channel to communicate with foreign leaders or American embassies without going through State, to have to use CIA or Defense Department communications. It now sent and received communications with U.S. embassies directly. Copies of cables in this back-channel traffic would be distributed to State and other departments only on the decision of Kissinger or one of his top aides.

When Kissinger became the president's chief emissary, the report of his talks with foreign leaders were sent only to the president and the NSC staff. Copies of his complete report were not usually sent to the responsible agencies. Thus when it came time for another negotiation with that country, only the NSC briefing memoranda could take account of all the previous exchanges. Even if a State Department representative had been on the trip, he rarely sat in on the meetings between Kissinger and the foreign leader. As a result, the NSC staff memorandum was the only complete record, giving Kissinger and his staff an unparalleled last word in American diplomacy and further weakening the hold of the State Department on U.S. foreign policy.

Under this unprecedently centralized gathering of governmental power Dr. Kissinger became less and less the neutral custodian, and more and more a strong advocate for policy positions, adding his own recommendations to all options papers he forwarded to the president, reinforced by frequent personal talks. He was always careful to present department views fairly, usually including their papers as back-up material to his covering memo. But it was no real contest.

(Kissinger later allowed that, in retrospect, he now believed the security adviser should keep a low profile, not see foreign diplomats, and keep out of the spotlight. With charming candor he admitted to having violated all three. As usual, Dr. K. had the best of both worlds—the enjoyable sin, followed by the redeeming confession.)[21]

[21]See Henry A. Kissinger, *White House Years,* introductory chapters, also interview in *Time Magazine* May 12, 1980, p. 24.

When Kissinger became secretary of state in September 1973, he took some of his trusted aides with him. The primary initiative for foreign policy moved to the State Department. Although Kissinger retained his role as head of the NSC staff until November 1975, the staff, then headed by Lt. General Brent Scowcroft, no longer served as the focal point for foreign policy business. U.S. foreign policy, during the decline of Richard Nixon and his eventual resignation in 1974, was wherever Kissinger was. It so continued during the presidency of Gerald Ford. But many observers saw Scowcroft's tenure as a refreshing reversion to the proper role of the security adviser and staff—anonymous, efficient, and supportive of the president without either undercutting the secretary of state or becoming a media star.[22]

Before Jimmy Carter became president in January 1977, he faithfully followed the pattern of his predecessors in firmly rejecting any idea of a "little State Department" in the White House, or of his assistant for national security affairs—ANSA—being anything more than an in-house staff aide—"a top conference staff person."

Carter shortly thereafter named Prof. Zbigniew Brzezinski of Columbia University, who told the press that he was not planning to be another Kissinger and that he would act purely as a facilitator, rather on the Bundy model.

But the naming of a bright and energetic intellectual and foreign policy activist meant that some of the old institutional strains were likely to persist. "Zbig," as his friends knew him, was an ebullient, wide-ranging, often brilliant political analyst and publicist who, as director of the Trilateral Commission, had been what one commission member, Georgia Governor Jimmy Carter, had called his "teacher."

Dr. Brzezinski's personal élan contrasted sharply with the modest and underplayed approach of the highly competent Secretary of State Cyrus Vance. Given the Kissinger history, it was inevitable that apparent differences would become public, indeed, sought out by the press. The situation was the product both of the system as it had evolved, and of the style of a low-key president who, with sporadic

---

[22]An interesting depiction of what might frivolously be called an "ANSA-free world" is found in the best written of novels by former presidential assistants who cashed in on the Nixon White House notoriety. William Safire in *Full Disclosure* (New York: Ballantine, 1978) demonstrated to his own satisfaction that even a *blind* president could function with the help of only his normal staff, *not* including a Bundy-Rostow-Kissinger-Scowcroft-Brzezinski-Allen. Considering columnist Safire's notorious disagreements with his former White House colleague Kissinger, we can speculate that in this novel Safire succeeded in retroactively doing away with his bête-noir!

exceptions, tended to be permissive and loose in his operation by contrast with a Nixon, who was uptight, close, and secretive. This was unexpected, given Carter's engineer's concern for preparation, detail, and order. Somehow that did not apply to relations with his subordinates.

The National Security Council again was a sometime thing, used for formal meetings only on the gravest of occasions and really once again living out its existence through the NSC staff headed by the assistant to the president (described in official documents as the senior supervisory officer of the NSC staff), and the NSC committee structure.

The Carter-Brzezinski approach to the latter represented another sharp change from previous practices. The elaborate network of committees under the NSC chaired by the National Security Adviser on the Nixon-Kissinger model gave way to two basic committees plus a variety of informal interagency subgroups. The NSC policy review committee (PRC) was set up to develop policy for presidential decision where basic responsibilities fell primarily within a given department, but where the subject also had important implications for the departments and agencies. The chairmanship of the PRC was determined in each case by the subject matter. This meant that the secretary of state, more commonly the deputy secretary of state, or sometimes the number three, the deputy undersecretary of state for political affairs would chair PRC meetings, which were held only where either final agreement had not been reached, or where it had been reached but it was desirable "to sprinkle holy water" over it.

Secondly, political-military committees earlier chaired by Kissinger were collapsed into something called the NSC special coordination committee (SCC) which was intended to deal with cross-cutting issues requiring coordination in the development of options and implementation of presidential decisions, in the area of arms control (the old verification panel function) and more commonly, crisis management (the old WSAG function). The committee was chaired by Dr. Brzezinski, and the effect was once again to impose White House control over the process by which the highest levels of government formulated policy for presidential decision on the most critical national security questions. The SCC reached a peak with the taking of the American hostages in the American embassy in Tehran in November 1979. The SCC then met every morning and was frequently attended by the secretary of state, secretary of defense, the director of Central Intelligence, and other top officials. When the Soviet Union launched its invasion of Afghanistan in December 1979, Afghanistan was simply added to the agenda, and the same crisis management committee continued to meet regularly. Under the SCC there was no formal structure, but it became a custom to have meetings at a lesser level known informally as "mini-SCCs," during which crisis problems were discussed by interagency officials, usually under the lead of Deputy Assistant to the President for National Security Affairs, David Aaron. The pathways to power in Washington are wondrous to behold, and one of them which many people would not normally think of, was the power to make the final version of the meeting's summary record to be submitted to the president. (Perhaps it is rather like having the right of "final cut" in editing a motion picture under preparation—a right jealously fought for by the various participants in the enterprise.) The NSC staff kept this privilege for itself until very late in the Carter administration when Secretary of State Edmund Muskie complained to President Carter about one or another example of Dr. Brzezinski's performance. It was then agreed that it would be appropriate to have Muskie review minutes of PRC meetings before the president saw them.

The NSC staff was shrunk considerably by Dr. Brzezinski, to approximately 35 officers, divided into eight so-called clusters: the regional issues were dealt by small staffs under the headings of Europe/U.S.S.R., North-South, Middle East, and Far East. The so-called functional issues broke down four ways: policy analysis (really the entire defense and military area, the largest in the NSC staff), global issues, intelligence coordination, and international economics. Dr. Brzezinski continued the Kissinger custom of having his own press officer, who, while a member of the White House press staff, was also in fact Dr. Brzezinski's press spokesman (this was one of the stigmata of the Kissinger-Brzezinski approach which was to be eradicated by the team that followed. See below.)

The general structure of operations continued somewhat as it had under Dr. Kissinger. A series of so-called presidential review memoranda (PRM/NSC) were issued "tasking" the State Department and other agencies to come back with analysis, policy options, and recommendations by a given date (the date often slipped, which was one of the persistent sources of tension between the two institutions).

When a bureaucratic recommendation had finally been completely staffed out and presented to the president and he made a definitive decision, a presidential directive (PD) would then be issued to promulgate his decision. This was often done in the form of a memorandum to the various cabinet officers, signed by the president's assistant for national security affairs, indicating what the president had decided.

The reference to "tasking" above is not inadvertent. Not only the president and his National Security Adviser but members of the National Security Council staff as well, would frequently prepare memoranda calling on the secretary of state, or other cabinet officers, or the director of Central Intelligence to take certain action, prepare certain materials, or analyze a given problem. These usually went to the appropriate cabinet officer over the signature of the assistant for national security affairs (or his deputy) and were known as *tasking memoranda* or, less formally, *taskers*. For low-level tasks to be laid on the agencies, the NSC staff memoranda would typically be addressed to the executive secretary of the State Department and signed by the staff secretary of the National Security Council.

So far as the incoming traffic was concerned, there was no change in the previous methods in that the papers from the agencies would be routed to the appropriate NSC staff members, who would then either get additional information, do some negotiating if that was necessary, or call interagency meetings in their office to review the matter further. The latter was often initiated by the NSC staff member before any papers were prepared, in order to generate interagency (or even single agency) action in response to a problem which the NSC staff felt required handling.

As before, the NSC staff member would transmit the final version of departmental papers to the president in the form of a cover memorandum from Dr. Brzezinski, covered in turn by a memorandum from the staffer to Brzezinski. The staff was very active in attempting to provide other points of view, including missing facts, and above all making sure that the president had sufficient options to give an adequate range of choices. It is a sad but inescapable truth that an agency, whether State Department or any other, when asked to provide options is likely to provide a rather limited range of options reflecting the policy conclusions which that agency has reached in its own process of deliberation. After all, like the U.S. government, it too is pyramid-shaped. For a final paper to come out of the top of that pyramid, headed for the president, means that an *intra*-agency discussion, clearance, and decision-making process has already taken place. It is rather unrealistic to expect that that end product will carry equally weighted representations of all different positions, including those rejected by the department, in a neutral tone of voice. This is another reason the president's policy-coordinating staff has a major task, however invisibly it performs that task.

In the 1960s and 1970s, the NSC staff became controversial when the president was presented with options including, but not necessarily limited to, those offered by the appropriate department or departments, and in addition received *specific policy recommendations* from the National Security Adviser. This role of *advocacy* rather than the coordinating function was the main source of the trouble.

It was, however, not the only source. The high visibility Dr. Kissinger acquired after about 1971—cover stories in news magazines, TV interviews, gossip column items, and a sort of worldwide media, and public following—was carried over to a limited degree in the Brzezinski era. Dr. Brzezinski had not only great expertise and the confidence of the president of the United States. He was also an unusually eloquent and energetic person who had a superb talent for shaping the often formless flow of policy events and decisions into coherent and persuasive strategic shapes which helped to explain presidential policy to the people.

Perhaps for that reason, President Carter permitted Dr. Brzezinski to be his public spokesman, and this too made for considerable friction with the secretary of state. Dr. Brzezinski gave press interviews as Henry Kissinger did, not always off-the-record. When Chinese Deputy Premier Teng Xiao Ping arrived in the United States in February 1979 for his path-breaking visit, that great media event began with a dinner at the home of—Zbigniew Brzezinski. Dr. Brzezinski's views were featured at the presidential summit meetings, and the president made him the administration's foreign policy spokesman, along with David Aaron, at the 1980 Democratic Party Platform Committee.

Two episodes created a particular stir. One was Dr. Brzezinski's ebullient performance on the Great Wall at Peking, in May 1978, at which he jokingly challenged the Chinese to a race, with Moscow as the prize. The other was his equally spirited performance at the

Khyber Pass clutching a rifle soon after the Soviet invasion of Afghanistan. Needless to say, the press was always interested, even when they played it straight and did not try to invent friction between NSC and State.

One unusual aspect of the Brzezinski NSC staff were the frequent press contacts which members of the staff had. These were invariably off-the-record, and faithfully recorded nightly in the extraordinarily useful "evening reports" which each *cluster* sent nightly to Brzezinski summarizing the day's activities and contacts, and were circulated to the whole staff the following day—a superlative form of staff interactive communication. But this openness to press also gave State Department officials the feeling that unfavorable press stories were leaked by NSC staffers—a suspicion fully reciprocated by the latter when they read the State Department's side of the story in the same newspapers.

Day-to-day relations between Vance and Brzezinski were in fact, quite civil even when put under occasional strain. On several occasions Vance went to the president for clarification of the two roles and, as stated earlier, the president occasionally let it be known that Vance was his number one spokesman and Brzezinski was being muzzled—but it didn't really happen. Both denied that a rift existed, at least until Vance resigned in 1980 and went public on his view of the proper relationship between the two functions (see Chapter 4).

Others also worried. The House International Relations Committee (later rechristened House Foreign Affairs Committee) wrote the president in spring of 1978 asking who was running the show. Secretary Vance certainly had daily access to the president, and was at his side at all appropriate events. His principal means of private communication with the president, apart from the telephone, was a so-called "nightly note," rather like the NSC staff's nightly report. Brzezinski received a copy of it but it went directly to the president—unlike virtually every other piece of paper from the secretary of state.

Coordination between the agencies was accomplished chiefly through the VBB (Vance-Brown-Brzezinski) Thursday lunches (sometimes breakfasts). Major issues that needed to be discussed by the three, as a kind of informal senior NSC minus the president, were prepared in advance by members of all their staffs and discussed on those occasions.

After Secretary Vance resigned in 1980, as a result of his distress over the decision to attempt a mission to rescue Iranian hostages (which failed), Senator Edmund Muskie became secretary of state. He entered the job with considerable confidence that his stature in the Senate and long experience with the bureaucracy would enable him to gain control of the situation. In the fall of 1980, a frustrated Muskie publicly spoke of the need for reform to eliminate a confusion of American voices.[23] Two months later, after Carter's defeat at the polls, Secretary Muskie sharpened his criticism and urged elimination of the NSC press officer and of official contacts between the NSC and foreign officials.[24]

President Carter was defeated after his first term in the fall of 1980 and we will never know how the National Security policy apparatus might have shaken down—if at all—in a second Carter term. What we do know is that the Reagan administration came in not only saying the same things previous administrations had said confirming the primacy of the State Department and the desirability of a low profile White House staff, but actually acting on that principle!

Before the 1980 election, Governor Reagan's chief foreign policy advisor, Richard V. Allen, defined Reagan's goal as "offloading" the policy formulation task from the White House back to State, and persuading the bureaucracy to become, in fact as well as in name, the lead foreign policy executor. This meant downgrading the National Security Council staff, which according to Allen had a clear-cut staff function of insuring that all options were put before the president, and which ought to function as an honest broker pulling together and collating the inputs of the designated agencies.[25]

When General Alexander M. Haig was nominated as secretary of state, he testified before the Senate Foreign Relations Committee at his confirmation hearings in January 1981 that the president needed a single individual to serve as the general manager of American diplomacy which would be himself, while the National Security adviser would fill a staff role.

So far that was familiar rhetoric. But soon the evidence of a genuine change began to appear. Secretary Haig moved quickly to seize the bureaucratic high ground, handing the president on Inau-

[23] *New York Times,* September 12, 1980.

[24] *New York Times,* September 23, 1980.

[25] See interview with Richard Burt in *New York Times,* June 29, 1980 and subsequent statements.

guration Day a twenty-page memorandum urging that key interagency committees function under the leadership of the State Department. This ploy was not accepted by the White House. But at the same time it was announced that the president's number one aide, Edwin Meese, would be Richard Allen's immediate supervisor, for the first time interposing an additional layer in the White House hierarchy between the assistant for national security affairs and the president. This would not necessarily work in high-speed crises. But nevertheless Mr. Meese moved into the spacious Kissinger-Brzezinski northwest corner office on the first floor of the White House West Wing, and Mr. Allen was consigned to the West Wing basement where Henry Kissinger had begun, and where his predecessors—but not his successors—had operated. Allen spoke of modelling his role after Gordon Gray, one of Eisenhower's low-profile policy aides.[26]

On February 21, 1981 the White House announced the new line-up of interagency committees, an important indicator, as we have suggested, of the geometry of power. The plan involved three separate interdepartmental groups, one on foreign affairs chaired by the State Department, one on defense matters chaired by the Defense Department, and one on Intelligence matters chaired by the CIA. State would set up interagency committees to coordinate foreign policy planning and operations under a Senior Group headed by the deputy secretary. None of those was under the president's National Security adviser. But the NSC staff would decide which issues should be assigned to which committee; that "traffic cop" function itself was an element of power. President Reagan placed crisis management (to the annoyance of the secretary of state) under the vice-president. The NSC staff still prepared the talking points for presidential conversations with foreign leaders, and in fact the NSC staff was increased in size. Some of the familiar White House-State sniping began again.

Where do we come out in this extraordinary history? The president clearly needs his own policy coordinating staff to get matters in shape for decision, and to make sure he gets all sides of the policy arguments that inevitably arise between departments. Neutral adjudicators are needed because other agencies do not accept State's (or Defense's) primacy. In high-speed crises, the president should not have to wait until all of State's bureaus have cleared every detail of a

---

[26]See interview with Hedrick Smith, *New York Times*, March 4, 1981.

paper—often a painfully long process (although as Kissinger once remarked, it is surprising how fast State can act when it wants a particular policy decision badly enough!).

The president must be able to employ what Richard Neustadt called the "action-forcing process." The presidential staff can in those cases helpfully expedite foreign policy making because it can act in the president's name (even if he is not always consulted.) And finally, the availability of a mind-boggling inventory of nuclear weapons at the command of the president gives many of his actions a portentous character that policy decisions forty years ago simply did not have.

Balanced against the benefits of a strong NSC staff are the costs in morale and commitment when State Department officials feel themselves outmaneuvered, criticized, and undermined by the president's men. There may be times to do that, in order to get something vital accomplished. But there may also be times when delay, prudence, and deliberate pace will prove to be better for the country.

Most ANSAs since the job was upgraded in 1961 have been extraordinarily bright and active men who would naturally be impatient with the cat's cradles of government institutions and their often molasses-like flow of policy ideas. As former professors they are used to having innovative ideas, and putting them into circulation. But most State Department officials are accustomed to operating within a career service that has seen White House idea men—and presidents—come and go (even though they often "role-play" NSC staffer when temporarily assigned there.) They may, as Secretary of State Dean Rusk put it when he took office, have the laudable goal of "getting foreign policy off the front page." But the president's political interests may require a media spectacular that shows him in heroic motion.

The ideal would probably be a system nicely balanced between competitive State Department initiative and presidential decision, aided by an efficient and self-effacing staff in the White House. As we have seen, the president must be able to act in an emergency, and his staff needs to ride herd on the bureaucratic process to keep it moving and to keep it sharp. But it should not preempt State by advocating its own preferred policies.

We need efficiency and bright new ideas in conducting our foreign affairs. But in a hair-trigger world full of turbulence, episodic violence, and uncertainty about everything except change itself, slow, if not small, should also be sometimes regarded as beautiful.

chapter four

DRIVING THE MACHINE: PRESIDENTIAL LEADERSHIP

THE SCOPE OF POWER

Before he became president of the United States, Woodrow Wilson said something that was true for a long time:

> The initiative in foreign affairs which the President possesses without any restriction whatever is virtually the power to control them absolutely.[1]

On February 20, 1979, President Jimmy Carter stated the obvious when he said that "the United States cannot control events within other nations."[2] His successor, Ronald Reagan, took office in 1981 on a more assertive and confident note. But even if the U.S. can manage external forces effectively, we have to ask whether the president can really control foreign policy making *within* the United States.

The U.S. Constitution, as we saw earlier, gives the president certain formal powers. He is "Commander in Chief of the Army and

[1]Woodrow Wilson, *Constitutional Government in the United States* (New York: Columbia University Press, 1961), p. 77.

[2]President Jimmy Carter, Address at Georgia Tech, *New York Times,* February 21, 1979.

Navy" (and now the Air Force); he can, "by and with the Advice and consent of the Senate," appoint ambassadors. Perhaps most important, he can "provided two thirds of the Senators present concur" make treaties with other countries that bind the U.S. to do or not to do certain things, and under Article VI, those treaties "shall be the supreme Law of the Land."

As we also noted earlier, the Constitution makes no mention of any of the other important and influential institutions in the United States that are involved in the making of foreign policy. It mentions neither the State Department nor the National Security Council. There is no mention of the steel industry, the AFL-CIO, the shoe lobby, the editorial writers of mass circulation daily papers, Wall Street lawyers, CBS News, or Texas oil interests.

Those and other American institutions are influential in one degree or another. The varied voices of the people—or of the main interest groups (which is not always the same thing)—find their daily expression, not in the White House, but in the Congress. If a president wants to carry the nation along on major foreign policy decisions, he must bring those varied interests together in a collection of what John Calhoun called "Concurrent Majorities." If the president does not do this, he is likely to fail as Wilson did when he triumphantly brought the Versailles Treaty and League of Nations Covenant back from Paris after World War I, only to see a recalcitrant Senate repudiate them, and him.

At the same time, over the years American presidents have interpreted their powers ever more broadly. For almost the entire history of the nation, executive powers in foreign policy have increased. The ink was hardly dry on the U.S. Constitution when a president delayed for a whole year submitting to the Senate the nation's first arms control treaty (the Rush-Bagot Treaty of 1817). Six years later, President Monroe ignored the Congress completely and simply proclaimed the Monroe Doctrine—one of the two or three basic U.S. foreign policy commitments.

In 1940 President Roosevelt reversed two decades of isolationism when he turned over to the beleaguered British fifty overage destroyers in exchange for a 99-year lease of British bases in the Atlantic. He made this momentous deal with a simple exchange of notes!

The most heated controversies arise over the president's ability to put the U.S. in a war. The Constitution reserves to the Congress the power to declare war. However, early in the post-World War II period, in June 1950, President Harry Truman committed U.S. military forces to the defense of South Korea over a weekend, and during the whole "police action" Congress never formally declared war. President John F. Kennedy sent U.S.-backed Cuban emigré forces clandestinely against Cuba in 1961, in an ill-fated counterrevolutionary attempt at the Bay of Pigs. A few years later President Lyndon B. Johnson dispatched into the equally ill-starred Vietnam War half a million Americans and untold amounts of U.S. military hardware (much of which was left behind and eventually used by the victorious North Vietnamese Communists to attack their neighbors). Johnson not only failed to follow the Constitution's allocation of war powers; he never even called it a war, apparently to minimize the domestic consequences.

Twenty-five years into the Era of U.S. Intervention the Congress finally rebelled and reasserted its foreign policy muscle. (In Chapter 5 we catch a vivid glimpse of those newly flexed muscles, including limits on any presidential commitment of U.S. troops abroad without congressional sanction.) But despite recent legislation the president is still the commander in chief, with unhampered authority to order U.S. forces into action, at least initially.

Our little scenario in Chapter 2 showed a worried (although fictitious) president abandoning a cabinet room meeting on food policy and going downstairs to the situation room, where he eventually issued an order sending thousands of U.S. soldiers, sailors, airmen, and marines scurrying forth on missions that could at least potentially cost them their lives and even involve the entire nation in war. No one could stop him, even under the new limits Congress has set on the unlimited initiative Woodrow Wilson celebrated (and tried to practice while in office).

Even apart from this special case of war powers, the presidency is unique in its concentration of power on a huge range of matters. President Carter brought from the Truman Museum the famous sign reading "The Buck Stops Here" and put it in the Oval Office next to a bust of Harry Truman. The moment of truth for a president comes when an undecided issue reaches the top of the governmental pyramid. It can only be decided by the solitary individual who sits alone at the summit.

All too often these days presidential decisions seem to fall, as Edmund Burke once put it, between the disagreeable and the intolerable. Theodore Sorensen, President Kennedy's closest aide, quoted Prussian Chancellor Otto von Bismarck, who may well have been the first modern administrator, on the toughness of top-level choices:

> Every decision a President makes involves uncertainty. Every decision involves risk. Almost every decision involves an element of prediction and at least latent disagreement with others. Bismarck believed that it was these "doubts and anxieties," not the burdens of the daily schedule, which were so wearing on a political official. . . . In the White House, the future rapidly becomes the past, and delay is itself a decision.[3]

An authoritative source on the same point is Bill Moyers, who performed similar functions for the next president, Lyndon B. Johnson. Speaking of the need for presidential staff, Moyers told an interviewer about

> the increased power and responsibility of the President himself—the sense of expectation that causes people to look to the President to solve all foreign and all domestic problems. It has a fallout effect on those around him. No one man can do everything that he, the President, is expected to do.[4]

A close observer of the presidency, former Secretary of State Dean Rusk, said it with due solemnity:

> . . . the President must prepare himself for those solemn moments when, after all the advice is in from every quarter, he must ascend his lonely pinnacle and decide what we must do. There are such moments, when the whole world holds its breath and our fate is in his hands. Then every fragment of his experience, all that he has read and learned, his understanding of his own nation and of the world about him, his faith, conscience and courage are brought to bear.[5]

The responsibility of the modern president is symbolized by the military aide who discreetly accompanies him with the daily code for

---

[3]Theodore C. Sorensen, *Decision Making in the White House* (New York: Columbia University Press, 1963), pp. 10–11, 30.

[4]Interviewed by the chief of *Time Magazine*'s Washington bureau in "The White House Staff vs. the Cabinet," *The Washington Monthly*, February 1969, p. 26.

[5]Dean Rusk, "The President," *Foreign Affairs*, April 1960, p. 369.

the firing of the U.S. nuclear weapons in that ghastly eventuality. This crushing burden, combined with the vastly increased complexity of world affairs, has had the effect of involving the presidency ever more personally in international diplomacy.

One diplomatic consequence of this trend has been an exponential increase in *summit meetings*. These (as we saw in the Introduction) are meetings at the level of head of government (or head of state) rather than at the level of secretary of state and his foreign minister counterparts. Under the American system, the president is *both* head of state and head of government. His meetings at the summit can thus be with kings, queens, emperors, presidents, dictators—or (as with the semiannual Western economic summits) with prime ministers and chancellors.

Summit meetings (unless they are purely ceremonial, such as laying a wreath or accepting a jewelled sword to give to the National Archives) have become a familiar way to conduct business between nations. A nation's top political leaders no longer stick to domestic matters except when it is a question of war and peace. Instead, they talk endlessly to each other about trade, inflation, oil prices, strategic weapons limitations, textiles, steel imports, regional conflicts, agricultural surpluses, and immigration across borders.

Without doubt the currency of summitry has been devalued. Things have reached the point when President A will not consider changing his position on textile imports unless Prime Minister B discusses it with him in person. Alternatively, Premier C will be offended if President D does not reciprocate the state visit he made five years ago, even if the only current topic on the agenda is the sale of half a dozen military aircraft.

Before he became secretary of state to two presidents (who, as it turned out, travelled much and summited often), Dean Rusk gave a series of widely remarked lectures at the Council of Foreign Relations, the first of which was published in the venerable journal *Foreign Affairs* (the other two were dropped as potentially embarrassing to the new Kennedy administration). In the one that was published, Rusk was highly critical of the spreading vogue of presidential jet-age summitry, arguing that

> visits to 20 or more countries in the course of a few months, interspersed by periods of preparation and rest, take too much out of the man and his office. A presidential system cannot easily

> adjust to an interregnum; a nation moving with such great mass and velocity needs the engineer at the throttle. . . . We can be jealous of his time and energy and resistant to every influence which comes between the man and his burdens.[6]

Of course some presidents seem to enjoy their power, and we should not feel too sorry for them. The mystique around the president comes from his awesome powers and responsibilities (particularly his ability to blow up the world), but it also comes from other more mundane aspects—the hush that falls on a room which he enters, the Secret Service men who surround him, the armored limousines flown ahead in advance of his travels, and the historic beauty and elegance of the White House.

If Jimmy Carter at his Inaugural in January 1977 tried to play down what Arthur Schlesinger, Jr. called the *Imperial Presidency*,[7] by walking from the Capitol to the White House, Richard Nixon designed Prussian dragoon-type uniforms for the White House executive police, set up the equivalent of summer palaces in which government business was conducted at his whim, and dressed his top aides in specially designed blazers whenever they rode "his" plane, Air Force One. Ronald Reagan's presidency featured a return to ceremony.

The evidence is compelling that presidents tend to find diplomacy not only fascinating, but far less vexing than, say, managing food prices. It may not be totally unfair to say that some recent presidents were not about to let their secretaries of state reap the glory of well-publicized trips abroad on luxurious jets with huge entourages, cheering crowds lining foreign streets, and worldwide TV beaming the symbolic message to the proud and grateful folks back home—in short, they didn't want the secretary of state to have all the fun.

One-time Presidential Press Secretary George Reedy, in an extraordinarily thoughtful book, suggested that we not feel too sorry for presidents. "A president, in a peculiar sense that does not apply to other people, is the master of his own fate and the captain of his own soul."[8]

---

[6]Ibid., p. 360.

[7]Arthur M. Schlesinger, Jr. *The Imperial Presidency* (Boston: Houghton Mifflin, 1973).

[8]George E. Reedy, *The Twilight of the Presidency* (New York: The New American Library, 1971), p. 37. Copyright © 1970 by George E. Reedy, reprinted by arrangement with the New American Library, Inc., New York, N.Y.

Theodore Roosevelt said it all when he described the presidency as a "bully pulpit"—a notion picked up and used effectively by President Reagan.

THE LIMITS ON POWER

If an "imperial" physical setting and increased personal involvement in diplomacy reflects one trend, equally striking are the feelings of frustration and even impotence by modern presidents, despite the vast authority invested in the presidency by the Constitution, and by the power inherent in America's world role.

Even presidents cannot pull rabbits out of the various hats symbolizing the current intractable world problems of war and peace, inflation, trade, money, or the environment. As we have already glimpsed, even a superpowerful president is constrained by a whole network of forces and influences. Perhaps most startling to the student of power is the notorious presidential inability to really control the executive branch over which he presides! If the external world is hard to tame, so—on the testimony of recent incumbents—is the president's own bureaucracy.

Richard Neustadt, who observed White House operations at close range under Truman, Eisenhower, and Kennedy, wrote a book that became obligatory reading for subsequent presidents the way Machiavelli's *Prince* was for Renaissance rulers.[9] The most appealing thing about the book to an incoming president was Neustadt's sympathy for and understanding of the limits of presidential powers, in contrast to most people's assumption that the president is omnipotent.

Neustadt quotes President Truman as complaining that "I sit here all day trying to persuade people to do the things that they ought to have sense enough to do without my persuading them. . . . That's all the powers of the President amount to."[10]

Truman went on to say something to Neustadt that has been even more widely quoted. Speaking of his elected successor General Dwight D. Eisenhower, Truman, tapping his desk for emphasis, said: "He'll sit there and he'll say, "Do this! Do that!" and nothing will

[9]Richard E. Neustadt, *Presidential Power: The Politics of Leadership, With Reflections From FDR to Carter* (New York: Wiley & Co., 1980).

[10]Ibid., p. 22.

happen. Poor Ike—it won't be a bit like the Army. He'll find it very frustrating."[11]

Neustadt's pathbreaking conclusion? The president's power to persuade "is the power to bargain . . . when a President seeks something from executive officials his persuasiveness is subject to the same sorts of limitations as in the case of congressmen, or governors . . . private citizens, or foreign governments."[12]

A classic instance of failure to persuade was supplied during the Cuban Missile Crisis of 1962. According to written accounts, at one point in the week of life-and-death deliberations by the president and his immediate advisers, U.S. Representative to the United Nations Adlai Stevenson suggested trading Soviet missile withdrawal from Cuba against removal of U.S. intermediate-range Jupiter missiles from Turkey.

President Kennedy informed Ambassador Stevenson that he had ordered those missiles removed from Turkey months before, and therefore they were not available for a deal. It took a brave subordinate to tell the president that his order had *not* been carried out and that the missiles were still in Turkey.[13]

Perhaps the most authentic (certainly the most inelegant) expression of presidential frustration came from the Nixon tapes, which—unfairly—faithfully show the feelings of impotence at the top (unfair because other presidents are spared the embarrassment of seeing their private conversations in print; of course, it was Nixon who shot himself in the foot, so to speak; also because it reflects unkindly on a man who later became secretary of state). "Well, God damn it, I'd told them two weeks ago not to put this out. See, Haig didn't follow up on it. Nobody follows up on a God damn thing."[14]

How can we explain this weakness amid enormous power?

First of all, I think the point, while suggestive, is probably exaggerated. Johnson's Presidential Press Secretary George Reedy said in that very readable book that "presidents glory in telling people that they are prisoners of a system and of circumstances beyond their

[11]Ibid.

[12]Ibid., p. 47.

[13]See, for example, Robert F. Kennedy, *Thirteen Days: A Memoir of the Cuban Missile Crisis* (New York: W.W. Norton and Co., Inc., 1969), p. 95.

[14]U.S. Congress, House, Hearings Before Committee on the Judiciary, 93rd Congress, Second Session, *Statement of Information,* Book VII, Part 2 (Washington: Government Printing Office, 1974), p. 877.

control." Reedy obviously does not agree and suggests that "this is probably the subconscious device by which the chief executive prepares his alibi for history."[15]

He may have a point. The world gets more complicated, and along with it the U.S. government. In some cases the world might be better off if presidents could exercise their full powers, rather than being frustrated by our complex political process. (I'm thinking of the sinful waste of petroleum by us Americans—one barrel in nine of the world's entire supply burned up on our own highways.)

But maybe it isn't such a bad idea after all that a president's every whim is not always catered to. Maybe staff assistants and cabinet departments *should* drag their feet sometimes, for instance: when the president issues an order that will foul up U.S. relations with all of Latin America (Kennedy's ill-starred invasion of Cuba at the Bay of Pigs in 1961); or an order that will blacken the U.S. reputation in much of the world (the 1970 Cambodia "Incursion"); or an order that violates the nation's laws (a number of Nixon's injunctions to his staff were mercifully ignored).

PRESIDENTIAL STYLES AND PERSONALITIES

American tradition has it that any boy (not girl) can become president, even if he is born in a log cabin. (More recently being born rich, like the Roosevelts and Kennedy, didn't hurt either.) The premise was that any normal native-born American could reasonably aspire to the highest office in the land, as his ultimate personal goal.

However, since 1963 one president has been assassinated, his successor driven from office by public turmoil, and *his* successor forced to resign to avoid being impeached. Those three—Kennedy, Johnson, and Nixon, were followed by the relaxed (but underqualified) Gerald Ford, Ford by the seemingly relaxed Jimmy Carter, and Carter by the obviously relaxed Ronald Reagan. But relaxed isn't really enough. My own conviction is that as presently constituted the job of president is impossible to carry out fully. One constant part of it—deciding whether or not to blow up the world—alone puts it beyond reasonable limits for any mere mortal.

[15]Reedy, *The Twilight of the Presidency,* p. 31.

Even campaigning successfully for the job is so bone-crushing a chore that only the hardiest—or most obsessively ambitious—are prepared to see it through. Senator Walter D. Mondale (later elected as Carter's vice president) was a popular entry in the large pack that started out in the 1976 presidential race. Mondale dropped out soon after, pointing out that he had no desire to spend the next year eating rubber chicken at banquets every day in a different city and sleeping in a different motel room every night, not to mention making hundreds of speeches, kissing scores of babies, and shaking thousands of hands.

Thus it is axiomatic that all presidents who are elected to the presidency get there because they ran a superhuman race, after deciding that of all Americans they were the best qualified. To get there, you have to want it very badly indeed. This eliminates the pensive, ambivalent souls (like the late Adlai E. Stevenson, who eventually ran—reluctantly—in 1952 and 1956). It also eliminates those who need a good night's sleep and prefer to spend evenings and weekends with their families. Moreover, it certainly cuts out the faint-spirited—like most of us—who prefer not to have spiteful opponents dig up every nasty secret from the past and convert the most private aspects of one's life into fodder for millions of breakfast newspaper readers and TV viewers.

If the aspirant to the presidency has had little or no administrative experience (like Senators Truman, Kennedy, and Johnson, and Congressman Ford), he none the less is expected to administer one of the world's most massive bureaucratic operations the morning after his Inaugural.

The point is that, unlike almost any other line of work, the presidency of the United States is uniquely placed to attract people with supernatural amounts of ambition, single-mindedness, self-confidence, and physical vitality.

But winning the star role does not necessarily imply any *professional* qualifications. One tries out for the part by showing or demonstrating, not that one can administer a huge government, but that one can win an election (plus dozens of state primaries beforehand). That is doubtless the way it should be in a political democracy, but the result is to gear the presidency to other qualities than demonstrated ability to resolve insoluble domestic and global problems. It may be that nobody, even the giants of the past, could really master inflation,

resource scarcity, or nuclear weaponry. However, my point is that in the TV age, the presidency goes to those best at running a man-killer of a high-speed marathon race with millions looking on. Many a president has found that (as Brazilian revolutionary Francisco Julião was said to have warned his fellow radicals) "to agitate is beautiful, but to organize is difficult."

Lord Acton's famous aphorism about power says that "power tends to corrupt and absolute power corrupts absolutely." The late Andrew Cordier, long-time under secretary general of the United Nations, privately improved on Lord Acton: "All power corrupts, and being out of power corrupts absolutely." The joke turns sober (if exaggerated) in the words of the great humorist James Thurber, who wrote in his later, blind years that "complete power not only corrupts but it also attracts the mad."[16]

The point *is* exaggerated because there are actually great differences between and among presidents. They all have to have the qualities mentioned—ambition, single-mindedness, self-confidence, endurance, but their styles vary widely.

I have mentioned the sign that Harry Truman put on his desk saying, "The buck stops here." Some other postwar presidents have delegated authority broadly. Some—Franklin D. Roosevelt and John F. Kennedy—acted as their own secretaries of state. Others—Harry S. Truman, Lyndon B. Johnson, Richard M. Nixon, Jimmy Carter—probed into the deepest recesses of policy questions. Some—Dwight D. Eisenhower, Gerald Ford, and Ronald Reagan—relaxed in the role of chairman of the board.

Some presidents have run the executive branch in a way an efficiency expert would call chaotic. Roosevelt, Kennedy, and Carter featured a kind of competitive policy making among their top people. (The first two were masters of razzle-dazzle and sly games with bureaucrats. Carter at first tried a wide-open operation, later clamped down on public displays of internal disagreement.)

Other presidents were team players. They cooperated with, and delegated clear authority to, their bureaucratic machine: Truman, Eisenhower, Johnson (except on Vietnam), Ford, and Reagan often deferred to bureaucratic expertise. On paper, Nixon was an excellent

---

[16]Copyright © 1962 Helen Thurber from *Credos and Curios,* published by Harper & Row Pub., New York, originally printed in *Harpers Magazine* as "The Future, If Any, of Comedy," December 1961, p. 43.

organization man, but unfortunately he (and his foreign policy *alter ego* Henry A. Kissinger) were also secretive to the point of keeping everything from all but a few trusted lieutenants. Nixon's distrust of, and fear of betrayal by, the bureaucracy were self-fulfilling prophecies, generating distrust and disloyalty.

Some interesting clues to these differences are supplied by the typologies of presidential character developed by political scientist James D. Barber.[17] He worked with five concepts that help explain presidents: character, world view, style, power situation, and climate of expectation. He then divided presidents into four basic personality types: *active or passive; positive or negative.*

The first pair—active-passive—indicates how much energy a president invests in his presidency. (Like Lyndon Johnson, does he work like a cyclone? Or like President Calvin Coolidge, does he sleep eleven hours a night and nap at midday?) Barber also asks how a president feels about what he does. Does he get fun out of his work, as Kennedy did? Or is it all pretty grim, as with Jimmy Carter?

Barber's ingenious analysis comes down to four basic combinations:

Active-Positive:	(productive, and loving the job)
Active-Negative:	(power-seeking, but with hostile feelings within)
Passive-Positive:	(agreeable, and at least superficially hopeful of achieving big things)
Passive-Negative:	(politics felt as a "duty," with only vague goals)

How about filling in the boxes yourself? (And by the way, where would *you* fit in as president of the United States?)

	Active	Passive
Positive		
Negative		

[17]James D. Barber, *The Presidential Character* (Englewood Cliffs, N.J.: Prentice-Hall, Inc., 1972), pp. 10–14.

Nine Thumbnail Sketches

Franklin Delano Roosevelt was elected to serve an unprecedented four terms. (The Constitution was later amended to a two-term limit, although none since Eisenhower has actually served a full two terms!) As a manager-administrator, FDR's style was chaotic; it was not inadvertent but deliberate. He pitted one cabinet officer against another, asked different people to take on identical assignments, often personally conducted diplomacy and other public business without the knowledge of the responsible cabinet officer, and by the end of his presidency had completely bypassed Secretary of State Cordell Hull in favor of Roosevelt's own friend the Under Secretary of State Sumner Welles.

It is worth noting here that in 1939 a major governmental reorganization created for the first time a White House staff (formally the Executive Office of the President) to help the top man handle the mounting business of the U.S. government growing out of the New Deal at home and the menacing rise abroad of Fascism and Nazism.

Under the old system, the president had been shielded from the department and agency heads, if at all, by a handful of personal retainers or old buddies (in the case of the dying President Woodrow Wilson, it was his wife). Now there would be a variety of White House high-level assistants with what was described at the time as a passion for anonymity. The new staff was to introduce into the presidential operation a new degree of professionalism in the form of unpublicized coordination producing teamwork and a smoother flow of papers, recommendations, and decisions. Forty-eight people were on the FDR presidential payroll (plus several loaned by agencies). That number shot up to 275 by the '50s, and 540 by the '70s.

(We can smirk at that phrase "passion for anonymity" when we look at some of the presidential assistants for national security affairs who in the 1960s and 1970s, at least in a couple of instances, came to dominate the world press, the TV screens, and in the case of Dr. Kissinger, even the popularity polls.)

The fateful step was thus taken to create what amounted to an additional agency of the government with a professional staff. If, as some believe, Franklin Roosevelt considered his cabinet officers his natural enemies, some later cabinet officers would be "forgotten but not gone," as a centralized White House decision-making apparatus bypassed them and left them beached like stranded whales in their great federal-style public buildings.[18]

Vice President **Harry Truman**, who succeeded Roosevelt on the latter's death on the eve of victory over Germany in 1945, was, at first, best known for having been left out of the White House action as vice president. When lightning struck and he was suddenly a wartime president, it turned out that he was unaware of the most important secrets of the government he was to administer, such as the impending atomic bomb and top-level relations with wartime allies Churchill and Stalin.

However, this bustling, feisty, self-educated, history-reading Missourian, ex-haberdasher-become-senator, took over with a vengeance and quickly got on top of the job. Roosevelt's Secretary of State, James F. Byrnes, had become the closest thing the nation ever had to a deputy president. Governor Byrnes treated the new president with ill-concealed disdain. Truman swallowed it humbly until Byrnes bypassed him in dealing with the allied victors at a foreign ministers' meeting, and Byrnes was soon gone.

During the same war, Army Chief of Staff General George Catlett Marshall had become the closest thing the nation ever had to a second George Washington. (Truman later made the comparison explicit.) As Truman's secretary of state, he treated the president with respect and ran foreign affairs with high competence. He went on to be secretary of defense before retiring. His successor at State, Dean Acheson, tall, aristocratic, mustachioed, looked to some resentful congressmen like a British Guards colonel who had swallowed a bad oyster. That was a bum rap, because he was bright (too obviously so for some in Congress), compassionate, effective, and like General Marshall, totally loyal to the World War I Battery B commander who had become his president. Truman's relation with both Marshall and Acheson was a textbook example of mutual respect and delegation that influenced, but was never quite recaptured by, their respective successors in office.

Truman's presidency set in place the basic organization of the U.S. government to conduct the Cold War with the Soviet Union. The new system took the nation through the Truman Doctrine of 1947,

[18]A fine book about the Roosevelt foreign affairs (that is, wartime) presidency is playwright Robert E. Sherwood's *Roosevelt and Hopkins: An Intimate History* (New York: Harper & Bros., 1948).

the Soviet blockade of Berlin and the Czech coup in 1948, the creation of NATO in 1949, and the U.S.-UN response to North Korea's attack on South Korea in 1950.

The National Security Act of 1947 created the National Security Council, about which we have already said a good deal. Truman made use of the new machinery, worked effectively with his key cabinet officers even as the White House staff began to build up, and after a shaky start never shrank from making fateful decisions. But particularly on key decisions in the course of the Korean War, he may have narrowed the useful critical advice available to him by confining advisers to their own areas of specialization.[19]

Truman was given rough treatment by the domestic opposition. Condemned by later "revisionist" historians for being an all-out Cold Warrior who deliberately antagonized the Soviet Union, it is ironic that Truman was savaged at the time by right-wing Republicans (such as then-Congressman Richard Nixon) for "giving away" China to the Communists, sheltering "Communists in government" from Senator McCarthy's attacks, and getting the U.S. into "Truman's War" in Korea. (One of the many ironies of Richard Nixon's later administration was his frequent glorification of two earlier liberals—Woodrow Wilson and Harry Truman!)[20]

Dwight David Eisenhower brought to the White House the habits of mind and working style of the successful supreme commander of Allied Forces in Europe during World War II (and of NATO forces after its creation in 1949). He was used to having problems "massaged" by well-organized staffs. He believed there should be general agreement on policy recommendations at the working level before a problem reached his desk. While in uniform he had been blessed with a top-flight chief of staff, General Walter Bedell Smith (later to be under secretary of state). In the White House he expected the same service from his civilian assistants. He made use of the NSC.

For his own role Eisenhower adopted the strategy of standing above the pulling and hauling of the bureaucrats and politicians, re-

[19]See Alexander L. George, *Presidential Decisionmaking in Foreign Policy: The Effective Use of Information and Advice.* (Boulder: Westview, 1980), p. 125.

[20]Harry S. Truman: Memoirs, 2 vols. (Garden City, N.Y.: Doubleday, 1955–1956) are neither very interesting nor historically reliable. Better on both scores (but unacceptable to the Revisionists) is Dean Acheson's elegant, comprehensive, and self-assured memoir *Present at the Creation: My Years at the State Department* (New York: W.W. Norton & Co., Inc., 1969).

serving to himself the final decision, stepping in where necessary as peacemaker. He delegated, although not as much as people thought.

Under his administration the NSC staff was expanded further, while still operating under a succession of able (and still "anonymous") men. The State Department under another strong secretary, John Foster Dulles, was still the chief source of policy recommendations and also actively contributed to the White House-level coordination by playing the lead role in the NSC Planning Board.

Dulles, a superbly well-informed, arrogant, insensitive, and sometimes hypocritical lay churchman, served Eisenhower for most of the decade of the 1950s, yielding after a fatal illness to the quickly forgotten (but uncommonly decent) Christian Herter.

This strong and willful secretary managed to cut the president's men off at the knees if they took public initiatives that in Dulles' view (a correct view, I feel, despite my criticism) are the prerogative of the secretary of state. Dulles did this with that eternal presidential hopeful, Harold Stassen, when as White House assistant for disarmament affairs Stassen seemed to be going into business for himself with deviant policy pronouncements.

Dulles pushed matters to their logical conclusion when he sounded out the White House on the possibility of having a sort of supersecretary of foreign affairs (as the Hoover Commission had recommended in 1949). It would, of course, be John Foster Dulles. The incumbent would be the president's chief adviser on foreign policy—which the secretary of state is, of course, *supposed* to be under our system, but he would also be running (or rather escaping from), the State Department by working physically in the White House. It apparently struck Dulles (as it later did Henry Kissinger) that to be close to the president, where the great decisions were made, was more fun than managing a large and unwieldy apparatus that was forever urging caution, creating delay, producing administrative headaches for the top man to solve, and for its pains being privately criticized by the NSC staff (and president as well) for sluggishness and lack of imagination.

Eisenhower, as a "Board Chairman," spent more time on the putting green than Washington workaholics found acceptable. However, he knew an unacceptable power grab when he saw one, and Dulles got neither the White House office nor the supertitle. (In 1981 Secretary Haig's early attempt to control the government's decisional machinery was similarly declined.)

Eisenhower, not a great reader, required that virtually all staff recommendations come to him in no more than one page, with a single recommendation for policy action to be checked either yes or no. (Compare that with the multiple options preferred by later presidents.) The one-page limit was really ludicrous for a complex and tangled policy problem, but on some matters it was a healthy corrective to bureaucratic loghorrea and pomposity. The single *yes or no* requirement meant that the bureaucracy had to work hard trying to cut a mutually acceptable deal. It also meant that some policies were served up to the president in very dilute form, all the sharp edges having been filed off in the quest for consensus between competing positions at the subpresidential level.[21]

John Fitzgerald Kennedy was young enough to be Eisenhower's son. He came directly from the U.S. Senate with a record of energy, political astuteness, visible concern for some global social issues (such as aid to India), a bad back, and the habit of using intellectuals to stimulate his thinking.

Unlike Ike, Kennedy was an activist *par excellence*, given to direct action regardless of bureaucratic organizational lines. His style was loose and relatively open. One widely remarked televised glimpse of the early Kennedy administration showed all sorts of personal assistants milling around in the Oval Office while Kennedy put through his own phone call to a Cambridge professor (named, as it happened, Kissinger). If Ike ran the White House the way he ran the army, Kennedy sometimes ran it like a Boston storefront political headquarters.

The dense network of interagency committees set up by Truman and Eisenhower to coordinate all aspects of foreign policy were, as we have seen, abolished. If Kennedy wanted answers to a question, he picked up his desk phone and called the responsible office within the agency, even if it was only an assistant secretary. That habit made for uncommonly alert responses to ringing telephones in the departmental labyrinths, but it also left some obvious gaps in the system of policy coordination.

Just after Kennedy was elected, his personal aides made a survey

[21]See Robert A. Divine, *Eisenhower and the Cold War* (Oxford: Oxford Univ. Press, 1981.) The reader might consult Walt W. Rostow, *The United States in the World Arena* (New York: Harper & Bros., 1960), Townsend Hoopes' *The Devil and John Foster Dulles* (Boston: Little, Brown, 1973), and of course Eisenhower's memoirs, Dwight D. Eisenhower, *The White House Years: Mandate for Change 1953–1956* (Garden City, N.Y.: Doubleday & Co., 1963).

of foreign affairs experts to solicit recommendations for the top jobs. Most people who were asked reportedly urged for the job of secretary of state Dean Rusk, a former State Department official who was then president of the Rockefeller Foundation. Many of those solicited also informed the Kennedy survey team that the brightest individual they knew was McGeorge Bundy, then Professor of Government at Harvard. Kennedy, who scarcely knew either man, interviewed them and chose both.

Rusk was a decent and thoughtful man who later became inexplicably locked into an increasingly dubious set of propositions about the monolithic nature of Asian Communism and the parallels between contemporary communist-nationalist movements and the aggressive Fascist dictatorships of the 1930s. His model for secretarial comportment was Secretary of State George C. Marshall. Marshall, with his towering stature among Americans, played an Olympian role of taciturn judge among the squabbling bureaucrats, reserving final judgment until he and the president were alone. By all reports Rusk tried to bring the same dignified approach to the uniquely free and easy Kennedy conclaves with his advisers. As a result, Rusk reportedly failed to make State Department inputs count when they mattered most. (Notable examples were State Department diffidence in opposing wrong-headed DOD and CIA forecasts before the Bay of Pigs, and later failure to push State's expertise on Indochina to counter favorite administration theories about the area.)

The point is doubtless exaggerated by Kennedy partisans, who scorned the aloof Rusk and derided the measured tread of State Department motion. Rusk, in fact, saw a great deal of President Kennedy, but the influence of State declined in proportion as real power (in the sense of influence over the president's thinking) flowed away from Foggy Bottom and toward the White House basement (and also toward the Pentagon under the dynamic Defense Secretary Robert S. McNamara).

In the basement of the White House West Wing there sat the president's special assistant for national security affairs, McGeorge Bundy, who with an initially small staff, plus consummate skill, converted the traditional interagency arguments into a series of ordered *options* for presidential consideration, rather than the watered-down *YES-NO* choice that reflected a compromise position agreed to by the agencies. Now the president would receive not only a faithful summation of agency views—which he did—but a more sophisticated array of boxes to check, each representing a different solution for a foreign policy dilemma.

The system did not necessarily produce better foreign policy outcomes, or even better policies. The new president's first meeting in June 1961 in Vienna with Soviet Premier Nikita Khrushchev was reportedly brutal, featuring some inexperienced presidential floundering in the presence of the tough, earthy Soviet leader. (Unlike American leaders who can run for office from any background, Soviet leaders are men who have risen through a monolithic party hierarchy with no genuine popular elections or provisions for succession when leaders die. The qualities which count in the tough road to the top in Moscow are personal influence, organizational skill, and ruthlessness.)

The disastrous U.S.-sponsored invasion by Cuban emigrés at the Bay of Pigs in April 1961 was in part due to the notion that Kennedy had to show Khrushchev how *macho* he could really be. In part it was also because of faulty U.S. intelligence predictions of mass uprising of the Cuban people. And in part it happened because the State Department (and Kennedy's own White House advisers on Latin America, such as Arthur M. Schlesinger, Jr.)[22] were bashful with their advice that an attempt to overthrow Castro would produce a disastrous setback in U.S.-Latin American relations. (Kennedy is reported to have said later that he would never again listen to the experts; it is not clear that he in fact ever did.)

The Cuban Missile Crisis in 1962 is believed by many—including the author—to show Kennedy as a wise, sober, and courageous leader in the face of what was undoubtedly the gravest threat of nuclear war during the postwar period.[23] But as I will argue in Chapter 8 in discussing the various "models" of policy-making behavior, the Missile Crisis is not a good example of how the government functions. On that occasion the government as a whole was almost entirely disconnected from the policy process, with the president and his top advisers

[22]See his account in Arthur M. Schlesinger, Jr. *A Thousand Days* (Boston: Houghton Mifflin, 1965), p. 296.

[23]There is substantial literature on the tragically brief Kennedy years, since the Kennedy entourage included numbers of literary-minded people. Theodore Sorensen's *Kennedy* (New York: Harper & Row, Pub., 1965) and Arthur Schlesinger Jr.'s *A Thousand Days,* are probably the best. (Dean Rusk, loyal and modest to the end, has stoutly refused any suggestion that he write what he has called "kiss and tell" memoirs.)

constituting an EXCOM (Executive Committee) of the NSC, never before in existence as such, but useful for the purpose.

Lyndon Baines Johnson succeeded Kennedy when the latter was tragically struck down in Dallas, Texas in November 1963. Johnson immediately announced his intention to continue Kennedy's work unchanged (as Truman had at a comparable moment). Actually, Johnson did better than Kennedy in pushing civil rights and other social legislation through the Congress. However, his dreams for a new economic and social deal for poor Americans of all colors (The Great Society) foundered in the quagmire of Vietnam, along with dreams of a strategic arms control agreement with the Soviets, and of being the peacemaker who would bring warring parties to "reason together."

Johnson was initially more open than Kennedy to systematic foreign policy making. In Chapter 2 we saw how he accepted the recommendations of General Maxwell Taylor for a fresh structure of interagency coordination in the form of units known as SIG-IRGs (Senior Interdepartmental Group and Interdepartmental Regional Groups).[24] As usual, genuine interdepartmental collaboration depended on whether the State Department people, dealing with, say, Asia or Africa, were interested in having collaborative policy discussions or tried to exclude others from sensitive questions of policy.

Another cause of failure was that other agencies with foreign policy concerns made end-runs around State directly to the White House. History seems to demonstrate that complexly structured coordination mechanisms rarely last through an administration. White House staff coordination, in the name of the president, turns out to be increasingly appealing to presidents who are fed up with what they and their assistants usually see as bureaucratic squabbling, sniping, and end-running.

The National Security Council rarely met under Johnson, but a less formal coordination mechanism "The Thursday Lunch," developed. It was attended by the president, the secretary of state (still Dean Rusk), defense (still Kennedy's "whiz-kid" Robert J. McNamara), the director of the CIA, and the president's assistant for national security affairs (now Walt W. Rostow, who had originally been Bundy's deputy, then went to State to run the Policy Planning Staff in the

[24]See Maxwell Taylor, *The Uncertain Trumpet* (New York: Harper & Row, Pub., 1960).

face of considerable disinterest and skepticism—see Chapter 9). In effect, the Thursday lunch was the National Security Council, meeting informally around a White House luncheon table.

This decision-making command group increasingly sealed out those growing elements of the bureaucracy who were losing their enthusiasm for the Vietnam War. Johnson, a basically insecure and suspicious human being despite his huge ability and experience, made fidelity to his Vietnam policy the acid test of membership in the closed circle. When in 1967 McNamara began to express doubts, he was cut out of the pack (and invited by Mr. Johnson to become president of the World Bank, where he went on to do a remarkable job).

President Johnson himself eventually became the closest thing to the U.S. government's Vietnam desk officer. He selected detailed targets for U.S. bombing runs, demanded information that would show the U.S. to be doing well, and defined ever-changing standards for judging success and failure. (Needless to say, people down the chain of command often biased their reports to comply with the president's predilections.)

Johnson's increasingly paranoid reaction to criticism, in a situation that was gradually tearing apart the internal fabric of the United States of America, provided a textbook example of "selective perceptions" on the part of political leaders who filter out the information they do not want to hear and distort incoming signals to fit into their own belief structure (more on this in Chapter 8).

On the testimony of Johnson's staff, he was personally a bully, with a high capacity for cruelty toward his subordinates accompanied by a sentimental streak of concern for their families, and a weather eye for his place in history. Toward many who served him, his strategy was the same as that toward his younger brother, Sam Houston Johnson: Keep him weak enough to take orders and strong enough to carry them out.[25]

In a sense, Vietnam destroyed both Johnson and his successor, **RICHARD M. NIXON**, but the record of Nixon's presidency is even more scarred by its traumatic ending of hasty resignation a step ahead of the sheriff, so to speak. In Nixon's case, the White House-orches-

[25]Johnson's memoirs, given the saltiness of his own personality and language, are extraordinary for their dullness. A fascinating glimpse into his head is supplied by Doris Kearns, *Lyndon Johnson and the American Dream,* written after his retirement on the basis of 5 A.M. interviews in her bedroom (apparently innocent) at the Johnson ranch on the Pedernales River in Texas (New York: Harper & Row, Pub., 1976).

trated coverup that followed the Watergate break-in compounded the number of "enemies" already acquired at home by his failure to end the Vietnam War. As with Johnson, Nixon's denouèment obscured some other important things that happened during his presidency.

Nixon put into effect a managerial revolution in the White House, under the direction of Harvard Professor Henry A. Kissinger as his assistant for national security affairs, the effects of which we saw in the last chapter. Suffice it here that the 1969–1974 White House, even before it was made a bastion against Nixon's own bureaucracy, had become the true center of power and influence in the U.S. foreign policy-making process, culminating the process of decision-making centralization accelerated by Nixon's two Democratic predecessors.

Communist parties around the world have always taught organizational skills to their cadres as a form of judo by which to manipulate and eventually topple the massive but soft structures of democratic rule. Kissinger, with Nixon's guidance and direction, used somewhat the same kind of organizational judo to bring to heel what both of them (Nixon through experience as congressman, senator, and vice-president, Kissinger through his studies of bureaucracy) recognized as the "warlordism," so to speak, of the great "barons" of the career foreign service in State, the career military officers in the Pentagon, the economists and monetary experts in Treasury, and the career spooks in Langley, Virginia (the neatly manicured rural home of the CIA.)

If LBJ kept people weak to manipulate them, Nixon chose weak people, such as Secretary of State William Rogers, to avoid having to deal with them at all. In the same spirit, one side benefit of the new system of presidential directives, designed to make the agencies study and report on a myriad of topics, was to tie up the bureaucracy for months at a time so Nixon, Kissinger, and the immediate White House staff could get on with the business of implementing their own diplomacy.

Influence and information—and ready access to the president and White House—are the hard currency of Washington. It wasn't long before leading foreign ambassadors with something to tell the U.S. government went directly to the White House, rather than to the State Department. Routine diplomacy continued to be conducted by State, and the great juggernaut of government gave the outward appearance of continuing as before. But the center of gravity not only shifted to 1600 Pennsylvania Avenue in principle, starting with Kennedy, but now it shifted in practice as well.

Back-channel strategic arms limitation (SALT) negotiations with the Russians and openings to China were both conducted in great secrecy by Kissinger, under Nixon's supervision. In the first case Kissinger was actually in Moscow for several days speaking to Chairman Brezhnev for the president of the United States without the American ambassador even knowing he was in town. In the second case Kissinger was also the emissary, in an elaborate deception involving rumored dates with glamorous women in Paris restaurants and mysterious flights from Pakistan. Even when U.S.-Soviet arms control negotiations for SALT I became routine, formally backstopped by the Verification Panel under Kissinger's chairmanship, a separate back-channel still functioned for private communications between the White House and the Soviets on the most crucial issues, with the U.S. delegation in Helsinki often unaware of changes in policy that were being discussed through that circuit.[26]

The Nixonian-Kissingerian passion for secrecy was even carried to the extreme of not taking an official American interpreter into some of the pivotal presidential talks with Soviet leaders, but rather relying on the official Soviet interpreters. The latter are darned good; but this was clearly a serious breach of responsibility both to the U.S. government and to history-reading posterity.

The policy results were nevertheless often spectacular, and those involved would argue that such secrecy and deception, along with the extreme narrowing of the official action circle, were necessary to bring about the turn-around in U.S.-Chinese relations (still spectacular) and U.S.-Soviet relations (obviously less durable).

As Watergate-plus-Vietnam moved the Nixon presidency to its final destruction, history provided a replay of Mrs. Woodrow Wilson running the U.S. government from the bedside of her paralyzed husband. This time the steadying hand was General Alexander Haig, called back by Nixon to be chief of the White House staff (and in 1981 made secretary of state). It is rumored that precautions were taken to

[26]For details see Henry A. Kissinger, *White House Years* (Boston: Little Brown, 1979), also John Newhouse, *Cold Dawn: The Story of SALT I* (New York: Holt, Rinehart, 1973), and Gerald Smith, *Doubletalk: The Story of SALT I* (New York: Doubleday, 1980).

ensure that the desperately beleaguered (and clearly neurotic) president would not, in a kind of Nixonian *Götterdämmerung,* do anything dangerously spastic.[27]

Gerald R. Ford was hand-picked by the fading Nixon to be vice-president of the United States after Vice-President Spiro Agnew was forced to resign or face prosecution for corrupt behavior in office. Ford became president when Nixon fled the office. If Nixon was hot, Ford was cool; if Nixon was paranoid, Ford was generously open; if Nixon was clever, Ford was simple (as he himself told the nation, "I am a Ford, not a Lincoln.").

It was not surprising that Ford, like Johnson on succeeding Kennedy, promised to continue the policy lines of his stricken predecessor. But unlike Johnson, Ford had a normal ego and thus in fact did continue the same general policies, both in bending to the post-Vietnam spirit of drastically reduced activism abroad, *and* in demonstrating *machismo* in the *Mayaguez* Incident to prevent underestimation of U.S. determination. Symbolic of the "deimperialization" of the presidency was Ford's change of language referring to the White House as the *residence* instead of the traditional *mansion* (continued under Carter), and from "Hail to the Chief" to untrumpeted entries into rooms (continued but then reversed under Carter).

Ford kept Henry Kissinger on as secretary of state, but soon yielded to mounting right-wing criticism of the Nixon-Kissinger detente policy and took back the White House hat Kissinger had continued to wear even after moving to Foggy Bottom. Kissinger's sucessor, his deputy Lt. General Brent Scowcroft, was made chairman of four of the key interagency committees within the NSC structure, although Secretary Kissinger continued to chair the Verification Panel backstopping the SALT talks, as well as the WSAG crisis management group. As for the NSC itself, Ford convened it for his *Mayaguez* theatricals, but otherwise generally followed the narrower staff channel favored by his predecessor.

Ford's foreign policy activity was fundamentally guided by Dr. Kissinger, who was the principal actor in formulating two major policy changes: on North-South relations (i.e. how the rich countries

[27]See Richard Nixon, *RN, The Memoirs of Richard Nixon* (New York: Warner, 1979), as well as the Kissinger memoir (*op. cit.*). The former is dull, the latter mordant and often brilliant. Also, for the fun of it, several thinly-veiled novels by Nixon staffers, notably John Ehrlichman, *The Company* (New York: Simon & Schuster, 1976) and William Safire, *Full Disclosure* (New York: Ballantine, 1978).

would help the poor ones) in 1975, and in U.S. African policy in 1976. But Ford's defeat in the November 1976 election curtailed any innovations that might have come from a Ford second term based on election as his own man.

Even more than Gerald Ford, **JIMMY CARTER** represented a major—if short-lived—reaction against the "Imperial Presidency." Georgia Governor Carter was soft-spoken, modest, low-key, uncharismatic—and inexperienced in federal affairs. Unlike virtually all his predecessors, Carter was trained in engineering (at Annapolis and Georgia Tech) and skilled in managerial duties (in business and the Atlanta State House).

But he came in to office in January 1977 determined to be his own foreign policymaker. Perhaps to compensate for lack of experience, he became famous for being a workaholic. In his own words:

> The first two years I was in office, I literally worked day and night. I got up every morning at 5 o'clock and I was working until 5 o'clock in the afternoon. . . I felt it was necessary because I needed to know the interrelationship among the agencies and departments in the complex structure of government, the relative priority of budget decisions that I had to recommend to the Congress. I had to know the identity and character of the nations and their leaders with whom I had to deal. I had to know some of the history of things right up to the present time, how it was modified or affected by Truman or Eisenhower or Nixon or Ford or Kennedy and Johnson. There was a breadth of knowledge that I felt that I had to have."[28]

Carter's desire to blur the awesome quality of presidential charisma was dramatically exemplified by his bareheaded post-inaugural walk from the Capitol to the White House. But in time he too yielded to the temptations—and pressures—to assume a personal role in world diplomacy, to listen more to his immediate entourage, and to opt for White House (i.e., NSC staff) rather than State Department policies on key issues.

Before he took the oath of office, Jimmy Carter promised a decision-making style different from that of his predecessors. He even proposed (quixotically, as it turned out) having his key cabinet officers answer questions regularly before both houses of the Con-

[28]Interview with Boston *Globe,* Aug. 22, 1980, by Martin F. Nolan "No Apologies for His Style," reprinted courtesy of Boston *Globe.*

gress in front of live TV, so that executive policymaking would be open to the Congress and the people.[29] Not a bad idea, if only for public education, but never tried. (Secretary of State Haig met with the whole Senate in March 1981, but behind closed doors.)

Despite signals that the White House was no longer going to preempt the cabinet, the NSC-State Department conflict became more fierce than ever. And despite a threat by one of Carter's closest aides that he would not serve in the White House if members of the dominant eastern foreign policy establishment such as Cyrus Vance and Zbigniew Brzezinski were brought in, Carter named Vance to be secretary of state and Brzezinski to be assistant for national security affairs.

Vance had inherited Dean Rusk's title as unofficial Grand Panjandrum of that same "Eastern Establishment." He had campaigned for Kennedy kinsman Sargent Shriver, but became a key Carter transition adviser. Professor Brzezinski had been director of the nongovernmental Trilateral Commission, and in that capacity became Commission member Governor Jimmy Carter's "teacher" (in Carter's words) and friend as well.

For a year or so, relations were smooth. As outlined in Chapter 3, the elaborate Kissinger White House committee structure was reduced to two key committees: the special coordinating committee for crisis management, chaired by Brzezinski; and the policy review committee, chaired by the State Department or whatever agency was most involved. Dr. Brzezinski also shrank the Kissinger NSC staff to about 35 professionals. But the power of the NSC staff over the government's foreign affairs community, rather than declining, continued to mount. This was due in part to Brzezinski's capacity to conceptualize foreign policy fragments into articulate and coherent overall themes. But it was also due to his activism, Vance's low-key and modest temperament, and the tendency of both men's staffs to reflect their bosses' relative positions in the real power structure. (Clearly, it was also because President Carter wanted—or tolerated—it that way.)

Differences surfaced publicly within a year, over Soviet military shenanigans in the Horn of Africa. Dr. Brzezinski increasingly argued for linking such misbehavior to the SALT negotiations; Vance (who

---

[29]*New York Times,* June 7, 1976.

was more committed to arms cuts) deplored such linkage. Other disputes hit the press. Vance eventually took his frustrations to the president, who several times was reported to have put his National Security Adviser under wraps. But new strains developed over Brzezinski's highly visible role as point man in the normalization of relations with China, and as the president's spokesman who was photographed pointing a rifle in the general direction of Afghanistan from the Khyber Pass shortly after the Soviets invaded that country. The breaking point came with the Iranian hostage crisis of 1979–1980. Carter's fateful decision to try a clandestine rescue mission (which failed) was made while Vance (who opposed it) was out of town. Vance subsequently resigned, and for the first time went public, saying that having three foreign policy spokesmen "created confusion as to what the policy of the nation is." He went on to say, "The national security adviser . . . should act as a coordinator of the various views. But he should not be the one who makes foreign policy or who expresses foreign policy to the public. That is the task of the president and the secretary of state."[30]

Carter himself, far from being content with acting as the board chairman model of foreign policymaking, was a detail man. The National Security Council, as such, rarely met, being in effect replaced by Friday morning breakfasts of the president with his top foreign policy team. When President Carter took personal charge of Middle East peacemaking, his intimate and continuous involvement in not only the policymaking but the detailed diplomacy as well could be compared only with that of Lyndon Johnson on Vietnam (except that Carter's virtuoso "Camp David Diplomacy" was hailed by all, except the Arab parties left out of the process).

Like presidents before and after him, Carter liked to helicopter to Camp David to think things out, alone or with only his chief counselor, his wife Rosalynn (an intelligent and serious person who did not deserve the occasional snide criticism of her advice on policy matters). But in Washington Carter drove hard, even if his critics claimed to find him often inept or disorganized.

Veteran Washington correspondent Don Oberdorfer fills out Carter's own daunting self-portrait with which I opened this vignette:

---

[30]Baltimore *Sun,* May 5, 1980.

> At 5:30 A.M. daily, when the Rose Garden and the South Lawn are in darkness and most of Washington is still asleep, Jimmy Carter sits down at a small, hinged table before a crackling fire in the Oval Office and makes decisions. For two hours before his day officially begins, he attacks stacks of papers with a felt-tipped or ballpoint pen in a clear, bold hand. He checks the option boxes on the decision papers, writes memos to senior aides, and adds to official reports his marginal notations and instructions: "be tough," "agree," "Let's move," and, occasionally, "nuts."
>
> Carter is a clean-desk man, whose personal rule is to act on all business reaching his desk within a day of its receipt. He is activist in his methods, ambitious in his goals, wide-ranging in his interests, restless in his tendency for comment or command regarding matters great and small. He is a man forever in motion, rarely at rest.[31]

The *Economist* provided a wry political epitaph at the end of Carter's brief—but by no means failed—presidency:

> He was an appealing, wholesome boy next door with a wall-to-wall smile that made you feel warm all over. He was just like you and me, except that he didn't have our shortcomings. In consequence, he has been too much like you and me to make a good president. The blemishes that his critics now bemoan are the qualities many admirers applauded in him four years ago. . . .[32]

If Jimmy Carter was the embodiment of a backlash "Populist" reaction to the Kennedy-Johnson-Nixon "Imperial Presidency," **RONALD W. REAGAN** presented himself to the electorate as a kind of "Restoration" chief executive.

Not that President Reagan was stuffy or pompous; on the contrary. Where Carter was tense Reagan was, in the best California style, loose, mellow, and laid-back. Where Carter was a self-confessed workaholic, Reagan was a deliberate nine-to-fiver (although that soon slipped to nine-to-six plus a full evening's reading). Where Carter insisted on dealing with policy at the level of detail, Reagan delegated authority to his subordinates. And where Carter gave National Security Adviser Brzezinski free rein to speak publicly in the president's name on a wide range of foreign policy questions, field an activist and

---

[31] Washington *Post,* February 18, 1979.

[32] The *Economist,* August 3, 1980, p. 11.

freewheeling staff, and win most of the basic policy arguments with the secretary of state, Reagan hired a strongman as secretary, and moved Adviser Richard V. Allen back into the West Wing basement where his predecessors had sat prior to Henry Kissinger. He favored cabinet meetings to the point where he matched the newly-revived National Security Council with other "councils" similarly drawn from cabinet membership. He delegated much to "Prime Minister" Meese.

In short, it looked like another Eisenhower-type "collegial presidency": a board chairman with a board (or series of boards) to share the load, a take-hold activist as secretary of state, and a quiet and self-effacing White House National Security Council executive and staff. But there was one important difference. Reagan, unlike Carter, had been a spokesman for strongly held foreign and strategic policy views for a very long time (69 years old on his Inauguration Day, he was the nation's oldest new President). The people around Reagan in his campaign and in the newly spruced-up Washington social and political order, took their policy cues from the top man rather than vice versa. This fact guaranteed that it would be a Reagan foreign policy, not a Haig or Weinberger—or Allen—one. That was surely different from that other "board chairman" president, General Ike, who gave Secretary Dulles enormous running room.

Nevertheless, General Haig resembled Secretaries Dulles and Kissinger far more than he resembled Secretaries Rusk, Rogers, Vance, or Muskie. Tough-talking, he had been fired in the crucible of Nixon's flaming White House (where, having earlier served as Henry Kissinger's deputy National Security Adviser, he later returned as Nixon's terminal White House chief of staff). On being named in 1981 to the senior cabinet post, he lived up to his reputation as an ambitious bureaucrat who knew his way around Foggy Bottom well, but, strangely enough, not in the inner pathways of the "palace" where key decisions would be made. Defense Secretary Casper Weinberger acted the part of "hawk," who reflected Reagan's general worldview. But would from time to time have to be reined in when their tough approach went beyond that of the president who, whatever his earlier rhetoric, had to be leader of all the nation, and of much of the non-Communist world as well. Haig himself became more cautious.

Like Carter, Reagan brought his vice president into the scene of power and out of the oblivion to which the nation's Number Two man was historically consigned. Carter's VP, Walter ("Fritz") Mondale, had kept his ornate second floor ceremonial office suite in the Old Executive Office Building, but worked in a West Wing office a few steps from Brzezinski—and from the president. The same pattern was followed by President Reagan with his VP George Bush, who had run against Reagan in the Republican primaries, and had previously served as permanent U.S. representative to the United Nations (under Nixon) and director of CIA (under Ford). Reagan went even further and put crisis management under the direction of his vice president. (He also set up an informal NSC Planning Group.)

We ought to be able to draw a few conclusions from this series of brief sketches of presidents as foreign policymakers.

Thinking back to James D. Barber's provocative typology of "active-passive," "positive-negative" presidents, it seems pretty obvious that "active" presidents choose relatively "passive" secretaries of state (Roosevelt-Hull, Kennedy-Rusk, Johnson-Rusk, Nixon-Rogers—but not Nixon-Kissinger—and Carter-Vance). But "passive" presidents who rely heavily on their staffs and cabinet officers often tolerate secretaries of state as headstrong as John Foster Dulles (Christian Herter was an exception in the waning Eisenhower years). That pattern was followed by Ford-Kissinger and Reagan-Haig.

Presidents willing to tolerate a strong secretary of state (like Dulles, Kissinger, or Haig) also tend to delegate to the State and Defense Departments the authority and responsibility to carry out their assigned mission. This happened with Truman, Eisenhower, "Nixon II," Ford, and Reagan—but not with Kennedy, Johnson, "Nixon I," or Carter.

The reciprocal effect is logically found in the White House staff, with active presidents featuring a strong righthand man, and passive ones using a low-key, low-profile National Security Adviser.

You should have enough facts now to decide for youself which combination seems to serve the country best. Whatever your verdict, you might also ponder the astonishing rate at which modern America chews up and spits out its presidents. The 22nd Amendment was passed so no president after Roosevelt could duplicate his astonishing feat of being elected to four terms. But the sad fact is that no president since Eisenhower has actually served out even two full terms. The great nineteenth century circus impresario P. T. Barnum once remarked that to keep a lamb in a cage with a lion requires a large reserve supply of lambs. At the going rate of depletion maybe we need to keep more presidents handy.

chapter five

THE SECOND BRANCH: THE CONGRESS

The "Constitution is an invitation to struggle for the privilege of directing American foreign policy."

Edwin S. Corwin

The Congress shall have Power

To lay and collect Taxes . . . and provide for the common Defence and general Welfare of the United States . . .

To regulate Commerce with foreign Nations . . .

To define and punish Piracies and Felonies committed on the high Seas, and Offences against the Law of Nations . . .

To declare War, grant Letters of Marque and Reprisal, and make Rules concerning Captures on Land and Water . . .

To raise and support Armies . . .

To provide and maintain a Navy . . .

Constitution of the United States
Article 1, Section 8

I am extremely indebted to John Victor Gano for his substantial research and writing assistance in developing material for this Chapter.

A DIALOGUE

Scene: The curtain rises on the "Hideaway" office of the Speaker of the House of Representatives in the United States Capitol. This office, more intimate and convenient than the Speaker's massive and ornate formal quarters, has for a long time been the scene of important, usually relaxed, after-hours chats between the Speaker and key members of Congress. (When Sam Rayburn of Texas was Speaker, he was famed for his "Five O'Clock Seminars" there over bourbon and branch water.)

Today the Speaker's guest is an outsider who has slipped in through a back entrance, unnoticed by the all-watchful Capitol Hill press corps. The visitor is the president of the United States. The president is there for three reasons.

First, he is disturbed—as most of his predecessors were—over the recent swing toward the Congress of foreign policy-making powers presidents usually dominate, if not actually monopolize. Secondly, he has long promised to engage the Speaker in a leisurely, hopefully friendly debate of executive-legislative relations on foreign policy questions. (He privately hopes to convince the Speaker of the need to mend Congress's meddling ways.) Thirdly, he welcomes the excuse to get out of the Oval Office for a couple of hours.

It does not matter if our imaginary president's name is Ron or Jimmy or Teddy, or if the fictitious Speaker is Tip, or John, or whatever. Both play their roles as foredained by those wily geniuses who wrote into the U.S. Constitution the balanced invitation mentioned in the often-quoted statement of Professor Corwin at the beginning of this chapter.

As the curtain goes up, the Speaker opens a small, hidden bar and pours drinks for himself and the president. They both take a sip, stretch their legs, and start talking at once.

President: (laughing) No, you go ahead, Mr. Speaker. It's your bar.

Speaker: Thanks, Mr. President. You don't usually let me get in the first word.

President: For good reason!

Speaker: But I'll accept your invitation. (He pauses, looking up at the framed facsimile of the Constitution on the wall over his desk.) It sometimes seems to me that our modern lawyers would have insisted on dotting all the *i's* and crossing the *t's* in that gloriously flexible document. And what a mistake that would have been! Those eighteenth century lawyers who did the drafting must have gone to a very special law school.

President: I'll bet it was in California.

Speaker: I doubt it! But if they had insisted on fixing up all the fine print, I don't imagine we'd have a Constitution today. Think of the "silences of the Constitution," as Arthur Schlesinger, Jr. calls them. Nary a single word about any foreign policy action except regulating commerce, or an act of war, or a treaty!

President: That's what I've been trying to tell you, Mr. Speaker. The Founders knew the Constitution would have to grow organically, like a tree. Look at all the interpretations put on it by our own predecessors and by the Courts. I'll even grant you some of those interpretations to save an argument.

You fellows in the Congress just kind of *developed* a whole bunch of powers, like the power to legislate on matters relating to nationhood such as immigration, or the rights of aliens, or diplomatic immunity. And consider this: Congress can acquire territory for the U.S. by joint resolution (which *I* am forbidden to do by the Supreme Court). You can pass *sense of the House resolutions* or *Senate resolutions,* or *concurrent resolutions,* or *joint resolutions,* on any foreign policy subject. And your joint resolutions are legally binding on me unless I veto them.[1]

You can do lots of other things. You can withhold funds. You can attach *riders* to appropriation bills to force executive compliance on certain issues (usually, I might add, ridiculously unrelated, like sticking into odd bills in the 1960s the requirement that the U.S. share of the UN budget be brought down to 25 percent).

Speaker: You're telling me how powerful the Congress has been—sometimes. As it should be! But everyone I know agrees that the *presidency* has achieved *even greater* power, sometimes by just taking it! Take a look:

You've got control over the information gathered by U.S. diplomats abroad. Up here we don't forget that your very first predecessor was quick to convert that advantage to a legal precedent for *execu-*

[1]Daniel S. Cheever and H. Field Haviland, Jr., *American Foreign Policy and the Separation of Powers* (Cambridge: Harvard University Press, 1952), p. 15.

tive privilege by refusing to turn over to the House documents on the Jay Treaty.

Don't forget, your control of foreign policy *execution* gives you a monopoly on formal contact with foreign governments. And by the way, I can't think of a single one of your predecessors who hasn't done something to develop that power further. I mean things like dispatching presidential special agents to conduct diplomacy. And I certainly mean the whole dubious business of dodging the treaty process by signing *executive agreements.*

President: (looking at his watch) I secretly predicted you'd start on executive agreements within fifteen minutes of my arrival and by God, Sir, you have.

Speaker: You bet I have—and I'm coming back to them again. Listen, Mr. President, I've got most of U.S. history on my side.

> *Item*—Our nation wasn't fifteen years old when Thomas Jefferson bought the Louisiana Territory—a third of the whole darned country—without any congressional authorization.
>
> *Item*—The impact on U.S. foreign policy of the Monroe Doctrine was greater than that of most treaties. But what was it? It was an *executive statement of policy* and thus required no congressional approval!
>
> *Item*—Abraham Lincoln, bless him, during the dark days of the Civil War used powers so extensive that no other president after him has dared cite his precedent to claim all of them. In the ten weeks after the attack on Fort Sumter, Lincoln delayed the convocation of Congress while he "reinforced Sumter, assembled the militia, enlarged the army and navy beyond their authorized strength, called out volunteers for the three years' service, disbursed unappropriated moneys, censored the mail, suspended habeas corpus and blockaded the Confederacy."[2]
>
> *Item*—President McKinley may have been reluctantly dragged into the Spanish-American War by Congress. But who decided to retain control of the Philippine Islands at the war's end? McKinley, that's who! You remember the famous story. While he "walked the floor of the White House . . . and prayed to Almighty God for light and guidance" Congress consented, although its advice was not solicited. And of course his Secretary of State, John Hay, announced and expanded the Open Door

---

[2]Arthur M. Schlesinger, Jr., "Congress and the Making of American Foreign Policy," *Foreign Affairs,* (October 1972), 99.

policy in China with similar disregard for the Congress.[3] And President "Teddy" Roosevelt took even greater liberties.

Item—President Wilson circumvented a Senate filibuster and on his own say-so authorized the arming of American merchant ships—an act which he considered "practically certain" to lead the United States into the First World War.[4]

President: And then when the war ended, he neglected to include the Senate in the peacemaking process and brought disaster on his head when the Senate rejected the Versailles Treaty and U.S. membership in the League of Nations. A mistake *I* certainly won't make!

And now that I've finally got the floor from you, Mr. Speaker, isn't your U.S. history just a wee bit selective? I'll grant you there have been times when the president has pushed pretty hard and had his way on foreign policy. That's the way it's supposed to be, though you probably won't agree. But just look back again. After that early period, when presidents *had* to act boldly to get the new ship of state off the building chocks and into the water, and following the end of Andy Jackson's presidency in 1837 until 1897, we had half a century (never mind the Civil War period) when Congress took practically all the initiatives.

Item—In 1843, the Senate rejected a claims treaty with Mexico by attaching unacceptable amendments to it.

Item—In 1868, the Senate changed the rules so it could add treaty amendments by only a simple majority.[5]

Why, from 1871 to 1898 the Senate ratified no important treaty at all, to the point where Professor Woodrow Wilson referred in 1885 to the Senate's treaty-making power as the "treaty-*marring* power," and future Secretary of State John Hay said he didn't believe "another important treaty would ever pass the Senate."[6] And then from Wilson's time to F. D. Roosevelt's, the pendulum swung back to the Congress.

[3]Cheever and Haviland, *American Foreign Policy and the Separation of Powers,* pp. 58, 60.

[4]Alton Frye, *A Responsible Congress: The Politics of National Security* (New York: McGraw-Hill, 1975), p. 184.

[5]Cheever and Haviland, *American Foreign Policy and the Separation of Powers,* pp. 48, 51.

[6]Schlesinger, "Congress and the Making of American Foreign Policy," 89.

Speaker: (mildly) You do remember that the membership of the Senate Foreign Relations Committee that killed the World War I treaties was stacked, 6 to 10, in favor of the so-called "irreconcilable" opponents of the League of Nations.[7] We could call that a kind of historical accident, couldn't we?

President: *But* for fifteen years after that the Senate delayed, and then rejected, U.S. admission to the World Court, passed the Japanese Immigration Exclusion Act (1924) against Executive advice, overrode a veto to press for Philippine independence, banned loans from American citizens to states defaulting on U.S. government loans, and passed the "Ludlow Resolution for a National Referendum on a Declaration of War."[8]

Wait a minute, that's just the start! Then the Neutrality Acts of 1935–1937 embargoed arms sales and loans to all belligerents in foreign wars, right in the middle of Hitler's rise. The executive was even denied the right to discriminate between aggressor and the aggressed. Why, with aggression on the march, the Congress legislated "permanent neutrality" as the keystone of U.S. foreign policy.[9] It wasn't till three months *after* the outbreak of World War II that the Congress bent the Neutrality Act enough to allow arms sales to France and Britain, and then only on a "cash and carry" basis. *And* it was a full year after the Battle of Britain (and a mere four months before America's entry in the war), that Congress renewed the Selective Service Act by the margin of only a *single* vote. (He pauses for breath.)

Speaker: That's a mighty powerful list, Mr. President. I'm certainly not going to sit here and defend the ostrichlike postures of those isolationists at a time when history's storm signals were flying. But isn't there just a *chance* that at least on some of those items the Congress was reflecting the sentiment of the people?

President: Of course. But once World War II began in earnest, it was clear that President Franklin Roosevelt had been right, and the Congress wrong.

Speaker: But did he have to go whole hog with his use (*I'd* say "abuse") of executive prerogative? Let me give you a few more "items!"

---

[7]Cheever and Haviland, *American Foreign Policy and the Separation of Powers,* p. 76.

[8]Ibid., pp. 81–88.

[9]Ibid., p. 90

Item—Roosevelt used executive powers to bypass Congress on a whole gamut of vital policies: the destroyer-bases deal with Britain on September 2, 1940; the U.S. occupation of Greenland and Iceland on April 10, and July 7, 1941; the unspoken declaration of naval war on Germany by using U.S. Navy ships to convoy goods to Britain with orders given on September 14, 1941 to shoot German U-boats "on sight."[10]

Item—FDR covertly ordered "the closest possible marriage" between the FBI and the British Secret Intelligence Service and kept it secret even from the Department of State. He secretly sanctioned the establishment of British Intelligence's headquarters in New York City, and told its chief (Sir) William Stephenson, "I'm your biggest undercover agent."[11]

President: Now we're talking about *war powers.* That's a whole debate in itself. In World War II the world had changed, and the American people changed with it. The war, and the postwar period, were a brand new challenge we had to meet.

Speaker: To the point where we on the Hill finally had to blow the whistle in the 1970s.

President: Now you're talking about Vietnam and Watergate. The 1980s are different.

Speaker: It was that, of course, but it wasn't *just* that. The whole balance of the constitutional system was going out of whack. Let me remind you of some devastating figures showing how *"Cold War powers"* (if I can coin a phrase) escalated right out of sight from World War II to the time the Congress began to assert its constitutional role. Ready?

Between 1789 and 1946, the Senate passed between 900 and 1,000 *treaties* (and killed a couple of hundred) plus 200 *executive agreements.* But from 1946 to 1971, while there were 947 *treaties,* there were *4,359 executive agreements.*[12] Why do you suppose we're so gun-shy up at this end of Pennsylvania Avenue?

President: Mr. Speaker, I know this isn't a popular argument up here. But you know as well as I do that the Supreme Court has repeatedly

---

[10]Schlesinger, "Congress and the Making of American Foreign Policy," 93.

[11]William Stephenson, *A Man Called Intrepid* (New York: Harcourt Brace Jovanovich, 1976), pp. 77–80, 101–102, 127.

[12]Cited by John B. Rehm, "Making Foreign Policy through International Agreement," cited in Francis O. Wilcox and Richard A. Frank, *The Constitution and the Conduct of Foreign Policy* (New York: Praeger, 1976), p. 127.

supported the expansion of presidential power in foreign policy. In that famous case *U.S. v. Pink,* the Court ruled that executive agreements bear a "similar dignity" to treaties ratified by the Senate.[13] It ruled in that other famous case *U.S. v. Curtiss-Wright Export Corp. et al.* that the president alone has the power to represent the nation in foreign affairs and that "into the field of negotiations the Senate cannot intrude. . ." Just listen to these words describing the "very delicate, plenary and exclusive power of the President as the sole organ of the federal government in the field of international relations."[14]

SPEAKER: What you're saying is that we were intimidated from the very beginning! I understand President George Washington came storming out of his very first advice-seeking session on Capitol Hill, vowing he would be damned if he ever went there again. Of course that swayed the Supreme Court. They knew he was the Father of Our Country!

PRESIDENT: My friend, your history is very instructive—but incomplete.

Just consider the lengths to which postwar presidents have gone—including yours truly—to include the Congress in foreign policy making. We've *learned* our lesson.

Sure, the Congress laid a lot of the groundwork. During World War II, the Fulbright Resolution and the famous "B2H2" Resolution (wasn't that named for Messrs. Ball, Burton, Hatch, and Hill?) set Congress on the road to international postwar cooperation. Senator Vandenberg's role as a leading Republican isolationist led to one of the really transforming moments in American political history. Who can forget that in the middle of World War II, he switched over to active U.S. participation in building the postwar order? His conversion made possible a bipartisan foreign policy, with Congress a partner in the peace process, and indeed in the whole set of postwar policies. Until, that is, Congress decided to tie the President's hands again!

But before you interrupt, I also want to remind you that *presidents* also set the stage for *cooperation* by Congress. When the time

[13] 315 U.S. 203 (1942) cited in Cheever and Haviland, *American Foreign Policy and the Separation of Powers,* p. 9.

[14] 299 U.S. 304 (1936) cited in Schlesinger, "Congress and the Making of American Foreign Policy," p. 79.

came to write the peace, the last thing Franklin Roosevelt wanted to be was another Woodrow Wilson (and the same was true of most of his successors). Even at the height of Roosevelt's wartime powers, he took care to forestall a peacetime backlash of congressional power of the kind that had fatally wounded Wilson. FDR's Secretary of State, Cordell Hull, put the Democratic chairman plus one Republican member of the Senate Foreign Relations Committee on his Advisory Committee on Postwar Foreign Policy. He eventually added five other senators and eight representatives.

FDR took great pains to involve influential members of both parties and members of both Houses of Congress in the early formulation of the UN Charter. He established a bipartisan committee of eight Senators from the Foreign Relations Committee, and appointed four congressional leaders as U.S. delegates to the San Francisco Convention that set up the UN in April 1945.[15]

Speaker: I can't argue with any of that. I am in no doubt that it paved the way for the overwhelming approval by the Senate of the UN Charter, and the opening of a whole new era of responsible U.S. involvement in the world.

President: And those early postwar foreign minister conferences with the British, Russians, and French—the secretary of state went abroad flanked on each side by a leading Republican and a leading Democrat!

And my friend, the same approach was used in *all* the key foreign policy moves that together made up our overall postwar U.S. posture. Before he presented his historic billion dollar aid to Greece and Turkey to Congress in 1947, President Truman met with congressional leaders of both parties to win their support. The Marshall Plan that rebuilt Europe had significant inputs from various congressional committees. Two things I'm talking about—executive-legislative cooperation and bipartisan Senate support—were right out front in May 1948 when the resolution "advising" the president to form a peacetime alliance with Europe—which became NATO—was written by Senator Vandenberg, then chairman of the Foreign Relations Committee.[16]

It's still going on. Presidents regularly appoint a member of the House and Senate to be on the U.S. delegation to the annual sessions

[15]Cheever and Haviland, *American Foreign Policy and the Separation of Powers,* pp. 101–104.

[16]Ibid., pp. 123–128.

of the UN General Assembly and to many other international conferences as well. And God knows how many thousands of hours the president's cabinet officers have put in testifying before all the committees dealing with foreign affairs up here. (Reaches for his glass.)

SPEAKER: How about a refill?

PRESIDENT: Put some water in it this time, would you? (Both laugh. Glasses are refilled, and the men stretch and reseat themselves.)

SPEAKER: Mr. President, you outdid them all when you hit Washington. We can't complain we weren't consulted. But, there's still formal *powers!* I guess we can't duck the "war powers" question any more, can we?

PRESIDENT: Ah, now we *really* get down to it. I guess you know my basic position is the same as all my predecessors. There are times when the U.S. has to respond to a challenge, and you just can't have 535 men and women in Congress debating it for weeks. American lives may be at stake. Allies may be attacked. Theoretically, I may have to give an order that will blow up a good part of the world (Lord, I hate that thought!) So how can a president have his hands tied when the country can be wiped out by missiles that take less than half an hour to arrive? How can he get consent in such a crisis, let alone 'advice'? The nuclear age has changed everything. You have to allow for instant decisions. And don't forget, knowing that a president has that power contributes mightily to the deterrence of potential attackers.

SPEAKER: Mr. President, no one will argue about the need to be able to respond in a total emergency. But some of us up here feel that argument has been a bit of a cop-out. I mean, thank God that in real life the problems usually arise in slow motion. Not always, of course. President Truman presented Congress with a *fait accompli* by sending help to South Korea when it was attacked in June 1950. Oh sure, there were some informal consultations with congressional leaders before U.S. troops went into action. And, of course, there had been formal UN Security Council approval. Truman justified his refusal to seek formal congressional authorization by calling the Korean war a *police action.* His Secretary of State, Dean Acheson, said it all when he claimed

> Not only has the President authority to use the Armed Forces in carrying out the broad foreign policy of the United States and implementing treaties, but it is equally clear that this authority

may not be interfered with by the Congress in the exercise of powers which it has under the Constitution.[17]

President: Sure, but didn't President Eisenhower go to the Congress in 1955 to get the Formosa Resolution authorizing him to employ the armed forces as he deemed necessary to defend Taiwan and the Pescadores? And in 1957 the Middle East Resolution authorized him to use troops to defend nations attacked by "communist controlled nations."[18] (following which he sent the Marines to Lebanon.)

Speaker: That was then. By the 1960s, things began getting out of balance. I was a great Jack Kennedy supporter. But in the two foreign policy actions for which he is most remembered—both of 'em in Cuba—his ties with Congress sure left a lot to be desired. The U.S.-backed invasion at the Bay of Pigs in 1961 was not a response to any attack, but JFK never sought congressional authorization. It was planned and supported by the Central Intelligence Agency, and let's remember at that time there was no formal Senate watchdog committee. So for a decade the CIA was a potent tool for presidential foreign policy actions that were often kept secret from Congress.[19] No wonder we set up special "oversight committees" in each House to keep CIA on the rails—*and* Congress in the picture.

In the Cuban Missile Crisis—the closest we've come to the nuclear nightmare—Kennedy short-circuited the whole governmental process. He consulted exclusively with a small, ad hoc executive committee that did not contain a single member of Congress. Mind you, I'm not criticizing his superb handling of the crisis.

President: If I'm not mistaken, Kennedy once stated as a *senator* that "it is the President alone who must make the major decisions of our foreign policy."[20]

Speaker: The whole process still went much too far. Lyndon Johnson invaded the Dominican Republic in 1965 on the pretext of protecting

[17] Schlesinger, "Congress and the Making of American Foreign Policy," 95.

[18] The War Powers Bill," Legislative Analysis, No. 19, 92nd Congress (Washington, D.C.: American Enterprise Institute for Public Policy Research, April 17, 1972), pp. 8, 55.

[19] *Background Information on the Committee of Foreign Relations, United States Senate* (Washington, D.C.: U.S. Government Printing Office, 1975), p. 8. CIA oversight was at the time informally delegated to an ad hoc subcommittee composed of three members each from the Appropriations and Armed Services Committees.

[20] Frye, *A Responsible Congress,* p. 187.

American civilians. He also stampeded Congress into the Gulf of Tonkin Resolution in 1964 giving him *carte blanche* to escalate Vietnam into a big war, without ever coming to the Congress to declare war under its constitutional authority.

President: There's a lot of controversy as to whether he faked you out or not. Some argue that he escalated the U.S. presence in Vietnam in a very democratic way.[21] Anyway, your colleagues passed the Tonkin Gulf Resolution by *88 to 2* and *414 to 0*. And don't forget you overwhelmingly supported earlier presidential requests for authorization to use force "as necessary" to keep the peace or stop aggression. I've already mentioned the congressional resolution about Formosa on January 28, 1955 and the Middle East on March 9, 1957. Let me add Cuba, September 26, 1962, and Berlin, October 10, 1962.

Speaker: But no one then dreamed that presidential power would be stretched to the point of Nixon's invasion of Cambodia in 1970. What was even more shocking to Congress was that Nixon made none of the usual excuses for unauthorized foreign intervention—you know, national security, appeal from an ally, congressional resolution, and so on. He justified his act as "the Constitutional duty of the Commander-in-Chief to take actions necessary to protect the lives of United States forces."[22] He also lied to the Congress and the American people about the months of secret bombing that preceded it. My God, even after Watergate and his forced resignation, Nixon still insisted that if the president does it, that makes it legal. (Picking up steam.) *Then* President Ford attacked Cambodian territory after the *Mayaguez* was taken—and freed, as it turned out. *Then* President Carter sent uniformed soldiers inside Iran in the ill-fated Hostage Rescue Mission in 1980 (OK, that was a "SWAT" squad, not a military action). And *then* President Reagan sent more U.S. military "advisers" into El Salvador in 1981 . . .

President: (mildly) I know, I know. And it won't happen again (*sotto voce*) at least for a while anyway.

Look, I'm not going to sit here and try to defend anyone who abused his authority from the Oval Office. But (a little wistfully) can you really quarrel with LBJ when he said, "There are many, many who can recommend, advise, and sometimes a few of them consent.

[21]Leslie H. Gelb, with Richard K. Betts, *The Irony of Vietnam: The System Worked,* (Washington, D.C.: Brookings Institution, 1979).

[22]Schlesinger, p. 102.

But there is only one that has been chosen by the American people to decide"?[23] And would you really argue in favor of the late Senator Bricker's attempt to hog-tie the president with his crusade in the early 1950s—fortunately unsuccessful—for an amendment to the Constitution which said: "An international agreement other than a treaty shall become effective as internal law in the United States only by an act of the Congress"?[24]

Speaker: (mischievously) Maybe it wouldn't have been such a bad idea at that . . .

President: (ditto) It seems to me that as a junior member of the House at the time, you spoke out powerfully against it . . .

Speaker: Touché! But history is history. By the late 1960s Congress was beginning to wonder why it even bothered to get up mornings and come to the Capitol. By the end of the 1960s, when President Johnson used the Gulf of Tonkin Resolution to claim congressional *authorization* for the Vietnam War, and when Under Secretary of State Nicholas Katzenbach called that resolution a "functional equivalent" of a declaration of war, Congress became positively incited.[25] We felt we'd been blindsided. I don't need to remind you of the backlash on war powers that began to snowball.

President: I guess it started with Chairman Fulbright's televised Foreign Relations Committee hearings in 1966 on Vietnam policy.[26]

Speaker: I think the first major assertion of Congress's desire to reclaim its foreign policy powers was the National Commitments Act of 1969 proposed by the same Bill Fulbright and passed by the Senate 70 to 16. Remember? "A national commitment by the United States results only from affirmative action taken by the executive and legislative branches of the US government."[27]

President: It wasn't legally binding on the president. I mean, when Congress finally voted to repeal the Gulf of Tonkin Resolution, the Vietnam War was full-blown, and President Nixon cited his commander'in-chief powers to pursue it.[28]

[23]Schlesinger, p. 101.

[24]Cited by W. Taylor Beverly in Wilcox, *op. cit.,* p. 128.

[25]Frye, *A Responsible Congress,* pp. 190–91.

[26]See Francis O. Wilcox, *Congress, the Executive and Foreign Policy* (New York: Harper & Row, Pub., 1971), p. 31.

[27]*Congressional Quarterly,* 1970, p. 14.

[28]Frye, *A Responsible Congress,* p. 191.

SPEAKER: Let me just quote my colleague Congressman George H. Mahon of Texas in 1969. "There was a time that any member of Congress would hesitate to vote against anything proposed by the Joint Chiefs of Staff because he might be subject to the charge of being soft on Communism." But because of the Vietnam War, "that day is over."[29]

PRESIDENT: In the light of history Fulbright was probably right. But he was also a darned obstructionist. He overstated things. Sometimes he did flip-flops. After all, he had argued in 1961 that "we have hobbled the President by too niggardly a grant of power." But a few years later in the early 1970s he was talking about the "Presidential dictatorship in foreign affairs."[30]

SPEAKER: Did it occur to Fulbright's critics that lots of other people changed their minds on Vietnam?

PRESIDENT: Don't ask me to justify Fulbright. I'm not going to justify Nixon either, or LBJ for that matter. God, how the Vietnam War devoured presidents. . . .

SPEAKER: . . . and countries.

PRESIDENT: Nixon really tilted the machine, and that made life harder for those of us who followed him.

SPEAKER: How about us? We really had to dig up here to uncover the commitments Nixon made to Spain. I mean, there was a commitment that the chairman of the Joint Chiefs called "a far more visible and credible security guarantee than any written document."[31] Or how about the unilateral presidential commitments also made to Thailand, Laos, and South Korea?[32]

PRESIDENT: I'm not going to defend that. And I'm certainly not going to justify the White House response to congressional pressure, which was to actually *decrease* voluntary data sharing, and invoke "national security" and "executive privilege" as grounds for denying disclosure.

[29]Wilcox, *The Constitution and the Conduct of Foreign Policy,* p. viii.

[30]Schlesinger, "Congress and the Making of American Foreign Policy," 99 and Senator J.W. Fulbright, "Congress and Foreign Policy," *The Commission on the Organization of Government for the Conduct of Foreign Policy* Murphy Commission, Appendix L (Washington, D.C.: U.S. Government Printing Office, 1975), p. 58.

[31]Frye, *A Responsible Congress,* p. 207.

[32]*Background Information,* p. 36 and Schlesinger, "Congress and the Making of American Foreign Policy," p. 101.

Speaker: Then we really came down hard on the president.

President: And I'm still suffering from the fallout.

Speaker: But I *can* defend our next steps—the Case Act, and the War Powers Act. Remember, the Case Act did something about executive agreements with a stiletto that the Bricker Amendment had tried to do with a bludgeon: "The Secretary of State (must) transmit to the Congress the text of any international agreement, other than a treaty, to which the United States is a party as soon as practicable . . . but in no event later than sixty days thereafter."[33]

It passed 81 to 0 in 1971.

But even with it presidents still had the clout they needed. They only had to certify that "immediate public disclosure" would be "prejudicial to the national security." They can confine their consultations to members of the Senate Foreign Relations Committee and the House Foreign Affairs Committee, and they can even keep that from being full, public, or immediate.

President: That limited the *executive agreements,* and you'll notice we're not going that route very often these days. But don't you think you fellows went a little overboard with the War Powers Act that came next? I mean, under that Act I am allowed to commit troops only in case of a declaration of war, specific authorizing legislation, or a "national emergency," defined as an attack on the U.S., its territories, or its armed forces. I have to consult Congress "in every possible instance." I have to report within 48 hours to the Speaker of the House and the president *pro tempore* of the Senate, in writing, any commitment or significant increase in troops abroad. These two officials are authorized to reconvene Congress, if necessary, to consider my report.

And in my humble opinion you *really* changed the balance by providing for an automatic termination of my troop commitment within sixty days (with one possible thirty-day extension) unless Congress expressly approves. You empowered Congress to direct the president to disengage troops at any time by a concurrent resolution immune to veto.[34]

Speaker: But would you have vetoed it, the way Nixon did (on October 24, 1973) on the grounds that it would be "both unconstitutional

[33]Wilcox, *The Constitution and the Conduct of Foreign Policy,* p. 130.

[34]*Congressional Quarterly,* 1973, p. 2741.

and dangerous to the best interests of our nation" and that it would "give every future Congress the ability to handcuff every future President merely by doing nothing and sitting still"?[35] Because if you had, I'll bet the House would still have overridden the veto the way it did—284 to 135, and the Senate by 75 to 18.[36]

President: (pensively) I see a mixed picture. I guess I have to agree with Arthur Schlesinger, Jr.'s ironic reflection that had the War Powers bill existed before, "it would surely have prevented Roosevelt from responding to Hitler in the North Atlantic in 1941, and would surely not have prevented Johnson from escalating the war in Vietnam."[37] (He pauses.) How times change! In the nineteenth century, two of our nation's five declared wars were instigated, not by a president, but by a war-prone Congress . . . (he stretches his legs).

At the time Congress was probably right to blow the whistle with the Clark Amendment when the president tried to keep the U.S. in another civil war—I mean the one in Angola—through indirect CIA help. That's only because I believe in doing things openly if you have the choice. I don't even mind having to send up to you practically every proposal I make to get military equipment to a friendly country. You probably did me a favor by making the SALT II treaty pretty obviously unratifiable. I'm not even objecting to the "legislative veto" you threatened on the fighter plane deal to Israel and Egypt in 1979 to sweeten them up for the peace effort, and to Saudi Arabia for Persian Gulf security. Because you later agreed!

But what bothers me is that once you fellows got the bit in your teeth, frankly I think you began to foul up American diplomacy. The Jackson-Vanik and Stevenson Amendments to the 1974 Trade Reform bill tied Ford's hands in dealing with the Soviets. The Symington Amendment in 1976 cut off all U.S. aid to potential nuclear proliferators. Fair enough, but the president needs flexibility.

Carter objected strongly to Congress putting the U.S. in violation of the UN embargo on Rhodesia for a couple of years for the sake of chrome. And I don't like to see us violate World Bank rules by specifying that our contribution can't be used to help certain countries

---

[35] Pat M. Holt, *The War Powers Resolution* (Washington, D.C.: American Enterprise Institute for Public Policy Research, 1978), p. 8.

[36] *Congressional Quarterly,* 1973, p. 2985.

[37] Schlesinger, "Congress and the Making of American Foreign Policy," 103.

that Congress is mad at. I think you were *way* off base barring U.S. arms sales to Turkey after the 1974 Cyprus blowup and crippling our diplomacy on NATO's southern flank. Don't get sore if I suggest that you would probably have put the ban on *Greece* instead of *Turkey* if Turkish-Americans had the lobby in Congress that Greek-Americans have!

SPEAKER: You're cutting pretty close to the bone, Mr. President.

PRESIDENT: Sorry! But if this trend continues, you're going to make it impossible for *good* executive branch policies to be carried out. I may not like Jimmy Carter's human rights policies. But in all fairness, when he took office in 1977 Congress had already amended both the Foreign Assistance and the Arms Export Control Acts to mandate the human rights test. Not to mention the congressional laws on U.S. aid to about 30 countries *by name*. You may wind up paralyzing the whole system!

SPEAKER: Oh, I don't think there's any danger of that! After all, by March 1979 President Carter had already begun nibbling at our restrictions. By certifying for the first time that "an emergency exists," he sent arms off to North Yemen, bypassing Congress for the first time under the Arms Export Control Act. And boy, is my arm still aching from the White House twisting it got for my vote on the 1977 Panama Canal Treaty!

PRESIDENT: But that was a treaty, not an executive agreement, right?

SPEAKER: Yes. But (present company excepted) why, oh why, is the White House usually so inept when it comes to *understanding* the Congress? Why do all those 'congressional liaison' people from the executive branch wait so long before putting us in the picture?

PRESIDENT: Why do so many congressmen and senators persist in logrolling dams and post offices for the folks back home as a cynical trade-off against vital foreign policy legislation?

SPEAKER: Why do presidents play politics by sending up campaign contributors we don't always think are qualified to be ambassadors or deputy secretaries of state?

PRESIDENT: Taking the gloves off, are we? Why do some members of Congress only understand as much of an important bill as they can learn while their legislative assistants brief them on that 30-foot walk from the elevator to the floor for a quorum call?

Speaker: Why can't your cabinet officers ever understand the importance to the legislative process of floors, ceilings, and cutoff dates?

President: Why is it true of Congress, as Scotty Reston of the *New York Times* once said, that "if you scare 'em they go crazy, if you don't scare 'em they go fishing"?

Speaker: Why don't we restore bipartisanship to foreign policy so politics can once again stop at the water's edge?

President: Why can't Congress understand the links between domestic and foreign policy in an age of interdependence that makes what you just said obsolete?

Speaker: Why don't you let us in on all the vital foreign policy secrets so we can have a real partnership instead of a resentful one?

President: Why can't Congress stop talking to the press on every occasion—including things we tell them in confidence, like the "detection" of the Soviet brigade in Cuba in 1979? That helped cost Carter his presidency.

Speaker: Why can't White House staff members stop doing the same thing and then blaming Congress for leaks? (And by the way, blowing the lid off that Cuba story didn't help Foreign Relations Committee Chairman Frank Church one bit, if you recall the 1980 election results in Idaho!)

President: Why can't you arrange for members to do the kind of homework that will make you better equipped to function in the late twentieth century, instead of polishing up the Senate spittoons?

Speaker: (slyly) Why did Winston Churchill say that democracy was the worst form of government, except for all others? (They both pause for breath, then burst out laughing.)

President: My Lord, look at the time. Does your budget run to a short one for the road? But then, I'm forgetting that, unlike me, you can vote your own budget and then spend it.

Speaker: (filling his glass) You're welcome.

President: Thanks. (Sips) Well, where have we come out? I'll admit without argument that you people up here *set broad limits to what the president can do.* And I really do believe that's the way it should be. As the man said, the president proposes and the Congress disposes.

Speaker: You're being too modest by half. What presidents usually want—and, alas, sometimes get—is to propose and then have the Congress roll over and softly bark "yes."

President: Well now, we're both men of the world and deep students of American history. Wouldn't you agree that in the very nature of things, the president and the Congress have quite different responsibilities—really, different *constituencies*? After all, you're close to your voters back home. You run for office every two years . . .

Speaker: The only really silly mistake made by our venerable forebears!

President: Of course I'm elected too—but by all the people. My responsibility is to them—and to the outside world I'm supposed to deal with. Even if we're catching hell abroad, you up here can still try to pass protectionist legislation and say you're defending American manufacturers and labor. The president has the dirty job of fighting those bills because he is trying to negotiate reciprocal tariff deals with almost 100 other countries. I mean deals that cut down *their* trade barriers too, so that *our exports* can be sold abroad. You know as well as I do that more than ever these days it means U.S. profits and jobs too. Yet Congress usually acts parochially and responds all too readily to special interests. And then I take the rap for saving you from yourself.

I'll give you another example—foreign aid. I try to salvage the U.S. reputation for generosity. (Did you know we are now about sixteenth on the list of donor countries in terms of per capita contribution?) Congress gets credit back home for sending money to the cities, the farms, or wherever, instead of wasting it on "ungrateful foreigners."

Speaker: Cool down, Mr. President. (And you're not that generous!)

President: Sorry. But what I'm saying is I have to work with *both* constituencies, foreign and domestic: Congress sometimes acts as if it has only the one. If the State Department is the lawyer for the foreigners we deal with—and sure, that sounds unAmerican—well, the president is in the same fix.

Speaker: Why did you run for the office?

President: Seriously, members of Congress should read Edmund Burke's Speech to the Electors at Bristol.

Speaker: I can quote it verbatim. Members should act on their consciences, in the larger national public interest, where it conflicts with the narrow interests of their constituents. But did you ever walk down the main street of your hometown the day after trying to act like just that kind of statesman in Washington?

President: Can we agree the perspectives are different from both ends of Pennsylvania Avenue?

Speaker: You bet. But I don't concede for a minute that our concern up here for the national interest isn't as valid, and as devoted, as yours. It's just sometimes *different*.

President: It sure is. Well, I have to get back to the salt mine. Thanks for the drink.

(Curtain)

chapter six

PUBLIC OPINION: CITIZENS, LOBBIES, AND PRESSURE POLITICS

Under the Constitution the U.S. government has three branches—executive, legislative, and judicial. We have seen how deeply involved the first two are in foreign policy making. (The courts get into the act only when a specific case comes before them, and even then they are usually allergic to second-guessing the president or getting between him and the Congress.) In the United States (though not many other countries) *non*governmental organizations and individuals also play a major role in the formulation of foreign policy.

THE FOURTH ESTATE

During the French Revolution the *press* came to be known as the *Fourth Estate.* That label acknowledged the unofficial, but none the less real, involvement of newspapers in the policy process. The media today include not only the printed word but also TV. Taken as a whole, they constitute a kind of massive communications bridge between government and people. In the U.S.—but not in all countries—the media not only report the news and editorialize about it, giving their own slant to what is happening, but also see themselves as watchdogs who guard the people from abuses of power by government. There is thus a kind of adversary relationship between media and government in the U.S. This has been at the same time one of the glories of American political life and a persistent thorn in the flesh of political leaders elected by the people to carry out the public business.

Journalists are correctly credited with uncovering the Watergate scandal. That and other revealed abuses of presidential power during the Vietnam War led to President Richard Nixon's unprecedented resignation from the highest office in the land. The trend for the rest of the decade of the 1970s was to open up government. The media remained splendidly unmuzzled so future abuses of power could not easily be covered up.

In the 1980s, as Watergate faded from view and as new foreign policy strains in a turbulent world tested the capacity of the U.S. government to conduct diplomacy and manage its national power, some began to worry that the pendulum had swung too far. Of course some people still demanded that government have no secrets—an absurd idea if foreign relations are to be conducted on the basis of mutual trust. Particularly during President Carter's administration it often seemed that the press saw only a negative role to play, that of inveterate critic and faultfinder. A watchdog role was one thing. It was another to be permanently cynical, insisting on seeing cheap political motives in every presidential act, and never giving people holding public office the benefit of the doubt. Perhaps it was time for the people—and the media—to give government a break, to have a little faith again that political leaders were capable of good motives, at least between elections. The difficulty in breaking the habit of cynical negativism was one of several pernicious legacies of the Nixon administration.

Lest it be thought we are talking only about contemporary America, I would remind you that the history books are full of battles between press and government from the earliest days of the Republic, with only occasional periods of national harmony, during major wars. It is instructive and sobering that one of America's most revered President, Abraham Lincoln, was probably more savagely caricatured and bad-mouthed in print than any other president.

For simplicity we might christen as the *Fifth Estate* that amorphous but nevertheless numerous, and often potent, body of Americans who are out to influence government to do or not to do things of concern to them. Generically, we are talking of *pressure groups* or *lobbies.* They are pressure groups because their aim is to bring pressure on both executive and legislative branches. *Lobbying* means influencing legislators to pass laws (literally, catch them in the lobbies of statehouses or the Capitol). But common parlance uses both phrases to mean any form of influence-seeking activity toward government by the private sector. In a real sense it means use of the "right to petition" guaranteed by the First Amendment to the Constitution.

Such pressure is far more effectively brought to bear on members of the Congress, in the House of Representatives and Senate, than on the executive branch. The reason is that Congress makes laws, while the executive branch carries them out. However, executive agencies often decide or rule on matters of profound interest to one or another group of citizens, so the so-called regulatory agencies are also lobbied intensively for favorable rulings.

The president, the Pentagon, the State Department, and all other agencies involved in foreign policy making are, of course, also targets of persuasion efforts by private interests, but generally there is less chance of getting a favorable executive branch decision slanted to favor a private interest. One reason may be that the executive branch operates in a fish bowl. The chief fish bowl watchers are, of course, the members of Congress. To stretch the metaphor, the president's men depend for their fish food (appropriations) on the Congress. They can always be called to testify under oath about what they did and why. (The president and his immediate advisers may *not* be so required, under the doctrine of executive privilege—see Chapter 5.) Also, everyone in the executive branch (except the president) has a boss, but members of Congress are responsible only to themselves—and to their constituencies at election time. The president has four years, and at least in the past normally eight, to do his stuff. A member of the House has only two before having to please the electorate. So pressures are, in general, more effective on Congress.

It helps to distinguish between different types of lobbies and pressure groups. One kind we do *not* bother with here consists of *individuals* who have a grievance, an idea, an invention, a relative in jail abroad, or a special immigration problem. These individuals can try to see their congressmen or senators, as well as officers of appropriate government agencies. If they are lucky they can, on the initiative of their member, get a so-called private bill passed which, say, makes a special exception to immigration laws in order to deal with a particular hardship case. There are also White House procedures whereby anyone who writes a letter of legitimate complaint or grievance or a request for information is assured of at least a reply from a government agency. At worst, of course, the citizen gets a runaround from the bureaucracy.

We *are* concerned here with *organized causes,* reflecting groups of citizens banded together because of a common interest. We are concerned with economic interests of business or trade groups and unions. We are also talking about religious or charitable groups who are concerned with a particular official policy.

If lobbying is pressure aimed at getting the government to favor one's special cause by having legislation passed by Congress or action taken by the president or the executive branch, what are the *issues* people lobby about? The list is incredibly long. The issue at stake can be *selfish*—preferential treatment for a business or union, or a tax break for one industry, or relief for one set of investors. Alternatively, it can be a *public cause*—electoral reform, school prayer, the UN (pro or anti), strategic arms limitation (ditto), gun control (ditto), and a host of others.

The exercise of private pressures on public officials raises some interesting philosophical questions about its meaning in a democracy. One key question is the conflict between special interest and general interest.

SINGLE-ISSUE POLITICS AND THE NATIONAL INTEREST

It has been a common complaint of political philosophers for centuries that parochial (or what we now call single-issue) politics are contrary to the common good. Edmund Burke's famous November 3, 1774 speech to the voters at Bristol, England is the classic statement of the politician's responsibility, not only to represent his constitutent's local interests, but also to be able to rise above those interests and take positions that may be unpopular in his home district but serve the best interests of the nation.[1] Some of the same criticism has been made over the years about lobbying.

Some label the present period an era of single-issue politics, but in actual fact, there have *always* been single-issue politics, just as there have always been private interests that favor one cause or another. The advocates of really narrow causes have a kind of tunnel vision which looks at only that portion of reality that reflects the viewer's prejudices or desires. Such partial interests are particularly visible in democracies like the United States. Their propagandists can be watched any day of the week in the halls of the Congress, statehouses, or local town halls.

Democratic theory holds that the government is accountable to the people (although, as Edmund Burke suggested, some feel it should be accountable to the citizenry *as a whole*, not to partial or local interests). In *non*democratic states, that is, dictatorships ranging from authoritarian to totalitarian, obviously public opinion does not play anything like the same role. In the Soviet Union, for example, public opinion seems to dwindle to invisibility, and the only permitted avenues of information (and thus of influence) are those in the hands of the state. However, even in the Soviet Union, special interests are at work—influential bureaucrats, ministries, professions, academies. Of course they all work for the state, and they operate behind closed doors, away from the public gaze. Just contrast the vast public dissent about U.S. involvement in the Vietnam War, with nightly TV coverage in full living color of U.S. military actions, with the silence of the media in the Soviet Union concerning Soviet military operations in Afghanistan a decade later.

Nothing so distinguishes the open democratic society from other societies as the influential role of general public opinion. A totalitarian state that controls all the organs of information can invade a foreign country and not tell its own people what really happened (as the Soviet Union did in Hungary in 1956, Czechoslovakia in 1968, and Afghanistan in 1979). In a democracy the government is far more

[1]Edmund Burke, Speech of November 3, 1774, *Works,* II 89–98, quoted in *Burke's Politics,* ed. Ross J.S. Hoffman and Paul Levack (New York: Alfred A. Knopf, 1949), pp. 114–117.

upfront, thanks to a free press and a nosy Congress or parliament. So democracy positively needs the undergirding of broad popular support for great national decisions, particularly those calling for a major sacrifice from the citizenry.

The role of government in such cases is generally to lead public thinking—as Franklin Roosevelt tried to do in the years before U.S. entry into World War II. Alternatively, it can (and does) follow. One anonymous definition of leadership says that the role of a political leader is to find out which way the mob is going and then get out in front. Whatever form the communication takes between leader and led, there is no doubt that a great ground swell of public opinion has been essential to carry out major American policies in the last several generations. In democracies such as the U.S., public opinion has the special role of acting as a broad, voluntary national constituency to give support to national policies.

It might even be said that to do so, *government lobbies the people.* A broad national consensus was essential to move away from nineteenth-century protectionism, aimed at shielding infant industries from cheap foreign competition. (A century later domestic industries were still clamoring for tariff barriers to avoid having to compete effectively in a vastly changed world market.) Given the huge economic stakes, you can see how important it was for the leadership to mobilize a large constituency in favor of free trade. In Edmund Burke's sense, the general interest had to be put ahead of the special interests of business and labor groups who wanted protection for the shoe industry in Massachusetts, the textile industry in New Hampshire, the cotton industry in the South, or whatever.

The first assault against traditional tariffs came in the 1930s. Under President Franklin Roosevelt's leadership the stultifying Hawley-Smoot Tariff was repealed and replaced by the Reciprocal Trade Act of 1933. It was not easy for Roosevelt and his Secretary of State Cordell Hull to persuade Americans to do this. It required an act of faith to believe that lowered tariff barriers would be a contribution to the peace of the world. The reasoning came straight from early nineteenth-century writers—the so-called utilitarians—who spoke of a "harmony of interest" that would come from a worldwide "division of labor." Few also remembered that George Washington spoke in his famous Farewell Address not only of avoiding entangling political alliances, but more positively of fostering trade with all countries of the world in a peaceful fashion.

Much has changed since the 1930s. Of course, domestic industries are still hurt by "cheap foreign goods" and "cheap foreign labor," but increasingly the reason is higher productivity and ingenuity abroad. Contemporary examples are the very serious cases of steel and automobiles. The U.S. used to be the undisputed leader in both but suddenly found itself practically driven out of the competition. The reasons included lowered American productivity, increased Japanese sophistication, and once-imaginative Detroit lagging behind the common sense of the American people in an age of growing petroleum scarcity. However, the fact remained that Americans lost jobs, and the "rational international division of labor" theory did not keep automobiles from being the number one issue between the U.S. and Japan in the early 1980s.

The U.S. national interest in free trade goes beyond a theory of peace. Consider the revolutionary fact that 30 percent of the best jobs in American industry are devoted to manufacturing for *export*. One-third of all the land in the United States devoted to agriculture is used for growing crops *for sales abroad.* The need for the U.S. to avoid slapping new tariff barriers against "cheap foreign imports" no longer rests on a philosophical abstraction; it is a matter of bread and butter for a growing portion of the U.S. population.

If this classic example of single-issue politics cannot stand up to analysis, should we conclude that similar lobbies cannot hack it any more when measured against the weight of deep and complex American interdependence in the world political and economic system? The answer, ironically, is "no": on other matters, single-issue politics have never been so strong.

American ethnic politics have long featured the "three Is"—Italy, Ireland, and Israel. Since the latter's creation in 1948 the pro-Israeli lobby remains a particularly potent element of the American political system. It can still generate pressures on the Congress and the president which result in taking or avoiding taking actions of grave concern to American Jews and other friends of Israel. That lobby is famous for its organization and mobilization skills, particularly when the time comes for the United States to stand up and be counted in a United Nations vote on Middle East questions or the Congress to put pressure on the president.

On a lesser scale, the same could be said of the Greek-American lobby which was instrumental in thwarting the intentions of several recent presidents of the United States by getting Congress, at least for a while, to bar aid to Turkey so long as its troops occupied a substantial portion of Cyprus.

To take an earlier, but even more dramatic, historic example, the Polish-American vote was a crucial element both in the construction of the post-World War II world order and in the falling-out with the Soviet Union over Yalta and other wartime agreements. The Polish-American community had a direct input into both largely because the chief political figure in the United States Senate who converted from isolationism to internationalism was Senator Arthur J. Vandenberg of Michigan, representing the greatest concentration of Polish-Americans in the United States. The price of Senator Vandenberg's conversion—which was absolutely essential for passage of the UN Charter and other building blocks of postwar international cooperation—was a presidential focus on Soviet control of Poland that was far more intense than with regard to the Soviet acquisition of control in the rest of Eastern Europe.

The enormous increase in expenditures for the American defense and aerospace establishment in the postwar years generated a steadily expanding population of industries and workers whose livelihood was associated with those policy sectors. At one time a U.S. senator from the state of Washington was referred to as "the Senator from Boeing." In the case of equally qualified bidders, more contracts seemed to be awarded to General Dynamics Corporation (with operations in Texas) at the behest of powerful Texans in both the executive and legislative branches.

However, it should not be forgotten that the growth of this defense lobby (immemorially summed up by President Eisenhower in *his* farewell speech as " the military-industrial complex") was paralleled by growth in organizations that lobbied *against* increased defense spending and *in favor* of disarmament and arms control measures. The great debates over the SALT treaties were, of course, rooted in central elements of the troubled relationships between the Soviet Union and the United States. The SALT II Treaty ran into trouble because of increasing irritation with Soviet-Cuban military adventures in Angola, South Yemen, and Ethiopia, culminating in the invasion of Afghanistan in late 1979, all during a period in which U.S. power was in retreat following Vietnam. However, in our sense the SALT debates were also battles between the two great domestic constituencies we have just mentioned.

A broad-based positive constituency was also essential for the post-World War II Marshall Plan for the reconstruction of Europe and the unprecedented programs of aid to the less developed countries in the 1950s and 1960s. In the early 1980s the U.S. aid program was in tough shape. The only thing that could revive it was a new coalition of Americans who acknowledged that their security was directly related to the insecurities of the vast majority of the world's population.

For those interested in probing more deeply into the political and philosophical issues of public opinion in a democracy, here are some paradoxes and conundrums. Only the reader can furnish satisfactory answers. (Satisfactory, that is, for the reader!)

SOME COMMON BELIEFS—TRUE OR FALSE?

The following four articles of faith appear to be shared by a sufficient number of Americans to call them the *conventional wisdom* about public opinion in a democracy:

1. *Foreign Policy in a democracy must, if it is to succeed, be based on broad popular consent.*

(I have already argued in favor of this proposition so it must be true!) As James Russell Lowell once wrote, "All free Governments, whatever their name, are in reality government by public opinion." As an article of faith this is incontrovertible. It has been expounded by even the most secretive and manipulative of presidents and secretaries of state. In his 1976 presidential campaign Mr. Carter contended that every time the U.S. has seriously erred in foreign affairs, the reason was that the American people were excluded from the process. After taking office he expressed his confidence in the good sense of the people, and spoke of letting them share in the process of making foreign policy decisions. To a degree—but only to a degree—this was true in his administration, and then a majority voted him out.

2. *Most Americans are not foreign policy experts, and live lives unrelated (or so they think) to day-to-day foreign policy. Nevertheless, the mass of the people, if sufficiently informed, will probably make better decisions than the experts.*

As Thomas Jefferson definitively put the point:

> I know of no safe depository of the ultimate powers of the society but the people themselves; and if we think them not enlightened enough to exercise their control with a wholesome discretion, the remedy is not to take it from them, but to inform their discretion.[2]

Three decades earlier, Jefferson went into the Constitutional Convention convinced that "the basis of our government (is) the opinion of the people . . . "[3] Abraham Lincoln frequently held that, over time, the majority of the citizenry invariably is right. A century ago, an Englishman, Lord Bryce, agreed, noting the "contrast . . . between the faults of the political class and the merits of the people at large." He went on to assert that "no such contrast exists anywhere else in the world."[4] Most Americans would probably agree.

3. *When Americans want to register their opinions on foreign policy, adequate channels of communication exist.*

Those channels include the Congress, the press and other media, and lobbies formed by the cause groups. In this nation of joiners, as that sharp French observer Count Alexis de Tocqueville remarked almost a century and a half ago, "Americans of all ages, all conditions, and all dispositions, constantly form associations."[5] Today some 2,000 nongovernmental organizations (NGOs) convey to each other, the people, and the government mass sentiment on foreign affairs. These groups range from church groups to local discussion clubs, UN associations, voters' leagues, granges, Rotary Clubs, and John Birch Societies, representing in their totality scores of millions of Americans.

4. *But of course, leadership is necessary to define the issues for the public, that is, to give them a policy they can support.*

All political leaders subscribe to this truism.

Each of these traditionally incontrovertible propositions has a flip side. You may not agree with the *contrary notions* that follow, but they represent weighty contentions. To the extent they are true, they

---

[2]Thomas Jefferson, letter to Charles William Jarvis, September 28, 1820, *Bartlett's Familiar Quotations,* 15th ed. (Boston: Little, Brown, 1980), p. 389.

[3]Jefferson, letter to Col. Edward Carrington, January 16, 1787, *Bartlett's Familiar Quotations,* p. 388.

[4]James Bryce, *The American Commonwealth,* Vol. II (New York: The Macmillan Co., 1916) p. 366.

[5]Alexis de Tocqueville, *Democracy in America* (New York: The New American Library, 1956) p. 198.

significantly modify the central ideological thesis of democratic participation in decision making we have just spelled out:

1. *Foreign policy in all countries, almost by definition, is a nondemocratic, elitist activity.*

In any society you can find a division of labor. In foreign affairs, the great mass of citizens either do not pay attention to foreign policy or feel helpless to affect it. Realistically, only a small number of specialists can and does work full time at the task of defining, ordering, and implementing a country's foreign relations, even in a democracy.

The practical effect of this is that you have an "elite sector" in the society; that sector is likely to develop what some people will criticize as an "elitist mentality." For that matter, the nongovernmental organizations are also joined by a relatively small proportion of the population, even though they often claim to be an authentic voice of the American grassroots. The sociology of popular participation is such that it is skewed (in words of a recent analysis) "in the direction of the more affluent, the better educated, those with higher status occupations."[6]

The gulf between insiders and outsiders is thus real. The American Left likes to argue that the gulf is the result of deliberately snobbish recruitment and class interests, but this is increasingly untrue. What really separates foreign policy insiders from foreign policy outsiders is the possession of *special information* and *experience.* That is what makes them a privileged class.

The great differences in expert knowledge create a deep communication gap no one has yet found a satisfactory way to bridge. The two sides simply do not speak the same language, in the sense of sharing the same perception of identical situations. Insiders have an abundance of information. They worry about short-term tactics in order to deal with pressures created by events or in order to respond by a fixed deadline. However, members of the general public are normally concerned with *political preferences and values.*

In this sense, the encounter between foreign policy officials and the public is never a fair fight. Officials try to explain to the public that things are tough, events not of our making must be confronted, and action has to be taken by certain deadlines—all true. However,

[6]Sidney Verba and Norman H. Nie, *Participation in America: Political Democracy and Social Equality* (New York: Harper & Row, Pub., 1972), p. 336.

private citizens usually are concerned with whether they *like* or *do not like* what the government is doing and whether they adjudge official actions to be *good* or *bad*.

Most of the time the government, on the basis of both its privileged facts and its hold on the levers of power, can shape policy decisions. However, when broad public concern develops as to whether a line of policy is *generally right or wrong,* there may ensue a powerful wave of what can only be described as the *democratic force.* It has sometimes proven capable of forcing transformation of an entire national strategy.

Many critics resent the elitist nature of foreign policy making. Yet the fact of life continues to be the natural narrowness of the circle of foreign policy expertise. The dilemma remains of how to pump into that small circle more authentic reflections of the public will.

2. *The American public, in fact, is usually massively indifferent toward foreign policy and can be directly engaged only at times of crisis.*

The general point can best be summed up by again quoting James Bryce, who said of the observably manic swings in American opinion, "Excitement at one time is succeeded by exhaustion at another."[7] He also reported the "one principle to which people have learned to cling in foreign policy is, that the less they have of it the better." The exception is the small minority of concerned outsiders, without special axes to grind, who form the State Department's only real constituency. Gabriel Almond, observing the mass of the population to be "neither interested nor informed," defined this minority as the "Attentive Public," a label that has stuck.[8]

This customary mass indifference except at times of crisis is compounded in the modern age by awesome complexities in the international scene. The fact that most people are, as a practical matter, "dropouts" who cannot be bothered by such complexities, leads some officials to the undemocratic conclusion that *people in the mass cannot be trusted to do the right thing or even to know what is a correct policy.*

Leadership as the correction of popular ignorance is well illustrated by a statement attributed to President Nixon on the eve of one of his speeches on Vietnam: "What this speech will tell is whether the American people can be led in the direction we have to go." There is

[7]Bryce, *The American Commonwealth,* p. 335.

[8]Gabriel Almond, *The American People and Foreign Policy* (New York: Praeger, 1965).

nothing new about presidential arrogance; Nixon's immediate predecessor Lyndon Johnson is said to have formed the opinion, well before entering the White House, that for the people or even the Congress to be permitted to determine the basic direction of foreign policy was "just plain wrong."

3. *The NGOs, special interest groups, and even the Congress are sometimes privately regarded by the foreign policy experts as biased, nonobjective, superficial, frivolous, and otherwise not to be taken too seriously.*

This cynical attitude unfortunately rests on some factual evidence. Its popularity among professionals is reinforced when the Greek-American lobby succeeds in hobbling U.S. security policy in Turkey; or the pro-Israeli lobby inhibits a sensible U.S. policy toward Palestinians; or the shoe manufacturers, or textile workers, or steel association lobby undermines efforts to liberalize trade. That insider prejudice is also reinforced when a national church board petitions the government to undertake unilateral U.S. disarmament, or a right-wing lobby calls for pulling out of the UN.

There is little doubt that parochialism and unprofessionalism on the part of many private citizens' organizations contribute to the traditionally disdainful attitudes of government professionals toward citizen involvement in foreign policy. Those built-in shortcomings reinforce the bureaucrats' preference for a closed policy system based on expertise, confidentiality, and a decision process unhampered by the drag of what they privately consider nonexpert, garrulous, or biased kibitzers from the private sector.

Perversely, government badly wants understanding and support for foreign policies from the same citizens' groups, on the sound premise that their active involvement in the process is required, as we have said, for the successful conduct of foreign policy in a democracy. There is most assuredly a paradox at work here.

THE DEMOCRATIC IMPERATIVE

Neither political ideals nor pragmatism supplies a clear answer to that paradox, nor to the profound moral question underlying it. The inherent conflict between an activist human rights policy and requirements for strategic arms control and security is only one illustration of the permanent clash between ideology and politics, confidentiality and openness, expertise and public feelings, leader and follower.

To be true to the democratic ideology, there seems no acceptable alternative to the conviction that, in general and over time, the values and preferences of the American people are the correct guides to foreign policy.

But if in that large sense the people are generally right, one still has to ask—*What people? How many of them?* and *Just what things are they right about?* Do you have to include in "the people" the *don't cares* as well as the *don't knows*? Are the relevant people only Almond's "Attentive Public"? How fixed a group do you have to concern yourself with? Or does it grow and shrink like an accordion, depending on how salient the issues are to what expanding or contracting circles of people, all of that depending, in turn, on whether one is fighting a war or considering a tariff on shoes? Hardest of all, *should decision makers be allowed to remain unencumbered by the constraints of popular sentiment just because foreign affairs often drop way down on the scale of public concerns?*

Democratic leaders must always seek to offset violent or irrational changes of direction that the nation would likely regret the morning after. The leadership's notion of policies that are "rational" and "responsible" has sometimes placed it in opposition to what turns out to be the authentic will of the sovereign people. The majority of concerned Americans in the late 1960s and early 1970s perceived the counterproductive character of further U.S. involvement in Vietnam before the president and his secretary of state did. This does not mean—as Lincoln acknowledged—that the people are always right, nor does it mean they (or, for that matter, Congress) can *administer* foreign policy. It means that their voices deserve great official respect, not just as a cheering section for the executive but as an authentic source of policy values.

Honesty compels asking the final paradoxical question: What if you and I *do not like* the majority will? What if the majority will is xenophobic, warlike, ungenerous, mean-spirited, selfish, racist, narrow—in short everything you don't like? There is no easy answer. Jefferson's precondition for popular democracy was education. We can hold as a legitimate article of faith that participation and honest information are the soundest prescription for sensible directives from the sovereign people. The alternative available to all Americans eighteen and over is to change leaders at the next election.

chapter seven

DIPLOMACY

> Ambassadors have no battleships at their disposal, or heavy infantry, or fortresses. Their weapons are words and opportunities.
>
> Demosthenes, 343 B.C.

A profession sometimes seems so remote from normal living that most people feel completely disconnected from it and treat its practitioners as if they came off a spaceship. One such profession is nuclear physics. Another is international finance. A third is diplomacy.

It might help to remember that diplomats really started off as *hostages. Embassies* were little groups of foreigners who bravely ventured into the enemy camp to deliver a message to the king from their particular ruler. Often, they remained there after delivering their tidings. In effect, then, they were held as hostages for the general good behavior of their own side or the fulfillment of a specific promise on the part of their masters. If the king they visited was truly displeased by the message they carried, the messengers might well lose their heads. (We are a little more humane these days—but only a little—to modern "messengers" who bring us bad news.)

Diplomacy really started a thousand years ago in Persia when diplomatic immunity became the commonplace rule that nations have followed ever since, even in wartime. The rule says that diplomats cannot be punished at the whim of their hosts; otherwise relations between nations would be intolerable and impossible. How ironic that it was modern Persia (Iran) which in 1979-1981 violated that essential rule and took the whole U.S. embassy hostage.

As the world got more complicated (I'm not sure I would say "civilized"), so did international diplomacy. States acquired separate sovereign identities about four hundred years ago in a series of events culminating in the Treaty of Westphalia in 1648. By the eighteenth century those states—mostly European—were represented by diplomats who wore fancy breeches, spoke French, and formed (as to a certain extent they still do today) a kind of separate trade union of international negotiators (and bearers of good or bad tidings.) Professional diplomats, even from systems as different as capitalist and communist, sometimes seem to understand each other better than do their own people back home. One sometimes represents another's interests. (As late as the nineteenth century it was not uncommon for a government to hire a bright foreigner to be its ambassador abroad, or even its foreign minister. Czar Alexander of Russia once asked German Chancellor Bismarck to do just that!)

Perhaps one reason the French people have such heady national memories of *grandeur* is that in Europe throughout that pre-Modern period not only did all diplomats speak French, but the French ambassador in a foreign capital often had what in diplomacy is called *precedence.* That meant he sat at the right of the ruler of the state to which he was accredited. His carriage led the way in diplomatic processions, and he often was spokesman for the whole diplomatic corps in that capital city. Today that spokesman is the ambassador who has been in town the longest (but note that he is formally referred to not as the *dean* of the local diplomatic corps but by the French word *doyen!)* In those days, as now, other ambassadors got their precedence according to the date when they presented their credentials to the host government. Some hilarious tales are told of mad rushes through city gates to get to the palace first in order to establish a prior date of precedence in the diplomatic corps, with horse-drawn carriages crushing each other as they tried to squeeze through the city gates together. (We are not told what happened to the ambassadors who happened to be sitting inside those carriages.)

The U.S. played a unique role among the big powers in insisting on a simple, nonfancy style of diplomacy for itself in a world of bemedalled diplomatic uniforms and hand-kissing Europeans. Benjamin Franklin, our revolutionary-era minister to France, won everyone's heart even while astonishing them with his plain homespun garb.

You will notice that I said "minister," not "ambassador." A kind of diplomatic inflation has set in and now virtually all diplomatic missions are embassies, headed by a person with the rank of "AE and MP"—meaning ambassador extraordinary and minister plenipotentiary.

But until 1893 the U.S. Government, proud of its rejection of European-style monarchy, kept all of its overseas missions to the status of "legation," rating only a minister at its head. Ministers usually had to wait in the anteroom while their colleagues with the rank of ambassador went in first. In London, at what is still called the Court of St. James, our minister never even got to shake hands with the monarch!

Is that what diplomacy is about? Precedence, protocol, dazzling embassy receptions complete with striped pants, medals, and sashes across gleaming shirt fronts? These are certainly the political cartoonist's favorite symbols of diplomacy. For that matter, worse things have been said about diplomats, such as Sir Henry Wooten's much quoted description of a diplomat as an "honest man sent abroad to lie for his country."[1]

Diplomacy is to an extent some of those things. However, it is really far more important than those superficial aspects, which is why it is an established feature of every government in the world. Even a revolutionary government discovers that diplomacy is not an effete class-system manifestation, but a way of conducting essential business. Leon Trotsky, on being named commissar of foreign affairs by Lenin in the new Bolshevik government in 1917 in Russia, is reported to have asked indignantly, "What, are *we* to have foreign affairs?" He added, "I will issue a few pronouncements and close up shop." Today the Communist regime in Moscow maintains one of the largest and most active diplomatic (and intelligence) services in the world.

[1]On the subject of lies, John Tyler Morgan was a respected U.S. senator in the nineteenth century who was admired for his wit. According to one account, he once told his colleagues in the Senate that "a lie is an abomination unto the Lord—and an ever-present help in time of need."

It helps to think of diplomacy as a process and a procedure. It is basically a means of *communicating* information about policy from one government to another, or from one government to the UN or other international organization—and vice versa. It is the means of conducting essential business between governments and with multilateral intergovernmental organizations, like the World Health Organization (WHO), or NATO, or OPEC. The topics may be war, peace, wheat embargoes, UN peacekeeping, steel prices, nuclear weapons, or eradicating smallpox (which WHO in fact did). But whatever the message, the *medium* of diplomacy provides a permanent network of communication so the world's official business can get done.

The forms which those communications take cover a wide range. The medium can be a formal diplomatic "third-person note" on heavy parchment-like bond paper stamped with official seals in wax, and full of antique (but universally used) salutations such as "excellency," and fulsome endings such as "Please accept, Mr. President, the assurance of my most distinguished consideration." At the other end of the spectrum would be a subtly raised eyebrow at a summit meeting.

There is one intriguing way of avoiding being committed in writing while still leaving a clear record of what you want to convey. It is the crafty device of a so-called "nonpaper." This is in fact what diplomats call an "aide-mémoire"—meaning just that—but on plain paper with no letterhead, no signature, nothing but the words. Which makes it "deniable" if necessary, but gets the message across.

Henry Kissinger tells the story of how President Nixon's reply to a formal invitation from the still-unrecognized Chinese communist leadership got around the obvious dilemma. The presidential response was typed on xerox paper with no letterhead or even U.S. Government watermark! (And typical of the Nixon-Kissinger White House operation, the State Department was not informed.)[2]

There is a whole flip side to the diplomatic process, devoid of fancy dress and focused not on high policy, but on the low but indispensable job of looking after a country's citizens when they get into trouble abroad. This is the Consular Service.

About ten million Americans travel outside the U.S. every year. Of those perhaps 10,000 will die overseas. Maybe one-tenth that number will wind up in foreign jails. American travellers who go

[2]As reported in *Time*, Oct. 1, 1979, p. 53.

broke need around $1 million in emergency funds to get home. 25,000 or so will lose their passports. All this requires Foreign Service officers assigned as consuls-general, consuls, and vice consuls, plus many local employees.

People sometimes blame diplomacy for failures in foreign policies. Of course, if one believes (as I do) that the *main objective of diplomacy is to find means of talking out and resolving differences between governments so that wars do not take place,* then certainly wars can be called failures of diplomacy. But that too is misleading. The problems of war and peace arise from the *policies* of governments and their peoples. A war is not often caused by the breakdown of the communication and negotiation process (that is, diplomacy). Such a breakdown happens as the attitudes, beliefs, and goals of two parties get on a collision course. (An outstanding yarn by historian Barbara W. Tuchman entitled *The Guns of August*[3] outlines the misperceptions and consequent "miscommunication" between the European powers who stumbled into the ghastly four-year carnage of World War I.)

It seems to me as silly to knock diplomacy as it is to criticize a laboratory beaker that holds a volatile substance, or to condemn the science of aerodynamics for the fact that cities are sometimes bombed from the air. The diplomatic process is a serious and essential feature of the landscape of the modern world that ought to be as well understood as the political process itself. The ordinary course of relations between the United States and 150 other countries, plus a couple of dozen important international organizations, involves a vast amount of diplomacy in the form of cables (about 1,000 per day from Washington to the "field"), conferences (over 1,000 per year to which the U.S. sends delegations), bilateral talks, trade flows, agreements, and, of course, disputes (which it is diplomacy's urgent business to resolve). Normal relations between two friends—and foes too—demand a great deal of interaction. It is in both parties' interest that it be conducted in an orderly and well-understood fashion. Whether one *likes* the other party is not really relevant, and the U.S. has succeeded in shooting itself in the foot, so to speak, by denying itself the benefits of normal diplomatic relations because it disapproved of a particular government. This was true from 1919 to 1933 in nonrelations with the Soviet Union, from 1949 to 1972 with China, and cur-

[3]Barbara W. Tuchman, *The Guns of August* (New York: Macmillan, 1962).

rently with Cuba, Vietnam, and several others. Virtually all other countries regard diplomatic relations as *not* connoting moral approval but simply common sense. If for no other reason, an embassy is essential to acquire authoritative information about what is going on, and to talk directly to people whose interests may clash dangerously with one's own. (Some legal eagles like to distinguish between *de facto* recognition, which technically just acknowledges the existence of a new regime, and *de jure,* which gives the seal of official finality. It's not a very helpful distinction today.)

One of the most striking facts of the modern political world is the change in *how* diplomacy is conducted. Ambassadors, whether in national capitals or at the UN, are far less free than they were to take initiatives and to broadly interpret instructions that come in from their own capital. Those instructions used to take a very long time to arrive compared with today's high-speed data-processing equipment and instantaneous transmission by satellite. In the nineteenth century, if you were an American minister (we had no ambassadors then) several thousand miles from Washington, and your instructions arrived in a diplomatic pouch carried by boat across the oceans and then by carriage across land, you had lots of latitude.

Not only was the *pace* of the diplomatic process more leisurely, compared to today's often frantic tempo. An envoy's judgment and sensitivity were extremely important factors that could make the difference between vital outcomes. Today the leash is short and the diplomat's independence of action is drastically reduced.

A story is told of President Lyndon Johnson's Ambassador to the United Nations, former Supreme Court Justice Arthur J. Goldberg. Even if the story is apocryphal it beautifully illustrates the point. During an important UN debate which was televised, Ambassador Goldberg, sitting behind the U.S.A. nameplate in the UN Security Council chamber, was observed by millions of television viewers being handed a piece of paper by an aide, and suddenly stiffening. Many people were scared to death that some portentous event had occurred that could bring disaster to everyone. The fact of the matter (so the story goes) is that President Johnson was sitting in the Oval Office of the White House watching his ambassador perform on television. The note from President Johnson to Ambassador Goldberg said: "Sit up straight!"

But ironically, Ambassador Goldberg was unusual in being in

personal contact with the president (a quirk of history resulted in our UN ambassador being a nominal member of the president's cabinet: Henry Cabot Lodge, named UN Representative in 1952, was an important defeated Republican and President Eisenhower gave him the extra perquisite—which stuck). The fact is that U.S. ambassadors, while technically personal representatives of the president of the United States, get nine-tenths of their instructions from an assistant secretary of state (or lower).

The truly revolutionary change came from the escalating complexity of international life described in earlier chapters of this book, in particular the vast range of economic-social-technological issues we lump together under the heading of interdependence. In addition are fantastic changes in military weaponry, in technical intelligence and information-gathering, and the increase in the number of independent world capitals since World War II from about 60 to about 160 today.

The practical effect of such change is that where an American overseas mission might have consisted of an ambassador, a couple of political secretaries (which means not typists, but diplomats of various ranks), some file clerks and a few code clerks, messengers, and drivers 75 years ago, today many U.S. embassies employ representatives from not only the State Department but over 40 other U.S. government agencies as well. Non-Americans employed at U.S. embassies abroad outnumber Americans by two to one. Of 25,000 Americans attached to our embassies abroad, only one-fifth come from the State Department (these are divided into four career *cones:* political, economic, consular, and administrative).

In Cairo, in 1979, the U.S. embassy had 61 Foreign Service officer positions, but also 111 additional officers, of which 97 were attached to the U.S. Aid Mission, and 14 represented a number of other organizations, such as the defense department, treasury, agriculture, commerce, CIA, and so forth. On the staff of the U.S. embassy in London are found representatives of 45 agencies. If you multiply this by the number of places in which the United States has embassies—approximately 140, including special missions—you are talking about thousands of Americans with diplomatic or consular status in Washington, New York, London, Paris, Moscow, and points east, west, north, and south. If you multiply *that* by the more-than-100 governments which conduct diplomatic relations with each other, the matrix adds up to an enormous number of individuals around the world who are engaged in the business of diplomacy in one form or another (not to mention the several thousand employees of the secretariats at the United Nations and its family of specialized agencies, along with regional organizations such as NATO).

This network of relations, and people conducting them, is essential to keep the planetary machine functioning. That is why diplomats have a special status making them immune from arrest in their host countries for any offenses committed in the course of carrying out their duties. Otherwise, in hostile situations any of them could be harassed and rendered incapable of carrying out what seem to the locals to be very unpopular functions. The seizure of the American embassy in Teheran in 1979 by a mob of young religious fanatics was a grave breach of this global fabric of custom and laws.

The shattering factor was not a mob that went on a rampage—mobs can be formed in many places by a demagogue in the streets. But the host government's solemn obligation is to protect the foreign diplomats no matter how bad official relations may be. If the two countries are at war, even then the two sides arrange to exchange their diplomats.

In Iran in 1979-1981 the intolerable act was that this kidnapping of an entire foreign embassy was aided and abetted by the Iranian government led by an aging and rigidly fanatical leader—the Ayatollah Khomeini. The reason virtually every government in the world objected to his act is that all of them have an equal interest in the observance of diplomatic privileges and immunities which have been imbedded in international intercourse for centuries. (In the same period mobs attacked the U.S. embassies in Islamabad and Tripoli. The difference was that there the governments furnished police protection, however belatedly.)

One of the charges hurled at the captured American embassy in Teheran by the so-called militants was "nest of spies!" The mob in the street, already inflamed by passionate utopian and hate rhetoric, was ready to believe the worst because the American embassy had people assigned to it whose duties were to gather intelligence. But that was simply another token of their ignorance.

Actually, intelligence-gathering is one of the prime functions of every country's embassy in every capital city of the world. Virtually all have one or more military attachés. The job of the latter is to report back home on military capabilities and activities—in short, military intelligence. The *secret* intelligence services, such as the American CIA, the Soviet KGB, British MI-6, and French Intelligence, normally assign their officers under a diplomatic cover, listing them as "attaché." The "station chief" who directs the embassy's CIA or KGB (or whatever) intelligence staff often has better contacts than the ambassador in the host country's society and politics. It is also fascinating to see the lowly embassy jobs in which Moscow often puts its senior KGB man—chauffeur, gardener, code-clerk—for a near-perfect cover from which unobtrusively to direct the intelligence function.

Even with the changes that have taken place thanks to satellite communications and jet planes, some things are constant. Personal character, integrity, patience, sensitivity, and intelligence are still crucial ingredients of diplomacy, along with technical and language skills. Sir Harold Nicolson gave the highest weight to the capacity of the diplomat to elicit *trust* and *confidence* from those with whom he (or she) is dealing. Nicolson also advised diplomats to separate emotion and sentimentality from the hard business of working out agreements that have to be ratified back home by both states, and said that diplomacy

> . . . in its essence is common sense and charity applied to international relations . . . immoral diplomacy defeats its own purposes . . . the worst kinds of diplomatists are missionaries, fanatics, and lawyers; the best kind are the reasonable and humane species.[4]

The advice is still sound. (Although lawyers would take exception.)

In important matters it is still valuable for diplomats to show initiative, intelligence, and imagination. But modern diplomats complain that these qualities are often stifled. In any informal gathering of American diplomats, an eavesdropper is likely to pick up a certain amount of resentment concerning the impending arrival by jet plane of an assistant secretary of state, secretary of state, or even the president, to handle some important matter that has arisen between the governments, and which the ambassador would normally handle. At a minimum he or she will sit in on the talks. But a record was probably set when Henry Kissinger spent several days in Moscow as President Nixon's assistant for national security affairs, closeted in intimate discussions with the leaders in the Kremlin preparatory to Nixon's momentous détente summitry, without the knowledge of the American ambassador until the very last day of the trip!

---

[4]Harold Nicolson, *Diplomacy*, 2nd ed., (London: Oxford University, 1950) p. 43.

Foreign Service officers in the political "cone" are nevertheless expected to be (or become) experts on the countries to which they are assigned, and today also fluent in the local language (although frequent reassignments cut into expertise.) They are expected to report honestly and sensitively to their own governments what they observe to be going on. At the same time they have to avoid the pitfall of becoming captives of the local government, in the sense of being excessively afflicted with what is known as localitis. It is *not* clear that U.S. diplomats in Iran in 1978 reported back correctly the Shah's fast-eroding popular support (although embassy political or intelligence officers may well have prepared such reports only to have a superior veto them).

Another reason for that eventual diplomatic catastrophe may have been the failure of the State Department to assign to Teheran during that fateful period the best available experts on Iran (some of whom were quite critical of the Shah's regime). According to Professor James A. Bill, it was no secret that Teheran in that period was the "professional graveyard of several fine Foreign Service officers." He went on to say

> Although State Department officials seldom deny this assessment, they do point out the real difficulties involved. How can American officials in fact get in touch with opposition forces in a country where they are first and foremost representatives to the government in power? How can Foreign Service officers with a minimum of training in the language, history and culture of Iran be expected to develop communication with Persian-speaking groups and classes? In such a labyrinthine society, how is it possible for a person to really understand anything in a typical tour of only three years? These are certainly legitimate queries, but they should not become stock excuses for an unfortunate state of affairs.

Bill concluded, "With the sensitive nerve endings of the American foreign policy-making system deadened this way, it remains impossible to transmit accurate signals to Washington. And when Washington has its own petrified view, the opportunities for any new perspective on this situation are slim indeed."[5] (In 1981 the State Department's Foreign Service Institute launched a promising new

[5]James A. Bill, "Iran and the Crisis of 1978," *Foreign Affairs,* Winter 1978–79, p. 340.

program of professional training for mid-career political officers aimed at bringing this important national human asset into modern times, so to speak.)

Americans have a particularly hard time wrestling with the issue of *public diplomacy*. That phrase is used increasingly to describe U.S. overseas information, cultural exchange, and propaganda services which often do a fine job abroad, if not always in Washington. But in the historic sense, what I mean here was defined by President Woodrow Wilson when he called for "open covenants openly arrived at." His demand reflected a thoroughly American revulsion against the secrecy and conspiracy in European diplomatic practices from which generations of Americans had fled. The theory was a nice one, but the trouble was that, as pointed out by a very experienced diplomat,

> Seated on a stage with the whole world as audience, statesmen are more likely to illustrate their virile nationalist fundamentalism than be caught in the flagrant act of concession. Compromise is the key to successful negotiation; and compromise, in essence, means that you accept today what you vehemently rejected as inadequate the week before.[6]

Former Israeli Foreign Minister Abba Eban then quotes the former Secretary General of the UN, Dag Hammarskjöld:

> The best results of of negotiations between two parties cannot be achieved in international life any more than in our private world in the full glare of publicity, with current debate of all moves, avoidable misunderstandings, inescapable freezing of positions due to considerations of prestige—and the temptation to utilize public opinion as an element integrated into the negotiation itself.[7]

I would go further and say that open diplomacy is a great idea, but like sex, even if one party wants to do it in public, the other may not. In both cases it takes two.

The U.S. Foreign Service "culture" is different from what it used to be. Young American Foreign Service officers represent a new breed of often independent-minded, broadly representative Ameri-

[6]Abba Eban, "Camp David—The Unfinished Business," *Foreign Affairs,* Winter 1978-79, p. 346.

[7]Eban, "Camp David—The Unfinished Business," p. 347.

cans, far from the exclusively white, eastern, middle-class Protestant males who characterized the Foreign Service of their grandfather's generation. The career is an attractive one for a young person interested in international relations and fascinated by foreign cultures.

The Foreign Service exam is given periodically in many U.S. cities, and is usually announced on post office and college bulletin boards (if it isn't, all you have to do is write the State Department for information). The exam is both written and oral. Those who pass get intensive training at the Foreign Service Institute, which is famous for its language training. First assignments can range from vice consul in a small city somewhere to assistant reporting officer in an embassy political or economic section. Promotion is based on merit, and about two-thirds of the American embassies abroad have a career FSO as chief of mission (ambassador).

So there's glamor—and tedium; hard work—and arid stretches. The late Adlai Stevenson, when he was President Kennedy's permanent U.S. representative to the United Nations, described the job of an ambassador as "one-third protocol, one-third alcohol, and one-third Geritol." Much of diplomacy's important business *is* conducted in informal circumstances such as a lunch, or a cocktail party, or after dinner, rather than in a stilted office setting. It sounds like fun, and it certainly beats heavy lifting. But just try sometime to draft a precise cable, complete with all the crucial points and nuances of an important conversation, in the late evening hours when after a full day's work in the office you have attended a couple of parties at which foreign officials conveyed things to you which your government must hear. If your cable is received with admiration and applause by the desk officers back in Washington (who do not get invited to as many parties), then you are just the kind of person the Foreign Service is looking for.[8]

[8]A good recent book on modern diplomacy is by an experienced bureaucrat and ambassador, William Macomber, *The Angels Game: A Handbook of Modern Diplomacy* (New York: Stein & Day, 1975).

chapter eight

EXPLAINING THE PROCESS: THEORIES OF FOREIGN POLICY DECISION MAKING

HOW THE SYSTEM WORKS

I have implied several times that, if we really want to know how things work in foreign policy making, formal organization charts complete with neat little boxes and lines can be misleading. They do show the *official* flow lines of information and advice running upward from the staff-level bureaucrats to the cabinet and White House-level officials. They also show the formal "lateral" relationships running across from agency-to-agency, all connected and coordinated by the White House. Moreover, they show the lines of authority running downward to the bureaucracy, transmitting the instructions that are to be carried out.

What I have just described is the ideal—the dream of every textbook writer, *and* every president. What really goes on is the interaction, not of a nest of empty boxes, but of flesh-and-blood humans. The moving parts in the bureaucratic machine are human, not inanimate (though they may sometimes look that way). Like everyone else, some bureaucrats are energetic; some, lazy. Some are fired by ambition; some dream of a sunny beach in the Caribbean. Some are honest; some, devious. Some are passionately partisan; some, coldly objective. Virtually all of them want promotion and other forms of recognition for the work they do. Sounds familiar, doesn't it? It describes any collection of people employed by an organization, public or private.

In the real world, the little boxes are not always linked in the way the charts show. The lines of communication are not always the same as the formal lines of authority and the lateral lines of coordination. In real life, people tend to try to work problems out with people they know and trust. Sometimes these are exactly the people the charts describe, but sometimes they are other people in the same area, perhaps a deputy, or assistant, or colleague, rather than the person officially designated. Action often takes place because informal *coalitions* or alliances have formed between key people in the system who share the same goals or interpret the national interest similarly.

Information is a form of power in governmental affairs. People who are "in the know" and have an "inside track" are sought out, even if they happen to be the great man's second assistant or belong in a different box on the chart. In this process of bureaucratic interaction bargains are struck, compromises hammered out, obstacles dodged (and brownie points sought with one's boss). Of course, the formally designated officials are centrally involved. But the *informal network* overcomes a lot of obstacles—including the obstacle sometimes represented by a stubborn or unmoveable official.

The value of this endless round of talk, give-and-take, and shifting tactics, is that a policy problem which might otherwise be frozen in stalemate can get dealt with, and the nation's business carried out.

Of course, the process can flatten out a problem and wind up settling on the lowest common denominator, defeating initiative and discouraging creativity. But if policy is a product of a lot of little strategies, this is not invariably a bad thing. As in any other walk of life, strategy is a plan of action to get something done. The process of seeking consensus always entails compromises and requires that every player not stake all his prestige on every issue: You win some and lose some. The alternative is a dictatorial system that would doubtless be more efficient. But when it chose wrong, the results could be calamitous.

Bureaucratic battles are won by the officials and coalitions who have not only the best argument, but the most influence on the top decision makers. Influence, like information, is power in government.

The hardest thing for well-meaning people to understand about complex systems of organization (and about international relations) is that *power* is an essential component of the process—in effect, the fuel that makes it go. Like the moving parts of an automobile engine, politics and bureaucracies also require a fuel. In a car it is gasoline or diesel oil. In politics, the element that fuels the system at every level is power.

This does not necessarily mean guns or tanks. It does mean empowerment *of* someone *by* someone in authority. If you are president of the United States or a member of Congress, you have been empowered by the electorate. If you are secretary of state, or a Foreign Service officer, or the president's National Security Adviser, you are empowered by the president.

The process of decision making simply cannot be understood without confronting the ever-present reality of power. Power by itself is neither moral nor immoral—it is neutral, and can be used for good or ill. At its best, power in government means influence over people who can get things accomplished by other people who have the best ideas as to how to do just that.

The flow of life and action through the foreign policy-making system comes from human forces joined together (or in battle with one another). The aim is to get something done *or* to see that it is *not* done. To be able to move and shape that kind of system, you certainly need a recognized place on a formal organization chart that others can acknowledge. But we have seen that this is not enough. You also need the ability to influence those who make the key decisions. Bureaucratic power comes from that kind of influence. This is the law of human organizations, of political life, and of the making of U.S. foreign policy.

CAN THE SYSTEM BE ANALYZED?

Students of government and foreign policy have looked at the system I have just described and have tried to explain it scientifically. Some have developed *theories* about its operation. That means trying to impose on this reality a form of *rationality*. The analyst looks at the *inputs* into the policy system—public opinion, Congress, acts of foreign governments, demands of world events, in short, the things that go into the foreign policy "in-box." The *outputs* of the system are decisions and actions in the form of U.S. policies and strategies. Between input and output, we can imagine a "black box." Inside it the actual decision-making *process* takes place. That black box has been the subject of great scrutiny. Many have tried to link together the elements of the process in a system that can be explained. (True science would require that the process could be *simulated* and its probable outputs predicted; see Appendix.)

President Kennedy's closest assistant, Theodore Sorensen, wrote while he was still in the White House that White House decision making is not a science but an art, requiring judgment rather than calculation.[1]

George Reedy, for a time President Lyndon Johnson's press secretary, wrote in a very impressive book called *The Twilight of the Presidency* these skeptical words about the futile quest for tidiness:

> It is assumed that there is something called a "decision-making process" which can be charted in much the same fashion as the table of organization for a business corporation.[2]

Perhaps the most extravagant commentary on collective decision making comes from that bizarre nineteenth-century German philosopher Friedrich Nietzsche: "Madness is the exception in individuals but the rule in groups."

I suggest we proceed on the assumption that there *is* rationality in the process, but not necessarily the rationality that takes place within the mind of an outsider trying to analyze the process, or the rationality that is natural to very different cultures from our own.

GROUP PRESSURES

Nietzsche's aphorism about madness being the rule in groups is obviously an exaggeration, but he was saying something important about the difference between the way an individual tackles a problem and the way a *group* discusses it and makes a collective judgment. One of

---

[1]See Theodore C. Sorensen, *Decision-Making in the White House* (New York: Columbia University Press, 1963), especially pp. 10ff.

[2]George E. Reedy, *The Twilight of the Presidency* (New York: New American Library, 1971), p. 30.

the famous experiments in psychology is the so-called Asch effect. Students in a lecture hall are led by the pressure of the social situation to defy their own senses and describe a line of the blackboard as being longer than another line, when obviously it is not. (The trick is to plant the professor's confederates among the very first students asked to say which line is longer. By the time the question comes to ordinary students they become torn between an objective assessment of reality based on their own senses, and peer group pressures not to look deviant or foolish.) Many a committee meeting in government (and elsewhere) demonstrates the Asch effect.

The normal, human, group pressures toward consensus can thus have a very distorting effect on the making of decisions. For this reason, Professor Alexander George of Stanford University recommended an approach he christened "Multiple Advocacy." Alternative courses of action are presented to the group and then challenged without anyone losing face or making the boss angry.[3] (See the Appendix for one technique—political gaming—that can bring out inconsistencies in official plans and weaknesses in policies but without the embarrassment or the pain of opposing a real-life group decision.)

The problem of running against the sense of the group is summed up by some advice out of ancient Persian history. A royal counselor is said to have warned of the impossibility, if no more than one opinion is uttered, to make the best choice. According to the legend he argued that then one is forced to follow whatever advice may have been offered. But if opposing arguments are heard, then a proper choice is possible.

MAKING THE CHOICES

One question that has received a lot of attention in management circles in government is how to allocate resources *rationally*. Rationally in this instance means choices tied logically to one's priority goals as well as to available supplies of things or money. (We recognize the old question of ends and means.)

Attempts have been made to adapt to foreign policy decision making some of the *cost-benefit* analytical techniques used in recent

[3]Alexander L. George, "The Case for Multiple Advocacy in Making Foreign Policy," *American Political Science Review*, September 1972.

years in many business and socioeconomic decisions as well as in weapons systems options under consideration in the Pentagon. (The PPBS—Program Planning and Budgeting System—became very controversial as a tool for rational defense policy decisions but is still used in varying forms.) Cost-benefit techniques in common use today combine the economist's utility-maximizing strategies with techniques of Operations Research employed in engineering and military problem-solving.

However, such approaches have proved tricky to apply to the foreign policy arena. A few areas do, of course, have numbers attached to them. Foreign aid programs involving specific dollar figures or assignment of numbers of staff personnel to one country can be quantitatively matched to a hierarchy of priorities derived from foreign policy objectives. But the toughest policy problems are, it turns out, issues of *competing values, ideas, and ideologies.* The expenditure of funds may not be relevant, and it may be impossible to *compare* tangible costs and benefits.[4]

The State Department in recent years has tried various modifications of the PPBS kind of analysis, with acronyms like CASP, PARA, Net Assessment, and GORM (none really worth remembering). It is fair to say that these never had a major influence on the big policy choices.

The question remains: How do we understand the process of choice between alternative courses of action where emphasis on intangible factors, in addition to the pressures of crisis management and the difficulty of access to secret records, weakens the power of formal cost-benefit analytical techniques?

One technique—gaming or simulation—can help to examine possible outcomes of policy debates by imposing artificially a "laboratory" analysis of political costs, diplomatic benefits, military implications, and negative consequences economists call *externalities.*

Another way to understand the process is through case studies of the behavior of the foreign policy-making system at times of crisis. Crises certainly make for more interesting reading than studies of the system at times when nothing is happening. They help give us a better sense of the kinds of decisions that are made under conditions of great stress.

---

[4]See testimony by Thomas C. Schelling, U.S. Congress, Senate, Subcommittee on National Security and International Operations, "PPBS and Foreign Affairs," 90th Congress, 1st Session (Washington: Government Printing Office, 1968).

However, crisis studies also have a distorting effect, precisely because in times of crisis *the system is not behaving normally*. The decisions made by President Kennedy and his immediate group of advisers during the 1962 Cuban Missile Crisis represented a deviant situation. The so-called executive committee of the National Security Council decoupled itself, so to speak, from the entire U.S. government. This is hardly a good way to study the normal, everyday workings of the bureaucracy (although it remains a favorite case study).

Other useful studies of decision making have their roots in the behavioral sciences focusing on individual behavior. That approach draws analogies from laboratory data about how individuals and groups behave under stress, and applies the findings to the real-life workings of the government system. Some excellent studies have emerged from this *genre* (see Suggested Readings).

MODELS OF THE PROCESS

It was not until the late 1960s and early 1970s that social scientists began seriously to theorize about the foreign policy process in ways that looked startlingly like the real-life system insiders know from their daily experience. The chief breakthrough came with analyses of events and decisions based on the so-called Bureaucratic Politics Model (sometimes called "Governmental Politics"). This model has rapidly gained popularity because it seemed to explain the hitherto mysterious process involved in foreign policy making. It also threw into sharper relief older models of the process that either had been unthinkingly accepted, or had been imperfectly translated from other fields such as economics (for example, the Rational Utility-Maximizing Model), or decision making through the behavior of business firms. It also had older roots in traditional public administration theory.

The rational actor model

This so-called Utility-Maximizing picture of organizational behavior presupposes a single ("unitary") decision maker whose logic could be readily understood. The idea came from formal decision theory, which in turn embodied "game theory" and bargaining theory. It grew from the notion of "economic man" endowed with full information and competing in completely self-interested terms for a predominant share of the market. As originally applied to international relations, it assumed a permanent desire to increase one's power at the expense of others—what is called a *zero-sum* strategy (your loss is my gain and vice versa). One had clearly defined goals, linked to appropriate strategies by a consciously deciding and purposeful mind. The same abstract rationality governed one's selection of appropriate policies and allocation of needed means. In this fairly antiseptic intellectual construct, policy is the realization of the decider's objectives by the process of adding rationality to purpose.

In philosophical terms, the rational method is both comprehensive and deductive—*comprehensive* in requiring awareness of values and objectives and information on all relevant factors; and *deductive* in proceeding logically from values and objectives to alternative policies by way of ends-means analysis.

In a way, this made perfectly good sense. Common sense tells us that much official staff work and decision making uses, in incomplete form, the Rational Model. The central difficulty with the Rational Actor Model was not in its emphasis on orderly analysis and action. It was in the confusion between accepting the model as a kind of intellectual *guide* and believing that it *accurately described* the process that actually took place.

Most recent theory about the process of decision making is based on a pair of quite different models of behavior—the Organizational Process Model and the Bureaucratic Politics Model.

My own hypothesis is that the Rational Model is generally followed by the *ultimate* foreign policy decision maker, such as the president or the secretary of state, at the point where his decision considers recommendations worked out at lower staff levels. However, in the process *below* the level of top decision maker, the behavior of the actors in hammering out their recommendations is far more likely to reflect the other two models.

The alternatives to the Rational Actor Model ought not to be seen as denials of rationality in the acts of bureaucrats. These other "explanatory models" help account for behavior in organizations, notably the way that lower levels must bargain their way up to the final decision maker. These other models illuminate the *nonrational* influences that bear on steps in the policy process, and acknowledge the compromises real-world people make when they work through the policy machinery to a point of decision.

The organizational process model[5]

This model also has a venerable ancestry, and certainly explains the positions taken by people who work for different government agencies such as the State Department or the Treasury. To get technical for a moment, the model envisages the *end product* of policy debate (which the Rational Model called acts and choices) as *outputs of the dynamic process* that takes place in large organizations which function according to regular and predictable patterns of behavior. The theorists call all that *organizational output*. In simpler language, people who work for organizations develop a tendency to identify with them. What eventually gets decided within organizations reflects that loyalty and set of habits. When representatives of, say, State or Air Force go to an interagency meeting, that's what they will express as their organization's best sense of the general or national interest.

Unlike the theory of pure rationality, this one recognizes that in real life people go only a certain limited distance in checking out all their possible options. Herbert A. Simon, who had much influence in this school, wrote of something called "bounded rationality" by contrast with the "comprehensive rationality" of ideal behavior. Simon came up with the idea of "satisficing," that is, of search routines that stop with the first "good enough" answer, rather than relentlessly pushing for the ideal—but unattainable—solution. He saw organizations as pursuing "uncertainty avoidance" as they went down the tried-and-true track of their SOPs—standard operating procedures.[6]

The policy option favored by each organization, according to this theory, inevitably and naturally reflects that particular agency's interest in controlling the decision-making process, rather than in what Model I considers objective choices. The standard bureaucratic joke is that organizations set forth their own preferred recommendation for action sandwiched in between two obviously ridiculous extremes. The president would have three choices: (a) all-out war; (b) what I propose; and (c) surrender.

---

[5]The most widely used work on foreign policy decision-making models is by Graham T. Allison, *Essence of Decision: Explaining the Cuban Missile Crisis* (Boston: Little, Brown, 1971).

[6]See Herbert A. Simon, *Administrative Behavior,* 2nd ed. (New York: Macmillan, 1957).

The bureaucratic politics model

Model III in a way is a refinement of the Organization Process Model (II). Here we really get down to the behavior of middle-level workers in organizations, and the games they play to get their way in resolving a contentious problem. Under this theory, foreign policy decisions are the outcomes of a *bargaining* process among players positioned in the hierarchy of government. They all play "decision games" in the process of transforming their bureaucratic pulling and hauling into decisions their bosses can act on (or send further up the line to *their* bosses.) Instead of that mythical abstraction the *unitary actor,* what we have here is a real pluralistic world of living, breathing human beings—players—whose stand on policy disputes comes from not only the parochial priorities of their agency—the Navy, Treasury, OMB, CIA, or whatever—but also from their own personal perceptions, goals, interests, stakes, deadlines, and perspectives.

So if you want to explain how a given foreign policy decision is made you don't ask, what are the objective goals, alternatives, rational cost-benefits, etc? You don't just ask, what agency is he/she from? You also ask, who's playing this game? what are the real reasons behind the stands he/she is taking? and, of course, how are those various stands all aggregated in the shape of the governmental decision which the public or foreign governments see?

The process of bargaining involves forming coalitions among players, and it is a familiar game for all bureaucrats down the line. Those coalitions cut across formal organizational lines and boxes. The process happens not at formal meetings but on the phone, by the water-cooler, or at lunch. Someone at one level may join up with someone at a different level, outside the chain of command, in different agencies, in order to create a coalition that can work things out to mutual benefit, then confront both bosses with an attractive policy.

Already the critiques of this school are emerging. But it at least partially explains recent bureaucratic history. And, of course, it has the metaphysical advantage of the "Haunted House Doctrine"[7] and is hard to refute! Detailed case studies to validate its propositions are often absent, but it rings true to many a battle-scarred bureaucrat and supplies a beguilingly sophisticated theory to the academic.

[7]If I say a house is haunted, and you go in and look around and don't see any ghosts, all I have to say is, "You see, they won't come out when you're looking."

I have suggested that the president of the United States is virtually the only rational actor in the system. He is able to select among various options without having to bargain with his peers, because he has no peers! This, of course, is not quite true either, since, as Richard Neustadt pointed out, the power of the presidency is the *power to persuade.*[8] As the (successful) Panama Canal and (unsuccessful) SALT II Senate ratification struggles in the late 1970s indicated, the president does have at least one set of peers that is nothing short of formidable—the United States Congress.

Below the president, Model II (Organizational Politics) seems best to describe the workings of the system. The departments and agencies are the central actors. Their behavior and advice is most predictable. Model II reflects the history, the loyalties, and the particular outlook of specialized units of government which, by definition, see things in terms of their own assigned missions.

And finally, below the level of leadership of the major bureaucracies, the Model III (Bureaucratic Politics) game is played by the action officers throughout the system in a way that is familiar to any experienced civil servant.

The sensible conclusion seems to me to take parts of each and use them to help explain a process that still contains all too many mysteries for the outside observer.

[8]Richard E. Neustadt, *Presidential Power: The Politics of Leadership with Reflections from FDR to Carter* (New York: Wiley, 1980).

chapter nine

ANTICIPATING THE FUTURE: FOREIGN POLICY PLANNING

Zbigniew Brzezinski, writing in 1969 after a two-year tour of duty in the State Department Policy Planning Council (as it was then called), was highly critical of the secretary of state for persistent neglect of his planners. Professor Brzezinski's recommendation was that the staff be "reduced in size, upgraded in status, and closely related to the Secretary."[1] The model, as in most subsequent American (and other) efforts at foreign policy planning, was George Kennan's pioneer planning staff of the late 1940s. That group—the original "S/P" (meaning: Office of the Secretary/Planning Staff)—numbered around six, was high in status, close to the secretary of state, and considered, erroneously as I shall argue, to personify a Golden Age of planning for others to emulate.

An even more critical view of U.S. foreign policy planning was advanced in the same period by another professor of government. Henry A. Kissinger wrote in 1966:

> What passes for planning is frequently the projection of the familiar into the future . . . Lip service is paid to planning; indeed planning staffs proliferate . . . since planning staffs have a

[1]Zbigniew Brzezinski, "Purpose and Planning in Foreign Policy," *The Public Interest,* Winter 1969, 63–66.

> high incentive to try to be 'useful,' there is a bias against novel conceptions . . . true innovation is bound to run counter to prevailing standards.[2]

However, after Professor Kissinger had become Secretary of State Kissinger, he used other words to describe the same function: "Our analytical and conceptual capabilities have been greatly enhanced by giving the Policy Planning Staff a central position in the organization and by staffing it with the best available talent."[3]

Whether wittingly or not, Secretary Kissinger adopted approximately two-thirds of the Brzezinski prescriptions. His planning chief, Winston Lord, was unquestionably close to the secretary of state, and S/P played an active role on a wide range of problems with a staff that was expanded to a record size of twenty-nine.

Secretary of State Cyrus Vance and his planning chief, Anthony Lake, decided early in the Carter administration to correct some of the defects, chronicled later, that had generally plagued earlier policy planning. But efforts to bring policy planning closer to the ideal of a speculative, wide-ranging, future-oriented, independent-minded, in-house policy critic were once again subordinated to the chronic and perverse pressures of short-run crisis management. Secretary of State Alexander M. Haig's planning director Paul Wolfowitz was, like Lake, close to his boss and involved in some of the most important current policy issues. But the short-term still invariably had priority over longer-range thinking.

Indeed, the history of official planning efforts, both in the United States and in many other countries, leaves one with nagging doubts about the possibility, even with the best will and brains, of fostering within *any* foreign ministry the ideal of policy planning to be found in textbooks, speeches by high officials, and State Department directives.

It should be emphasized that the problem is not the failure to produce some kind of master plan to be slavishly followed. That is neither possible nor desirable. A reasonable definition of policy planning asks: what qualities that are most needed for a better policy

---

[2]Henry A. Kissinger, "Domestic Structure and Foreign Policy," *Daedalus*, Spring 1966, 503–529.

[3]Henry A. Kissinger, speech, June 27, 1975.

process are most *absent* from day-to-day diplomacy?[4] I would argue that there are three: speculative projections into the medium- (two to five years) and long-term (eight to ten) future; government-wide (rather than agency-bound) analyses of crosscutting global interdependence issues; and built-in challenges to established premises of foreign policy—a need underscored by self-created policy disasters from the Bay of Pigs to the Vietnam War. But in the real world, even when such criteria are acknowledged, they have a habit of bending to the universal bureaucratic imperative of maximizing influence with busy operating officials who are committed to carrying out policies dictated by the elected leadership.

The failures in recent years of the United States and other major governments to anticipate, let alone forfend, major convulsions in the international system correlate disturbingly well with the direct testimony of policy planners about weaknesses in their own efforts. Both support the conclusion that foreign policy planning, whatever else it has achieved, by and large has failed to emphasize the qualities that most distinguish it from the normal policy-making process. The universal nature of this failure strongly suggests that its cause is not to be found in the quality of the people involved, which is often extraordinarily high. Rather, it would seem to lie in the very nature of foreign policy-making institutions and their bureaucratic processes.

EARLY EXPECTATIONS

S/P was originally set up in 1947 to perform four main functions: (1) to formulate long-term programs for the achievement of U.S. foreign policy objectives; (2) to anticipate problems for the Department of State; (3) to study and report on broad politicomilitary problems; (4)

[4]Few analysts have sought to develop objective criteria for foreign policy planning. Perhaps the best treatment in political science literature is found in I.M. Destler, *Presidents, Bureaucrats, and Foreign Policy: The Politics of Organizational Reform* (Princeton: Princeton University Press, 1972), and Robert Rothstein, *Planning, Prediction, and Policy Making in Foreign Affairs* (Boston: Little, Brown, 1972). A different kind of analysis is found in "Organizing for Foreign Policy Planning" by the present author in *Report of the Commission of the Organization of the Government for the Conduct of Foreign Affairs* [Murphy Commission], (Washington, D.C.: Government Printing Office, 1975), Appendix F, Vol. 2.

to evaluate and advise on the adequacy of current policies.[5] Let me take these briefly in turn.

1. "Long-term," if it is to mean anything beyond a year or two, has, on the testimony of many planners, little or no respectable place in the official scheme of things.[6] Planners have in practice invariably limited their time horizons to six months to a year or so. A few have, of course, tried to project trends and events much further into the future. However, their pains were often rewarded with such epithets as "theoretical," "unrealistic," or "irrelevant"—to cite words used over and over again in interviews with planners (and nonplanners) in country after country.

The reference in mission 1 to "objectives" surfaces another problem. With rare exceptions, broad U.S. policy goals tend to be spelled out in cliché form, and the search by operating agencies for clearly defined policy objectives to guide them often ends in frustration. Policy ad hocery that assumes everyone knows what the goals are works well enough when there is a broad domestic consensus. It does not when overall national priorities are controversial, as they increasingly have been since the late 1960s. Nothing could be more dangerous than to fill this gap by defining various regions as *vital* to the United States on the basis of where Air Force One happens to be at a given moment.[7]

2. As for anticipating problems in an effective way, some recent transformations in the external world have clearly caught Americans flat-footed.

The towering contemporary issues of economic and functional interdependence, along with acute North-South alienation, were long foreseen by some policy planners (and by even more outsiders). But it is sobering that in the 1950s S/P included only one economist and had no organized way to analyze scientific and technological changes. Until the 1970s the (then) Atomic Energy Commission was responsible for basic international planning in the nuclear field, and pressed its bias toward ever-expanding nuclear uses rather than analyzing

[5]Department of State Order of May 5, 1947 establishing the Policy Planning Staff.

[6]See the author's report of approximately three dozen interviews with past and serving planners, predominantly American, but also including several British, French, and other planners: "Policy Planning Redefined: What the Planners Think," *International Journal*, Autumn 1977, 813–828.

[7]Or, it might be added, where some Cubans happen to be.

their long-range security implications and consequences. The Treasury Department was long the designated official worrier about the "dollar gap"—and sponsor of "shocks."

With minor exceptions, planners in State during the 1950s and 1960s simply did not go deeply into issues of energy, food, environment, or monetary policy, in the crucial sense of focusing top-level attention on projections and forecasts aimed at anticipating system-wide disorders. By the first half of the 1970s, studies of food, energy, proliferation, and other crosscutting problems were made, but only after they had become foreign policy crises. It took the Middle Eastern War of 1973 to focus top officials on the exigent "Interdependence Agenda."

One reason for S/P's uneven focus was the historic allergy of secretaries of state and their political deputies to other than political-security matters. That bias invariably inclined the departmental pecking order in favor of the traditional geographic bureaus. The planners, tied as they have had to be to other people's notions of what is important, tilted accordingly. A better balance began to develop in the top-level agenda with Kissinger's important speech in 1975 to the UN 7th Special Session;[8] nevertheless in the 1980s the Arab-Israeli conflict, Southern Africa, and superpower relations remained dominant, while North-South and "functional" politics were still clearly secondary to presidents and secretaries of state. Planners had to juggle their deep involvement in North-South issues alongside the pressures to come up with ideas on the priority areas.

This biasing structure of policy priorities was often accompanied by a lack of independence to tackle taboo subjects. During the Dulles regime through most of the 1950s, China policy, French anti-Americanism, military force composition and weaponry, human rights covenants, and commodity agreements were all off limits to State Department planners. Over the entire two decades prior to 1971, China policy was not something planners ventured into more than once (nor was the deepening Vietnam involvement). Even the PARA system,[9] an interesting experiment in quasi-formal planning techniques, excluded from its coverage the most policy-sensitive foreign countries.

---

[8]"Global Consensus and Economic Development," Bureau of Public Affairs, Department of State, September 1, 1975.

[9]Policy Analysis and Resource Allocation.

3. In one prime sector—politicomilitary affairs—the planners have been very active and often influential. S/P gets an *A* for its sustained earlier efforts to coordinate planning with the Department of Defense. Indeed, the *only* continuing interagency liaison established by S/P over three decades was with the Pentagon, through lunches with the Joint Staff, exchanges of personnel, and in-house expertise. Some might argue that this emphasis contributed to distortion of overall U.S. policy perspectives, but most of the time top-level U.S. policy perspectives *are* predominantly politicomilitary.

4. Current policies have rarely, if ever, been systematically evaluated within the government with the independence of mind that is essential to produce responsible first-order critiques of current national strategies.[10]

Doubtless that is natural. However, it would be difficult to contend that anything resembling consequence-oriented planning or high-level adversary debate went into misguided policy initiatives ranging from the Eisenhower Doctrine of 1957 that astonishingly misread Mid-East realities, to the disastrously ill-conceived 1961 Bay of Pigs invasion, from the 1965 Dominican Republic intervention and the 1970 Cambodia "incursion," to the 1971 Connally-Nixon shocks, from the neglect and patronizing of European allies, to the shortsighted periodic support of losers and racists in Africa, from the protracted involvement in a disastrous Indochina war no official dared to challenge, to overconcentration on military aspects of local conflict at the expense of indigenous root causes in the early 1980s.

THE U.S. EXPERIENCE

Clues to the puzzle of planning can perhaps be found by examining its three-decade-plus history. In April 1947, George F. Kennan, who had been detached from the National War College to work on the sudden and urgent problem of aid to Greece and Turkey, was instructed to set up a planning staff without delay. The reason for

[10]With rare exceptions, government analysis invariably accepts as *given* the first-order premises of policy ("the United States should have a continuing military presence in Europe/Asia"; "socialism is contrary to American values"; "Congress will never support purely humanitarian programs"; "the triad is essential to strategic deterrence"; "the United States cannot accept a Palestinian state until Israel does," and so on). Analysis normally focuses on implementation, tactics, and on second- or third-order options.

urgency was the desperate situation in Western Europe. Secretary Marshall emphasized that if the United States did not take the initiative to improve matters, others would. Kennan was ordered to assemble a staff, and to make recommendations within ten days or two weeks on U.S. actions regarding Europe. The only advice the general gave him was to "avoid trivia."[11] The Kennan planning staff has ever since been taken as a paradigm of planning.

Paul Nitze, who succeeded Kennan, was close (as Kennan had not been) to Secretary Acheson, and under his direction S/P drafted NSC paper 68 which, whether one agrees with it or not, nevertheless laid out a comprehensive Cold War posture for the United States that came close to being an integrated policy plan.[12] Nitze's special relationship with Acheson also engaged him in current policy situations, most notably negotiations to end the 1951–1952 crisis of Iranian oil precipitated by the lachrymose Premier Mossadeq. This pattern of cooptation of planners for real-time crisis operations has recurred many times; ironically, it meant that top officials found the planners to be too valuable to "waste" on planning.

As the Cold War unfolded, the locus of foreign policy planning shifted to the National Security Council. In the 1950s S/P became essentially a staff operation for the secretary of state in his capacity as a leading NSC member, and the NSC Planning Board tended to preempt the planning function.[13] Nevertheless, planning chief Robert Bowie accompanied Secretary Dulles to most international meetings and was frequently invited to Dulles's house on weekends to discuss broad issues "with no holds barred," in Bowie's words.

Secretary Herter, whose tenure was brief, was prepared to make use of planners (and also encouraged outsiders to help them).[14] But

---

[11]George F. Kennan, *Memoirs 1925–1950* (Boston: Little, Brown, 1967), p. 313.

[12]See *Foreign Relations of the United States*, 1950, Vol. I (Washington, D.C.: Government Printing Office, 1977), pp. 234–292.

[13]Robert R. Bowie, *Shaping the Future* (New York: Columbia University Press, 1964).

[14]Herter expressed great interest in the new technique of political gaming and asked the author, then newly at M.I.T., to include members of S/P in our adaptations of the so-called RAND game, while ruling out in-house State Department games for fear of incurring congressional ridicule. S/P members participated in all ten senior M.I.T. POLEXes. Only one subsequent S/P chief, Walt W. Rostow, ran the risk of sponsoring a full-blown in-house "State game." See "Games Foreign Policy Experts Play: The Political Exercise Comes of Age" by the present author and Cornelius J. Gearin, *Orbis*, Winter 1973, 1008–1031.

Herter's planning director, Gerard Smith, on his own testimony, had "no use for the ivory tower."[15]

The NSC precipitately declined under presidents Kennedy and Johnson, but planning did not consequently flourish back at State. In the early 1960s, rival centers of planning sprang up both in the NSC and in the Office of the Assistant Secretary of Defense for International Security Affairs (DOD/ISA).

Secretary Rusk's first planner, George McGhee, took particular pride in his contribution to settlement of the then burning West New Guinea (West Irian) conflict—like Nitze's Iranian negotiation a useful fire-fighting exercise but hardly "planning." In that period the staff was also preoccupied with the mounting Berlin crisis.

Walt Rostow, who succeeded McGhee, placed a substantial emphasis on his major specialty, developing nations (plus its ultimately deformed twin, counterinsurgency). In writing of his work in S/P, Rostow also stressed "expansion of work done with the military and in politico-military planning . . .," arguing that "the traditional sharp distinction between diplomacy and the application of military power has ended."[16] This argument (which some would claim contributed to an eventual distortion of American policy) was entirely consistent with the view of Rostow's superiors. What is less certain is the interest of the secretary of state in the planning efforts of either Rostow or his successor, Henry Owen.

In early 1969, State Department planning underwent a temporary metamorphosis. The new Republican secretary of state and his under secretary found themselves attending White House meetings equipped with departmental positions inferior in quality to the superlative staff preparations of President Nixon by his new special assistant, Henry Kissinger. Between the notional value of twenty-one inherited policy planners, and the felt need for coordination of the department's scattered policy process, it was no contest. For four years the broader policy planning function became a vestigial appendix to the new Policy and Coordination Staff (S/PC). William Sutterlin, who ultimately replaced William Cargo as S/PC director, recom-

[15]This and subsequent statements, when not accompanied by a citation, were made in conversations with the author. The unfortunate lack of literature in this area has required the use of this imperfect form of scholarship.

[16]Walt W. Rostow, "The Planning of Foreign Policy," in *The Dimensions of Diplomacy,* ed. E.A.J. Johnson (Baltimore: The Johns Hopkins University Press, 1964), p. 153.

mended that the planning function be restored and the coordinating function be assigned elsewhere.

The Policy Planning Staff was revived under Secretary of State Kissinger, who named as its head one of his most trusted assistants from the NSC staff, Winston Lord. Opinions differ within the State Department, and even among Lord's planners, as to how much of what S/P in fact did could properly be called planning. However, there can be no doubt that Kissinger placed an extraordinarily high value on Lord's services, and at the close of the administration in an unprecedented action, he bestowed the department's Distinguished Honor Award on the entire staff. I have already referred briefly to the same ambivalence in the two administrations that followed, under Secretaries Vance and Muskie from 1977 to 1981, and under Secretary Haig.

Presidents themselves are not immune to the illusory dreams of leisurely long-range planning as distinct from operations. When President-elect Richard M. Nixon presented Professor Kissinger to the press at the Hotel Pierre headquarters on December 2, 1968, he emphasized that his new assistant would spend much of his time in long-range planning, and Presidents Carter and Reagan said much the same thing of their prospective National Security Advisers. But experience suggests that the NSC staff is no more able to do leisurely planning than State. In the case of Reagan, by actually pushing much of the foreign policy action back to State he at least left it open, depending on Secretary Haig's preferences, for planning-type activities to be attempted.

Some inescapable conclusions emerge from these vignettes. First, "successful" planners are those considered most "relevant" by the secretary of state and other policy makers. Second, whether planning ever approximates the ideal model is entirely up to the secretary. Third, to be relevant, and thus "influential," planners simply cannot (or will not) get too far out of line with established policies. Two supplemental points: Inside information is a form of power in bureaucracies and therefore, to be in the know, planners have to remain close to operations. And to foster that relationship, they eschew experimental, theoretical, or methodological unorthodoxies, or flights into the future that in the Foreign Service subculture would invariably brand them as unsound.

The end result has been that many a planner has volunteered

(or has been drafted) to help with current crises and to perform operational tasks. Other planners, correctly perceiving that they were out of the mainstream, either retreated to write "think pieces" few operators would take seriously, or lowered their sights and assumed a low profile, cautiously steering between the regional bureaus that might feel threatened by competition, and a seventh floor chief impatient with concerns remote from his daily pressures. The Planning Staff, often as not, has tended to become a high-grade pool of spare hands, available to take on some chores on current policies which the operating bureaus are too busy to handle. With this drastically amended definition of the planning function, most planners can point to substantial accomplishments in the form of policy innovations and solutions.

However useful those things, we can legitimately ask: Is it policy planning? How could its original model have, in Secretary Kissinger's words, so "fallen into disuse"? It is not always remembered that the part played by the Kennan S/P in the dazzlingly successful Marshall Plan involved neither adversary challenge to top-level policy nor tensions between present needs and future orientation. In the case in point, the Kennan staff contributed as a *first-class task force* to a *one-time job* for which there was a clear and present need—and thereafter lost momentum.

It is not always recalled that two years and some months later, George Kennan resigned from his post in protest over losing direct access to the secretary of state, by then Dean Acheson. He recorded in his private diary some conclusions about the planning process that are worth rereading:

> Pondering today the frustrations of the past week, it occurred to me that it is time I recognized that my Planning Staff, started nearly three years ago, has simply been a failure, like all previous attempts to bring order and foresight into the design of foreign policy by special institutional arrangements within the department . . . The reason for this seems to lie largely in the impossibility of having the planning function performed outside of the line of command.[17]

In this reflection on his days as, in his inimitable phrase—"Court Jester"—George Kennan surfaced problems that have chronically

[17]Kennan, *Memoirs,* 1925–1950, p. 467.

beset the planning function, and which remain essentially unresolved: the dilemma of isolation versus involvement; the necessity for a conceptually minded secretary of state; and chronic uncertainty as to the planner's influence.

POLICY PLANNING ABROAD

Over the past two decades a number of planning staffs have been established in foreign ministries around the world, most of them in imitation of the American model.

In 1957 the British Foreign Office[18] set up a policy planning function which in 1964 became a full-fledged planning staff. It was charged (in the words of the Plowden Commission) not to "make plans" but to foresee choices Britain might face over a five-year stretch, and to formulate broad lines of policy. To give it a structured place, it worked through the permanent under secretary's Planning Committee attended by all the deputy under secretaries and other senior officials. That committee meets monthly to consider papers prepared by the planners.

The British planning staff, unlike S/P, decided to remain small (around five). Like S/P, it has worked on some major policy issues. (Indeed, it recently acquired an extraordinary means of weighing policy priorities, through a rule that no new funds may be approved in the international sector without the planners' comments.)

Nevertheless, like S/P, the FCO staff has generally had to function within a definition of relevance that is congenial to nonplanners. In London, as in Washington, policy planners tend to gravitate toward involvement in current problems. The British staff (like S/P) has enjoyed some success in focusing its operational colleagues on consequences of current government decisions, but its influence is uncertain, and there remains a strong sense that at least until recently, British policy planning has been a tender plant growing in an alien environment.

An interesting contrast is found in the Central Policy Review Staff (CPRS)—the so-called "think tank"—set up by Prime Minister Heath under the direction of a brilliant and unorthodox biologist at

[18]Since 1968 the Foreign and Commonwealth Office (FCO).

Cambridge University, Lord Victor Rothschild, with a staff of twenty-four.

In many ways that group came close to realizing the ideal model of a planning staff, complete with unorthodoxy (even heresy), continuous tension with the bureaucracy, and strong in-house challenges to policy. (Its terms of reference were written by the then cabinet secretary, Sir Burke Trend, in a way that, in the words of a British admirer interviewed by the author, was "characteristically lucid but incomprehensible," thus guaranteeing flexibility.) Its record on foreign policy has been mixed.

Initially the head of the think tank had an unquestioned pipeline to the prime minister and other cabinet ministers. The staff busied itself with complex trends and interdepartmental issues (such as the Concorde) which, in its chief's words, "tend to leave the cabinet confused," and became deeply involved in the country's choice of nuclear reactors. Indeed, until a ministry of energy was created it provided most of Britain's official forward thinking on energy.

Lord Rothschild required that his planning papers review what the government said it would do; what in fact it did; what it did not do; and what to do about it—a striking example of the *postaudit* which surely should be included among planning functions. Confronted with a new and less sympathetic British government, Lord Rothschild decided that four years was enough. His replacement by a man of different style suggests that the feeling may have been mutual.

Yet the iconoclastic tradition dies hard. Two years later the CPRG under Sir Kenneth Berrill generated a storm in the stately precincts of Whitehall with a 442-page report recommending the virtual abolition of her Majesty's diplomatic service on grounds of irrelevance to Britain's shrunken role and the priority need for specialists to work on the complex interdependence issues of trade, energy, and resources.[19]

The French, perhaps because of the newness of their experiment (or perhaps because planning is more congenial to the Cartesian than to the muddling-through tradition), may have had a more positive experience than the Anglo-Saxons.

Following establishment in the 1960s by Jean Laloi of a hybrid group to focus on East-West relations—a group successfully absorbed

[19]See *The Economist,* January 21, 1978, pp. 25–26 and January 28, 1978, p. 24.

by the Foreign Ministry bureaucracy—a proper planning staff was organized in 1973 under Foreign Minister Jobert, based on the Kissinger-NSC model, but also inspired by the successful Commissariat du Plan. The disappearance from the scene of "the Big Planner"—General de Gaulle—had left a vacuum: The energy crisis furnished the occasion to challenge conventional analysis. Jobert recruited planners (known familiarly as the "Joboys") who could take advantage of their newfound leverage to demonstrate the outmoded thinking of others and the necessity that the Foreign Ministry get involved in economic policy. The first chief was a professor of economics at the École Polytechnique; the other two original members were a systems analyst and scientist. Even the name suggests a more avant-gardist approach: *Centre d'Analyse et de Prévision.*

The staff, subsequently grown to nine (a mix of outsiders and insiders), aimed at integrating national, international, and multilateral components of policy. Like other planning staffs, the French one was excluded from certain of the most crucial questions (since the United Kingdom entered the European Community, the French prime minister had been the main coordinator of France's European planning). However, its members are often influential.

Other experimenters have had a less successful time of it. The Japanese Foreign Ministry, after several abortive attempts, decided in 1960 to concentrate a policy planning function in the office of the deputy vice minister. Ten years later, in the same quest for better planning, the International Data Department of the Foreign Office was substantially upgraded. However, Japanese observers note that the regional bureaus (like their counterparts in Foggy Bottom) are jealous of their bailiwick.[20] The Australian Department of External Affairs, which set up a planning staff in 1971 to think beyond normal boundaries, ran afoul of the same issues of turf and became absorbed into the Executive Secretariat.

In the late 1960s a preplanning staff was set up in the Belgian Foreign Ministry in much the same spirit: *Someone* in the diplomatic establishment should be freed to look ahead, take a broad view, and challenge policy. Alas, there too it failed. The top operating officials saw no need for long-range planning. In their off-the-record words,

[20]See Haruhiro Fukui, "Foreign Policy-Making By Improvisation: The Japanese Experience," *International Journal,* Autumn 1977, 791–812.

any thinking that had to be done could be done perfectly well by the operators. (Belgium took a shot at trying it again, this time with some interest in quantitative approaches.)

Canada, in August of 1969, established within the Department of External Affairs a Policy Analysis Group, "to develop and analyze major foreign policy alternatives for Canada, with particular attention to long-range considerations." The PAG group had much going for it—a compact size (five); location in the hierarchy directly under the permanent head of the External Affairs department; and a verbal commitment from Prime Minister Trudeau to a planning and systems approach to policy matters.

The PAG has devoted recent attention to defining Canadian goals and—innovatively—to domestic problems (such as unemployment) having international significance. However, in Ottawa as elsewhere planners experience the dilemma of overinvolvement versus irrelevance.[21]

The Dutch planning staff of five, set up in late 1971, analyzes long-term trends in foreign affairs, proposes policy alternatives, and, like many other planners, also writes speeches and performs odd chores for high officials. Norway's six-person staff (which worries that it is too large) took the lead in setting Norwegian policy guidelines on North-South and other interdependence questions, as well as on human rights. But its director recently devoted approximately half his time to serve as chairman of the U.N. Commodities Stabilization Committee in Geneva.

Many of their counterparts' frustrations have been encountered by Sweden's foreign ministry planners (unaccountably located in the division of disarmament and nuclear export affairs). But like the British, the Swedes have experimented with a higher-level think tank charged with introducing into political decisions a better sense of the long-term. The Secretariat for Future Studies was created by the prime minister in 1973 with a staff of four that included a mathematician, scientist, and educator. They too report that busy politicians have little time for, and are not easily accessible to, "thinkers." However, that unit shows an enthusiasm rare for frustrated planners (ex-

[21]See also Daniel Madar and Denis Stairs, "Alone on Killer's Row: The Policy Analysis Group and the Department of External Affairs"; and G.A.H. Pearson, "Order Out of Chaos? Some Reflections on Foreign Policy Planning in Canada," both in *International Journal*, Autumn 1977, 727–768.

cept for a few like the new, young Malaysian policy planning staff which takes pride in its recent ten- to twenty-year regional projections).

Indeed, most planning staffs, at least in their candid moments, admit to a mixed record at best; at worst to living proof of the pervasive foreign office belief that, at root, planning and operations are essentially inseparable. When a genuine success story is encountered (such as the role of Germany's then planning director, Egon Bahr, in the late 1960s in formulating the *Ostpolitik*), it often turns out to involve, not a planning exercise in the strict sense, but a first-rate *task force* product—like the Kennan S/P's Marshall Plan. The FRG record since is described as "mixed."[22]

Even Peking shared the common experience. Zhou Enlai is reported to have included in his newly reconstituted Foreign Office in 1949 a policy planning staff under the direction of Qiao Guanhua (who later became foreign minister). However, in 1952 it was dropped because, according to reports, it did not seem "useful."

One might imagine the genuine article ought to be found at least in Moscow, the home of The Plan, and undoubtedly planning *is* done where power and initiative is located, that is, in the Central Committee staff. It is reported that there are also around eighty fairly high-level planners in the Foreign Ministry (in a section entitled "Administration for Foreign Policy Actions"). However, the kind of planning they do is what might be called *operational;* the same is said to be true for policy planners in the German Democratic Republic (and in a perverse sense, from time to time in the United States as well). Operational planning connotes coordination and action responsibility, rather than anything resembling futurism, cross-bureaucratic integrative thinking, or—*a fortiori*—challenges to current policy.

Ironically, Soviet experts seem to have assumed that it is the Americans who have mastered the art (or science, as they would say) of foreign policy planning. Just as Soviet leadership reached out eclectically in the 1920s for American assembly line know-how, and in the 1940s for more powerful U.S. models of economic behavior, so in the 1960s Soviet analysts intensively studied supposed American policy planning methods, with particular emphasis on innovative techniques

[22]On the FRG's experience, see Ernst W. Gohlert, "Planning in German Foreign Policy," ibid. 769–790.

of analysis and forecasting.[23] The further irony is that official U.S. planning remains largely innocent to this day of social science methodology, including most assiduously studied by its Soviet counterparts.

THE PLANNER'S DILEMMA

Even this brief survey of some foreign experiences reassures us that the problem is not distinctly American, or a reflection of inferior American talents. For in one foreign office after another, the logic is inexorable. Politicians and diplomats are busy and focused on short-term problems. Policy planners, to be influential, must do what their bosses find relevant. Relevance is defined by policy makers as that which helps them to deal with their burdensome agendas, their exigent heads of government and critical publics, and their crushing deadlines. The planner's success, more often than not, varies in direct proportion to his willingness to help solve current puzzles, to present ideas in ways congenial to the operator's idiom and mind-set, and to be loyal to the basic policies of the administration. This enables him to gain influence. However, the more successful he is in gaining influence, the less successful he becomes as a planner. Like a clergyman in a rich parish, he comforts the afflicted but rarely gets around to afflicting the comfortable, except in minor ways.

Now and then planners do fulfill the ideal, but that cannot be relied on, since planning is defined by the whims and style of one individual for whom the alarm clock always seems more relevant than the calendar. Real-life planning functions range across a limitless continuum from philosopher to analyst, to speechwriter, to prophet, to kibitzer, to negotiator, to dreamer, to staff coordinator. Planning is what someone labelled a *planner* happens to be doing at any given moment. The consequence is that most of the time a Gresham's law is at work, with operations consistently driving out planning.

So long as this situation continues unchanged, planners will usually remain marginal people, tolerated by the system so long as they do not become irritating, valued to the extent that they make the

[23]See for example Vitaly V. Zhurkin, "The United States and International Political Crises," *USA: Economics, Politics and Ideology* (translation), no. 12, December 1970.

operator's life easier, not harder, and ignored when they start to become intellectually rarefied, methodologically unfamiliar, or politically heretical.

Some experienced diplomats have cautioned that planning is not really possible in foreign affairs. A legitimate fear of excessive rigidity moves professional diplomats to argue against contingency planning. (Former Secretary of State Dean Rusk cautions that "policy planning must be in the subjunctive mood."[24]) Sometimes of course that argument is a convenient way to sweep under the rug the whole idea of improved analytical tools. Yet, as Sir Harold Nicolson put it, "Nobody who has not watched 'policy' expressing itself in day-to-day action can realize how seldom is the course of events determined by deliberately planned purpose . . . "[25]

The circumstances in which policy planning was created, given the high military component of policy in the 1940s, suggests the possibility that General Marshall (and all others since then who have tried to establish foreign office planning) were misled by the relatively successful history of military planning. It is universally accepted that war plans require definition of potential adversaries, identification of contingencies to be prepared for, and logistical wherewithal. The plans may be disastrously wrongheaded, the strategies left over from previous wars, the anticipated contingencies irrelevant to the future. Nevertheless, the military cannot land on a beach without extensive advance planning. However, a political leader can land on the front pages—or in a war—with no preparation, lead time, or plan.

It is the inherent nature of foreign policy making institutions that makes it so difficult to isolate a planning function in a way that would be natural and obvious in, say, an army or a post office department. In fact each desirable quality of planning is contravened by

[24]Letter to the author dated August 21, 1974. From a subsequent letter dated June 9, 1978: I think I would have to say that the notion of planning is an essential ingredient in any policy maker's mind—at whatever level in the policy making he or she might work. Most foreign policy decisions, for example, are about the future—trying to shape the course of events somewhat more in one direction than in another. But Providence has not given us the capacity to pierce the fog of the future with accuracy, and so the planning point of view must involve a continuing process of revision and adjustment. A brilliant plan which is no longer relevant is not much help; however, the planning effort may be an invaluable experience for those who participate in it and who look over the results. It does help, for example, to discover the questions which might otherwise be ignored.

[25]Harold Nicolson, *The Congress of Vienna* (New York: Harcourt Brace Jovanovich, 1946), p. 19.

a distinctive institutional feature of the foreign office system, which is hierarchical, politically loyal, careerist, traditionalist, and incrementalist. More simply put in the form of Bloomfield's law, "Nothing happens until it has to."

Of course, if a desk officer is doing his job well, he should in a real sense *be* his own planner. In carrying out day-to-day line responsibilities, a good operating official should be constantly evaluating trends in his sector, forecasting future area developments, and drawing the attention of superior officers to pitfalls and opportunities, all from the standpoint of understood national interests, goals, and objectives. Those interests, goals, and objectives are often hard to find (which is one of the central problems in planning). However, even if they have to be invented, the action officer—like the planner—is expected to articulate them as a foundation for policy recommendations. "In the final analysis," said a definitive report on foreign policy making, "a top executive must do his own planning."[26]

None of this is to say that in the postwar decades there were not either major policy successes, or that policy planners were not often of major assistance in helping resolve particular policy dilemmas. Yet we are left with the nagging suspicion that foreign office planning may be doomed, by deep structural flaws in its very conception, to perpetual shortfall in living up to its officially defined purposes. The question is inescapable: Is there really a unique task to be performed by people called planners, in contradistinction to other intelligent and thoughtful people who bear operational responsibilities?

THE CONTINUING NEED FOR A GENUINE PLANNING FUNCTION

It is tempting to conclude from this gloomy recital that at least for the United States the time has come to strip the veil from the policy-planning myth, call a spade a spade, and release the planner to seek gainful employment. But logical as that may seem, nothing could be more damaging to the future conduct of American foreign policy.

[26]U.S. Congress, Senate, Committee on Government Operations, Subcommittee on National Security Staffing and Operations, *Administration of National Security: Basic Issues,* 88th Congress, 1st Session, 1963 (Washington: Government Printing Office, 1963). p. 6.

The conclusion that the policy-planning function is unworkable and should be scrapped is logically correct—but wrong.

Equally powerful logic argues that today, when uncertainty and complexity have expanded beyond recognition as never before, the case for proper policy planning is far more compelling than it was thirty-plus years ago when the world looked two-dimensional. The multiple interconnectedness of global life gives an increasingly unrecognizable face to foreign affairs. It is not traditional forces which have created potent expectations for the world's majority, and paralyzing instabilities for its embattled minority. Foreign offices are full of experts on diplomatic relations, not interdependence. Crisis managers take justifiable pride in their capacity for rapid response. But it is the over-the-horizon problems, left unanalyzed and unintegrated into present policies, which guarantee incessant surprises for the "practical" diplomats.

Professor Thomas Schelling of Harvard once posed the dazzling riddle of how to make a list of questions one would never have thought to ask. Such a task eludes both conventional organization structures and specialist mind-sets. No organizational form or professional specialty exists today that knows how to deal effectively with the linkages between trade, investment, food, and military security; how to integrate the mind-boggling capacity for electronic data manipulation with levels of human misery and intercultural antagonism; or how to tie warm homes and electoral votes in northern climates to war and peace in the Middle East, the South China Sea, and the west coast of Africa. When enormous political and social stakes ride on food supplies, the state of recent intellectual and conceptual arts was typified by the admission that U.S. government analysts had "no methodologies to alert policy-makers to adverse climatic change," and "no tools to assess the economic and political impact of such a change."[27]

It is overwhelmingly apparent that foreign affairs henceforth need to be dealt with not just in vertical segments, one compartmented from the other, but horizontally, across traditional agency and subject lines—and across the even more rigidly guarded boundaries between "domestic" and "foreign." Responsible powers

[27]CIA working paper entitled "A Study of Climatological Research as it Pertains to Intelligence Problems," declassified May 1976.

must, if they are to act rationally, be equally guided by integrative thinking across the barriers of agency, tribe, state, region. Large and small powers alike need new mental and conceptual tools for their survival in a world essentially beyond their control. Rather than being embarrassed at seeming "unrealistic," planners must be formally mandated to work within time frames well beyond the ken of day-to-day diplomacy and strategy.

Traditionalists argue that the future is unknowable, random events change history, and, as an anonymous wit put it, life is what happens while you are making other plans. But this shortchanges what can be done in an age in which the future is daily mortgaged through fateful decisions by investors, weapons designers, and determined groups aspiring to political power.

Trend-lines look different depending on how one projects them[28]—and on what one then decides to do to try to alter the outcomes. Econometric analysis is not always right, but it predicts better than Adam Smith or Karl Marx was able to. Political gaming and other social science tools cannot tell one what will happen, but if done well, they put the official mind into a believable future long enough to subject favorite policies to strain and to raise with participants hitherto unexamined alternatives.

An equally compelling case exists for doing that which most runs against the smooth grain of the bureaucracy: challenging first-order policy premises that may be reinforcing a faulty policy edifice. Justice Holmes pointed out that men naturally try to suppress opposing views. Writing of one of America's most traumatic cases of officially imposed policy myopia, Barbara Tuchman observed that "to halt the momentum of an accepted idea, to reexamine assumptions, is a disturbing process and requires more courage than governments can generally summon."[29] In the present era, a whole succession of later-regretted policies was accounted for by President John F. Kennedy when, after the Bay of Pigs fiasco, he acknowledged having made a grievous mistake in which not only were the facts he used wrong, but

---

[28]Examples are given in "Short-Order Futures" by Lincoln P. Bloomfield in *Forecasting in International Relations: Theory, Methods, Problems, Prospects,* ed. Nazli Choucri and Thomas W. Robinson (San Francisco: W.H. Freeman & Company Publishers, 1978).

[29]Barbara W. Tuchman, *Stilwell and the American Experience in China 1911–45* (New York: Macmillan, 1971), p. 354.

the policy was wrong *because the premises on which it was built were wrong.*[30]

In sum, in a global political atmosphere that often seems to resemble a gas-filled coal mine, modern governments cannot afford not to create and nurture a role, sharply distinguished from that of the workers battering away at the coal face, for the canaries who give early warning of potential disaster.

SQUARING THE CIRCLE

If the preceding analysis is accepted, planning will be defined in terms of two different functions, neither of which has been done well. The first distinctive task is to study the unfolding future—short, middle, and long term—free of agency bias, with the aid of modern analytical tools to supplement the experienced diplomat's *fingerspritzengefühl.* The other is enough independence of mind—and the clout to back it up—so that, particularly as an administration ages, bad news about the leadership's favorite policy assumptions can be delivered without the messenger returning to the planning office with his head tucked under his arm.

Yet it is painfully evident that an official planning staff, even if it wished to, cannot go beyond certain now-familiar bounds in trying to fulfill these functions. Long experience in the United States and elsewhere confirms that planners are unlikely to even try any of them if a particular secretary of state or minister of foreign affairs chooses not to acknowledge their value. Ideally, then, foreign policy planning should not be confined to an organizational setting in which, for deep structural reasons, it cannot realize even an approximation of the ideal.

A superficially tempting way out of the dilemma would be to transfer S/P from the State Department to the White House, so that it could embrace the entire executive branch, including primarily domestic agencies doing things which increasingly affect, and are affected by, foreign relations.[31] One can envisage an Americanized ver-

[30]See *New York Times,* May 17, 1970.

[31]Other options, along with elaboration of the recommendation that follows, are found in the author's "Organizing for Policy Planning," which appears in the *Report* of the Murphy Commission. Appendix F, Vol. 2.

sion of the British think tank, generating two-tiered official planning, with government-wide planners challenging State Department staffs and vice versa. Indeed, were it not for constitutional constraints, logic might even commend joint executive-congressional policy planning in order to prepare the U.S. government for the monumental agenda of crosscutting problems that lies ahead.

The 1975 Murphy Commission report was, however, probably correct in concluding that the function had best be left in the Department of State—but improved. However, the commission did not go far enough in breaking new ground demanded by the implications of its own analysis. Several linked propositions mark the path to a solution.

Planners inside the government must obviously give top priority to helping policy makers with their current headaches. Someone else, then, should be available to go further than S/P can in criticizing, thinking unthinkable policy thoughts, and peering into the longer-term future.

In-house planners must operate in private if they are to have the trust of their colleagues. Someone else, then, should be available to help think about the same range of issues in freer contact with public opinion groups, members of Congress, and the academic and intellectual world. Inside planners must respect the government's division of labor. Someone else must be free to tread on forbidden turf when necessary to do greater justice to planning problems that know no agency bounds. *What is needed is a combination of inside and outside.*

If S/P supplies to the secretary of state and the principal seventh floor officers a kind of "loyal opposition" to keep them alert to implications and consequences of current policy decisions, S/P in turn needs a loyal opposition to help it go beyond the well-known constraints of in-house planning, in the direction of the ideal.

In-house planning must maintain its vital link to policy and to action authority which alone can implement the planner's insights. Outside help, less tied to the hierarchy and more tenuously linked to authority, could, if adequately plugged in to S/P, ensure greater scope, more flexible and imaginative time horizons, freer methodological experimentation, and insistent independent-mindedness.

Outside counterparts could help keep the insiders intellectually honest. Inside planners would, in turn, help to keep the outsiders reasonably—but not bureaucratically—earthbound.

My modest proposal, then, is that a group of knowledgeable individuals of independent mind, with secure home bases outside of the government, be added on to the official planning function as a kind of outside wing. Their mandate would be to help the policy planners in ways that will maximize the possibility of fulfilling S/P's only partially achieved goals.

An outside wing of part-time planners would be small (and S/P itself might consider a further slimming down). Its members would be appointed as consultants, where possible without pay, with the understanding that they were independent of government. The wing would be so organized (for example, three-year appointments) as to ensure that it would not be eliminated when the policy going gets rough.

Contacts with S/P would be regular, preferably as often as two days of intensive meetings every month. The group would bring in others as needed, ad hoc, but its members would be fully cleared so there would be no inhibitions at the regular discussions.

Such an outside wing would appraise planning papers; suggest reordering of planning priorities when those priorities excessively reflect current operational needs; propose planning agenda items that from the inside might seem too distant or irrelevant; help supply more unorthodox inputs into planning (which, like the rest of the foreign policy establishment, tends to feature white males); and provide perspectives on policy issues which draw on non-State Department and domestically oriented concerns.

Such an outside planning wing could itself do or oversee tasks inside planners virtually never do: make long-range projections, and conduct post mortems on past planning products from S/P files in order to supply a more systematic learning experience that might throw new light on planning successes and failures. While primarily a "creative critic" of official planning, to the extent it was part of the political process it might at times act as a political ally of S/P through influence on top officials on behalf of good planning ideas (or to warn top officials against obvious misuse of their planning staffs).

Individually members would exploit their home bases, whether research institutions, businesses, labor, public organizations, universities, or whatever, to bring to the effort specialized knowledge about potentially useful and relevant work done elsewhere. To the extent possible, members would themselves try to translate and process that work in order to convey it in usable ways to in-house planners.

The outside wing would on occasion meet together separately to brainstorm certain of its ideas before taking them up with S/P, but it should not form an outside cabal, and members could bring individual contributions to S/P.

One additional potential contribution of the add-on function would be to focus foreign office planners on methods and techniques of analysis of which, on a virtual worldwide basis, they tend to remain ignorant and toward which they are often hostile.

Much theoretical and methodological work in the social sciences is unfortunately irrelevant to the needs of real-world planning, either because it is not applicable, or is still in the theory-building stage, or because some of it is excessively primitive and even shoddy.

Other work, I would contend, is potentially relevant but remains underutilized. The reason is that planners do not know how to use such tools, or because the work is not intelligible to any but a handful of academic cognoscenti, or because scarce official resources invariably favor projects with the highest short-term payoff. Some useful external research has been commissioned by the State Department at the behest of the Policy Planning Staff, and some contacts with scholars are regularly maintained by both planning and research units of the State Department. However, policy planning the world over is notoriously laggard in using or applying social science research tools, even the potentially valuable ones.

One such technique is mentioned with some diffidence, since I have been personally associated with it. This is the so-called political game. Assuming it to be well designed and aimed specifically at policy-planning purposes,[32] a game can, if conducted properly, constitute a stimulating technique for pretesting, so to speak, proposed policy strategies, as well as for examining in depth inadequately considered alternative policy outcomes. Political games can be a powerful tool for eliciting more useful reactions to the planner's central question of "what if?" than conventional discussions or individual analyses. Apart from well-known group pressures for consensus, usual methods have no systematic way of introducing either the clash of antagonistic

---

[32]The design, methodology, and results of efforts to tailor the political game for planning purposes are reported in *Anticipating Conflict Control Policies: The CONEX Games as a Planning Tool* by the author with C.J. Gearin and others, M.I.T. Center for International Studies, Pub. No. C/70-10, Cambridge, Mass. A summary is found in "Games Foreign Policy Experts Play."

wills or the dynamics of moves beyond the first action and reaction—undoubtedly the two chief features of games.

It can be speculated that the negative German and Brazilian reactions to the Carter administration's abrupt demands to cancel the agreed nuclear fuel cycle deal might have been better anticipated had the move been "gamed out" in advance; similarly, the negative Soviet reaction in the same period to substantial changes in SALT II (the hazards of which Moscow had specifically cautioned the newly elected leadership against in the fall of 1976). The same could be said of some hasty early Reagan initiatives.

One could conceive of simple but provocative games centered on decisions about weapons, or politics in countries in volatile regions, in order to get a sense of possible regional consequences that go beyond the usual short-term assumptions of stability or balance.[33]

In fact virtually all U.S. government political gaming has been conducted by the Pentagon, perhaps because it has far more funds than the diplomatic branch. Not unnaturally, since 1961 (when the Joint Chiefs of Staff set up an agency for government-wide political and military gaming), the emphasis has been on predominantly military crises. However, today what is needed are planning exercises on issues that have *not* become crises, as well as on nonmilitary sectors such as food, energy, and civilian technologies, which we now know can have profound security implications. The Pentagon's gaming effort should be purposefully redirected to become a far more effective tool for policy planning, perhaps by assigning S/P the guiding role in developing scenarios and insisting on more rigorous techniques of design and evaluation.

To give another example, computer systems are being widely developed outside the government for a broad range of activities including, for example, early warning of international conflict. Apart from some abortive experiments in the late 1960s and early 1970s,

---

[33]Again, with apologies reference is made to an M.I.T. report, which the government paid for but never made serious use of, containing important game-experimental findings concerning the possible effects of introducing arms assistance in various ways into local conflicts. See *Anticipating Conflicting Control Policies.* A review of all senior political games put on at M.I.T. from 1958 through 1970 (many of them comparable in problem and participants to the Pentagon's) showed that *forecasts of future events embodied in the scenarios* were almost uniformly wrong, but that, once given a certain genre of crisis, *the intragame* developments were uncannily correct in light of history.

little or no support has been given by the State Department to bringing this effort to a stage of usability by those officials who are trying to do complex planning tasks using pencil, paper, and imperfect human memories. Many otherwise interested officials have been turned off by excessive claims. Unfortunately, some computer enthusiasts see their machines as substitutes for experience and judgment, rather than as fast, efficient—and stupid—aids to intuition. The result has been to leave our diplomatic arm, apart from sophisticated communication mechanisms, a decade behind other sectors of American society.

It is not hard to think of many potential defects and weaknesses of the proposal for an outside wing. There is no dearth of external critics; why not just listen to them? Universities and private research organizations can obviously do some of these things. The proposed wing might not have had any effect on some policy failures. Official roles are focused on action; outsiders are often unrealistic about what is possible and not possible. If too tied to the system, outsiders may become co-opted by it, pull their punches, and meanwhile be downgraded elsewhere as "administration people." Regardless of what top officials say early in an administration, they may want to disregard *both* inside and outside critics when the time comes for hunkering down against the inevitable policy storms.

Such criticisms can be readily acknowledged as at least partially valid. However, after all is said and done, the gulf remains between the "thinking" side and the "doing" side of foreign policy making, as does the obligation to seek new remedies.

appendix

LEARNING THROUGH GAMING

The room was tense as everyone watched the president reach for the phone. To his right the secretary of state busied himself with the draft of a press statement. Across the table the secretary of defense was drawing up orders to be transmitted to U.S. military commands in three continents on nuclear "Defcon" alert since the upsurge of fighting in a Middle East country.

The president signalled for silence. "We have a hot-line message to Moscow. Yes, that's right. And it must go right away. You already caught it on the closed-circuit TV? Okay, what do we assume for delivery time? Right. Thanks."

He leaned back, lit a cigar, and said in the voice of a man desperately short of sleep but determined not to show it, "That's all we can do. The U.S. is not intervening, and we can only hope the Russians don't misunderstand and start mixing in. If they do, we have no choice but to go in."

The vice president of the United States looked up. When he spoke, his voice was perhaps a shade too loud. "Dammit, Mr. President, we did the right thing. We probably avoided another Bay of Pigs and another Vietnam, and that's the way the American people and the Congress want it. What if the Russians do get involved? Why should we?"

The argument that had waxed and waned for two days and part of a hectic night seemed to be starting all over again. Three members of the National Security Council executive committee opened their mouths to join battle once more over whether America should respond militarily, when the door opened and a secretary walked into the room, carrying a tray of sherry. "Control says it's time for lunch, and would you please fill out your questionnaires before you come downstairs?"

The scene, it will now be clear, was not the White House situation room; rather it was Endicott House, M.I.T.'s country house in Dedham, Massachusetts. The "president of the United States" was neither Jimmy Carter nor Ronald Reagan. He was, rather, a distinguished business executive with some presidential pretensions and vast firsthand experience of government. His "secretary of state" was not Henry Kissinger, or Alexander Haig, but *was* a high-ranking State Department official, just as the "secretary of defense" was a real-life senior Pentagon official.

What, then, was all this about? It was a *POLEX*—political exercise (or game, or simulation)—put on by M.I.T., which during recent years acquired an international reputation for "gaming out" with real-life government officials (and scholars and students) important issues of foreign policy.

The same kinds of political games—POLEXes—have provided a splendid chance for students in thousands of classrooms, in the U.S. and around the world, to learn about international relations and foreign policy decision making in the most vivid way possible—by taking part in the process themselves.

DEFINITIONS

Let's back up to get some definitions straight.

The words I used above were *simulation, games,* and *exercises* (I could have added *game theory* and *model*). Games are informal names for what we are talking about. But if we want to be rigorous, a game really means a competition in which, through skill or chance, one can win or lose according to clearly specified rules; international politics have few such rules. Game theory comes out of mathematics via economics; it means a theory of competitive interaction in which numerical payoffs are specified for strategies chosen by each side to minimize losses and maximize gains; that bears some relation to reality—and to the POLEX—but is too formal for our purposes. Simulation, technically speaking, means a model that can be formally expressed (for instance, in mathematical terms), that enables one to represent reality dynamically, preferably on a computer. The POLEX does not mean that.

As my M.I.T. colleagues and I developed the POLEX (originally conceived in the Rand Corporation), these definitional obstacles convinced us to substitute the loose word *exercise* (thus POLEX, for political exercise). But as such exercises became popular for teaching, research, and even government policy purposes, the word *game* crept back in, as did the word *simulation.* My advice is to relax—as we are doing here—and call them *Political Games,* or even *simulations.* Everyone will know what we mean.

However, we *should* become a bit clearer as to why we sometimes call the POLEX a "model." In fact, a political game is interesting because it is an *operating model of reality.* The reality is that of the political world, international or domestic. The POLEX models the process of decision making in ways that emulate decision making in the real world. But like all models, it is a form of *reductionism,* meaning that it reduces to manageable proportions the infinite complexity of reality.

Thus we can never hope to duplicate in a classroom the real White House, or Kremlin, or United Nations, or Middle East. We cannot reproduce the full complexity of the real world. But we can pick several *crucial variables* from the millions of variable factors found in reality. We can simulate (or model) a *simplified* reality by putting into motion in our "laboratory" those few important aspects that we really need to care about for our purposes. Our purpose in the POLEX is not to *do* the president's job. It is to *learn* more about his job as part of our education. It can also be to contribute to research on foreign policy decision making.

The POLEX is really no different from familiar models which, for teaching or research purposes, reduce other forms of complex reality so they can be experimentally manipulated. Maps, wind tunnels for aerodynamics testing, computer simulations of elections or of the economies of countries, war games and computer-simulated jet fighter duels, buyer-seller competitive markets (as in business school games), or (as in many colleges and high schools), model UNs—all those are models that reduce reality to manageable size for experimental purposes. Indeed, *everything* except reality is a model.

In this spirit, a political game or exercise is a dynamic interaction between two or more groups of human players (or, in theory, computers) acting the roles of decision makers. Unless it is a war game, the POLEX, to be realistic, is not played to "win," for one rarely "wins" definitive victories in real-life international relations. Its aim is to see what can be learned about alternative foreign policies, likely reactions by other actors on the international scene, and policy outcomes that one might never have anticipated simply by reading a book, writing a paper, or listening to a lecture.

Political gaming is thus very different from *war* gaming, where the object *is* to win a decisive victory, at the expense of the other side—the enemy. Diplomacy's chief purpose, as I argued in Chapter 7, is to keep things from ever getting to that fateful point.

Nevertheless, the ancestry of the POLEX turns out to be the *Kriegsspiel* (war game) played in the eighteenth century by Prussian cadets and officers as a training substitute for large-scale, expensive maneuvers. War gaming got a little closer to political gaming when, prior to World War II, German strategists adapted the *Kriegsspiel* to examine the political as well as military consequences of alternative courses of action.

The POLEX has other ancestors as well. One is the business or management simulation. Games are now very common in business schools to train executives in information processing, decision making about market competition, and operating under pressure. Similarly, moot courts are used in law schools to give students experience in mock competition.

Simulation has also been used by psychologists and other students of decision theory as a research tool. Individuals roleplay by reacting to simulated problems under laboratory conditions, so researchers can study the behavior of individuals or small groups in simulated crises. (It is also used for group psychotherapy.)

In the last couple of decades political games of varying types, drawing on these various ancestral forerunners, have been employed in classrooms, from primary school to university postgraduate levels, to teach international relations and foreign policy. Increasingly, gaming has also been employed by governments to train diplomats and senior officers, and by researchers to study policy problems.[1]

---

[1]For a brief review of this recent history, see L.P. Bloomfield and Cornelius J. Gearin, "Games Foreign Policy Experts Play: The Political Exercise Comes of Age," *Orbis*, Winter 1973; 1008–1031; also John R. Raser, *Simulation and Society* (Boston: Allyn and Bacon, 1969).

It can be seen that one vital component of the POLEX is the use of *people* to model reality. Some simulations use only computers, but obviously if computers are the players, the game cannot be used as a classroom device to give students a firsthand experience with the feel of foreign policy!

One hybrid *has* been widely used in classrooms—the Inter-Nation Simulation (INS) first developed by Professor Harold Guetzkow at Northwestern University, and widely elaborated by many of his former students.[2] The INS features hypothetical rather than real countries, leaving the choice of national identity up to the players. It assigns to the teams numerical units of military and economic capabilities and checks their competitive moves against a validation program, embodied in a computer, to determine wins and losses. No experience in world affairs is necessary, since the purpose is to learn about theories of international relations by illustration in laboratory experiments, so to speak.

THE POLEX

The POLEX, on the contrary, depends entirely on the psychological phenomenon of role playing in which players themselves are the models of real world decision makers. Their own knowledge (or instincts), as they put themselves into the shoes of a decision maker, provides the action of the game.

Indeed, in *professional*-level POLEXes it is precisely *because* there exists no good, formal, or written theory or model of the top-level foreign policy decision-making process, that experienced experts are asked to be players. The model of decision making in the professional POLEX is based on what might be called the *implicit* model of the real-world decision making and bargaining system which such professionals have, through their experience, built up inside their heads, as it were.

In the same way, in a classroom game the more homework a student does in advance on the game role he or she is assigned to play, the better model of the real world will be available to all the players and the richer the game *and* the learning experience.

The all-human (as contrasted with computerized) simulation of

---

[2]See Harold Guetzkow and others, *Simulation in International Relations* (Englewood Cliffs, N.J.: Prentice-Hall, Inc., 1963).

national security or foreign policy decision making originated in the U.S. at the Rand Corporation in 1954 and was subsequently developed at M.I.T. by the author and others for teaching and analytic purposes.

The so-called Rand-M.I.T. game uses role-playing techniques which simulate as accurately as feasible the real-world environment of the decision maker. That is, teams of participants consciously "act out" the policy and strategy they believe would be (or in some cases, *should* be) pursued by real-life governments. What makes the game interesting and dynamic is what might be called the *sequential interaction of conflicting strategies, based on the clash of antagonistic wills.* That means that A makes a move; B reacts to A's move; A reacts to B's reaction; C looks at both and introduces a new element; A and B have to react to that, and so forth. An umpire, or *Control Team,* supplies the initial problem to the players and then sees that the rules are followed. A and B may be friends or allies, or they may be suspicious adversary countries. An interesting variation is to make them competing cabinet-level officials in the top decision making level of a single government.

For the simplest kind of game, there will be only two teams representing adversary governments plus a directing Control Group. The teams can consist of as few as one player each—or as many as ten (three to seven seems best). The structure of simple games that focus on U.S.-Soviet relations looks something like this:

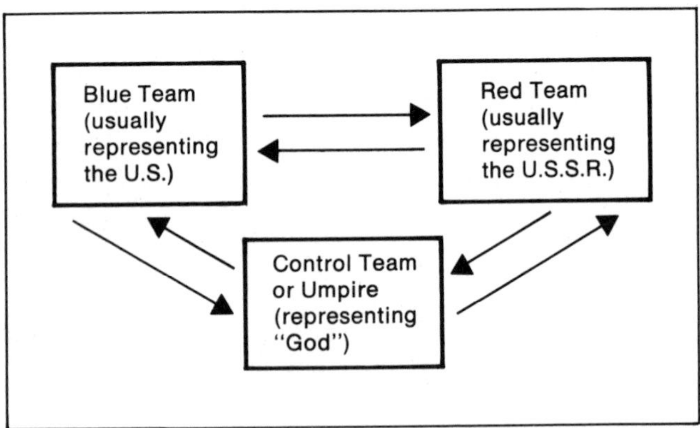

FIGURE A.1

As more teams are added, the games become more complex:

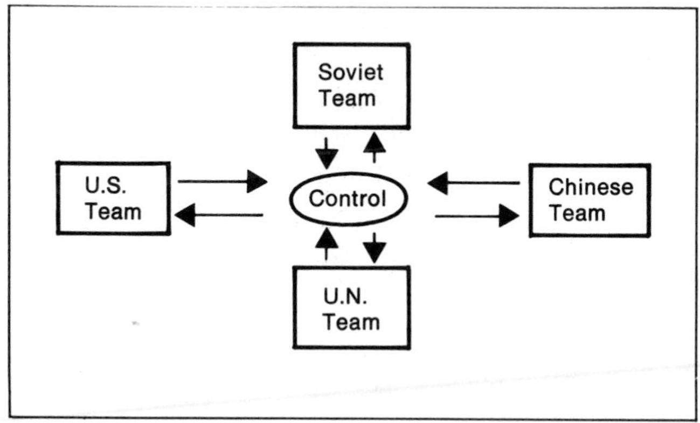

FIGURE A.2

In this particular game all contact between the teams is through the Control Team.

The most dramatic games simulate crisis situations that involve great powers on the verge of conflict. The rules are simple: do what you think "your" country would do when faced with the problem the game designers have given you. The result is a flow of free and largely unstructured interactions. The benefit is usually an increased understanding by the participants of some complex issues, as well as some feel for the pressures and stresses on people in positions of national responsibility.

Although not of immediate interest to us here, it is worth pointing out that some analysts have tried to use games to get at the heart of the always-difficult problem of future planning. (I argued in Chapter 9 that political games have been sadly underutilized for real-world policy planning.) Experience shows that political games can do several useful things: (a) throw light on policy makers' *assumptions,* by examining them in the crucible of a realistic simulation; (b) pre-test proposed policies by trying to anticipate probable reactions from other governments, or groupings; (c) discover contingencies and alternative policies one might not otherwise have taken seriously, by putting people's favorite policies (and premises) under strain, thus loosening up frozen assumptions in their minds about the way events will probably turn out; (d) examine closely one particular line of plausible interaction, and learn as much as possible about its fine bone structure and anatomy.

Early games in the U.S. were political-military, reflecting the Cold War atmosphere. The M.I.T. POLEXes increasingly brought in private citizens who could add a fresh perspective to the sometimes stereotyped—though highly expert—approaches of government officials and experts. The Pentagon (which still runs political-military games for the U.S. executive branch) experimented in the early 1960s with the use of outside personalities as role players, but soon closed their games to all but officials and cleared consultants. (One reason might have been the participation by a famed comic-strip artist, who subsequently shared his experience with the millions of readers of "Steve Canyon.")

How a POLEX actually works

First, a policy problem is chosen. It can be a current world situation, a future crisis, or even a past event. A *scenario* is written for the players to react to. It can be anything from one paragraph up to a dozen or more pages in length. In it a hypothetical—but *plausible*—series of events—say, a revolution, threatened invasion, terrorist act, oil embargo, or food crisis—is depicted to the game players, either in brief or in detail. The scenario-problem will start the game, and be the basis for the interaction between the teams (or between the teams and the Control Group) for however long the game runs. (Additional pieces of scenario or scenario updates can be fed to the teams at different times as the game progresses.)

Second, teams are decided on, and their leaders named. The teams can be "governments," or alliances, or interest groups, or different parts of one government. The teams are selected on the basis of the problem: is it mainly a U.S.-Soviet problem? is NATO a key part? China? Cuba? Mexico? (More than three or four playing teams gets very complicated for Control. Also, the number of people available will help determine how many teams.)

Third, the details of the game—*time, place, duration*—are decided on, depending on availability, convenience, and the purpose of the game. A classroom game can be played in one class hour, or over a weekend, or once a week for a semester, or whatever suits the class best. (But I'll say again, the key is adequate advance homework by the player.)

These basic steps of game design should be carried out by the game designer with his/her objectives clearly in mind. Game designers can be teachers, individual students, or groups of students. The game designer often will become the Control Group once the game gets under way.

Game Designer's Objectives

1. To expose students to the dynamics of international relations and foreign policy through participation in a simulated decision-making process focused on a major problem of foreign policy.

2. To give students an in-depth educational experience by concentrating their energies and attention through the technique of role playing.

3. To engage the students in a sequential interaction process that focuses on a specific policy problem, enabling them to observe how alternative courses of action are chosen and how political outcomes can vary depending on unpredictable factors.

4. To get a vivid glimpse of the process of international relations and foreign policy, the frequent absence of clear-cut wins and losses, and the uses of diplomacy to avoid war.

Problem-Scenario

1. The problem to be gamed out should be one that either draws on the participants' prior knowledge, or is one on which they can readily brief themselves before the game, through readings and discussions.[3] *The success of a game depends largely on the participants' having some accurate knowledge* of the particular area, the past policies of the real-world countries involved, and the realistic limits of geography, travel, communications, and the like. You can see that this means boning up in advance of the game on general background knowledge each team member ought to have mastered.

2. The simplest form of POLEX focuses on a *crisis* situation. The reason is that a crisis, by its nature, creates an atmosphere of urgency, engages the players, and supplies the pace necessary for a dynamic simulation of the action process. However, a crisis game needs to be managed in such a way that it is not ended in the very first move by a

[3]Students have found it profitable to communicate with the Washington embassy or New York UN Mission of the country they are role playing, to request recent foreign policy statements and other appropriate documents. This should be done well in advance.

devastating war (or maybe it never gets beyond move one because everyone becomes cautious and no one will commit themselves to take any action!).

3. Thus the problem-scenario should be presented to the players in a form that requires them to develop their general strategy, that is, their assessment of the situation, basic objectives, and so on, *before* they can make detailed policy moves. There must thus be enough leeway in the problem they are given so they are not forced to make drastic first moves—but at the same time it should carry enough urgency so they cannot just limit themselves to asking for more information (a human tendency particularly among experts!). It is useful to require that the first move by each team be a brief paper answering the following questions:

How do you define the problem you have been given?
What are your major objectives and goals?
What alternative strategies are open to you to achieve your goals?
What strategy will you follow?
What initial moves will you make to carry out that strategy?
What do you think the response of others will be to your strategy?

Schedule

Let us suppose two full days and evenings are available. The illustration on page 205 is what a game schedule might look like.

On the evening before or morning of the game all team members, Control personnel, and administrative staff attend an orientation session in which the game designers remind them of the purposes, scope, sequence of events, and rules of the exercise, concluding with administrative announcements. Team members can be given part or all of the final scenario at that time. But it is a good idea to save distribution of last-minute "crisis details" in the scenario until the game actually begins on Day One. This is so those details will hit the player when they are actually getting into their roles, and they will react far more directly. One item that should not be neglected is a *map* of the region in question. Big ones can be posted in each team room, or xerox copies can be provided each player.

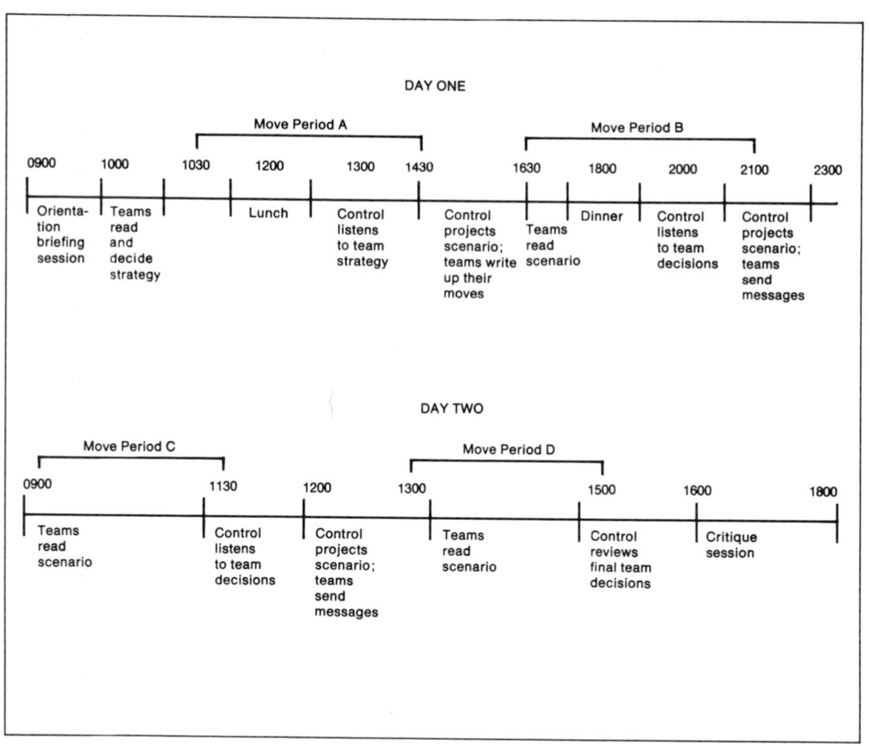

FIGURE A.3 This and other diagrams are adapted from Lincoln P. Bloomfield and Cornelius J. Gearin, "Political Games: Experiments in Foreign Policy Research", *Technology Review*, Oct/Nov, 1974.

When the teams meet in their assigned rooms they discuss the situation until lunch, and wind up with the short paper described earlier containing their general strategy and major implementing policies. To save time, even while one member may be committing to writing the results of the discussion, team chairmen should consecutively appear before Control to give it a short oral summary of team strategy and programs, so Control can get to work without awaiting the written message. The Control Group can then prepare a brief update of the scenario that takes into account the stated plans and opening moves of the teams. The update is handed to the teams at the beginning of the next move period, and they react once more. This process is repeated for each of several move periods.

All team moves should be in writing, however simple the message, and should flow through Control, which acts both as arbiter and message center, distributing messages to other teams, updating the scenario-problem, ruling on implausible or frivolous moves (but exercising its power sparingly), and acting as a source of news it invents to enrich (or complicate) the background against which the teams make their moves. A duplicating machine is absolutely indispensable for Control.

Another function of the Control Group is to provide the game inputs on behalf of relevant *secondary* actors (other governments, Islamic Conference, etc.), for which there is no playing team (you don't want too many teams, or the communication system will become hopelessly overloaded.) One M.I.T. game used "sub-teams" of one or two people each under the supervision of the Control Group. They wrote up plausible messages from their "country" or "faction" when asked to do so by Control, that is, they "half role played," as confederates of Control:

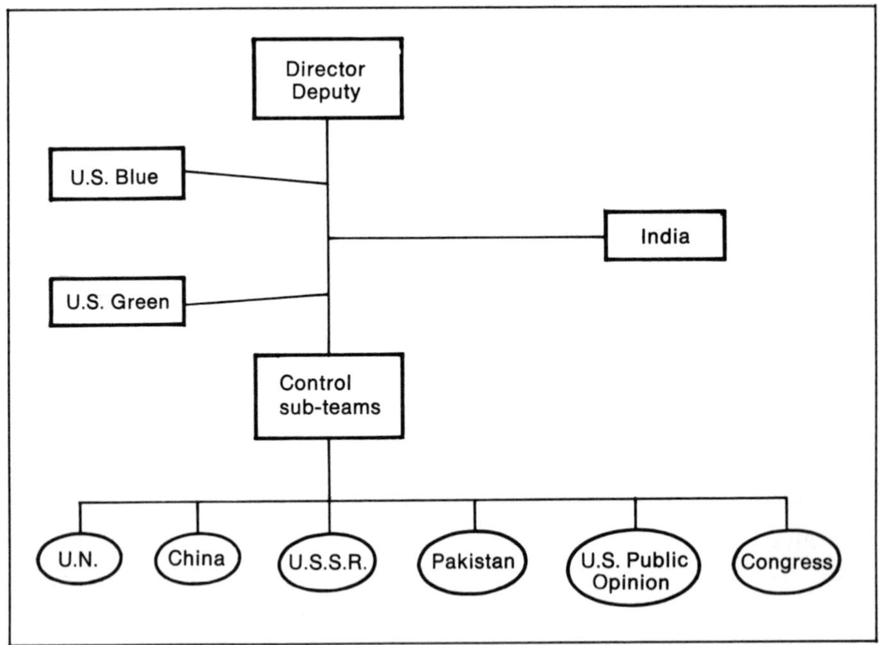

FIGURE A.4

The exercise is concluded with a *critique*. This is an important part of any game. It consists of brief explanations by each team chairman of the major elements of their respective strategies, general criticism of the exercise format and process, and discussion of relevant policy issues and what was learned about them—and about games.

Layout

What about the physical setup? It can be as simple as putting two teams in two corners of a large classroom, where they cannot listen in on each other. At the other end of the scale, you can have a complex (and expensive) layout of the kind sometimes used for senior-level policy games, such as this one, complete with closed-circuit television:

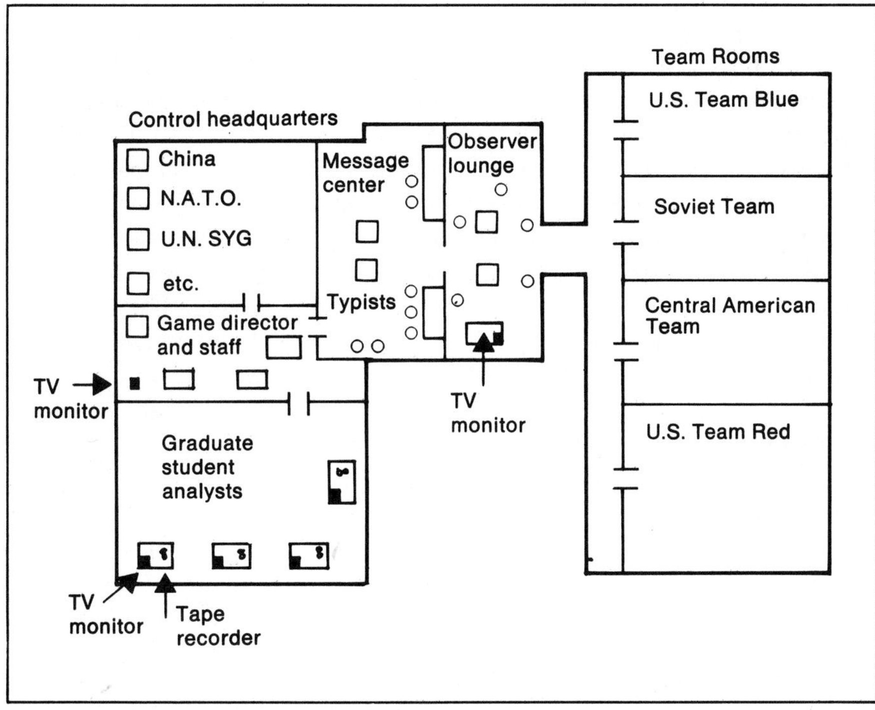

FIGURE A.5

Not everyone can afford luxuries like closed-circuit TV, but televising team sessions to Control is a great help. It minimizes distractions to team members from having Control people popping in and out of team rooms, and allows Control to anticipate questions and team moves. (By the way, there is no evidence that the small camera and microphones, positioned unobtrusively in the team rooms, have any really inhibiting effect on deliberations.)

If one really wants to get fancy—as we did in the M.I.T. professional-level game—computers can be used for high-speed, controlled communications between Control and teams, and between teams. In a game called CONEX IV, we experimented with such a system. Our other games had relied on a manual system which required all game messages to be typed on a color-coded form, reproduced in many copies, and distributed by messenger. Handling a hundred or more messages reproduced in fifty copies in an eighteen-hour exercise was a terrific burden, and also unhelpfully delayed delivery times.) Since game time is sharply compressed from reality (hours of the former often representing days or weeks of the latter), we became concerned that this physical limitation might artificially limit team interaction.

A bright M.I.T. student designed a computer program whereby secretaries assigned to each team (and Control) could type a high-priority message on a small console connected to the M.I.T. Compatible Time Sharing System. The message was instantaneously transmitted over a telephone data-link to any desired combination of recipients. The program was designed to block unwanted transmission of messages, providing for storing (buffering) any given message until the addressee's console was free, and then transmitting. The system functioned well and has excellent potential for expediting game communications.[4]

In that particular game we had not one, but *two* U.S. teams, which proved fascinating. We set up two similarly constituted, parallel U.S. teams, each unaware of the other's actions (or even existence) until the game ended. Our purpose was to see whether they would react differently to the same scenario-problem if *one variable* (say, access to special information) were changed for only one of the two. (As it turned out, they so faithfully reproduced typical U.S. government responses that their chosen strategies were virtually identical!) The game looked like Figure A.6 on page 209.

Even in the simplest classroom games, it can deepen the participants' understanding to do one other thing that costs nothing but an investment of imagination. The game director can assign one or more people to act as analysts, making a *decision tree.* Such a diagrammatic analysis shows the general profile of the game, that is, the major alternative policy options considered and chosen, but also those *not*

---

[4]For details of more sophisticated techniques and procedures along these lines, the serious gamer is referred to L.P. Bloomfield and C.J. Gearin, with J.L. Foster, *Anticipating Conflict-Control Policies: The CONEX Games as a Planning Tool* (M.I.T., Center for International Studies, C/70-10, February 1970).

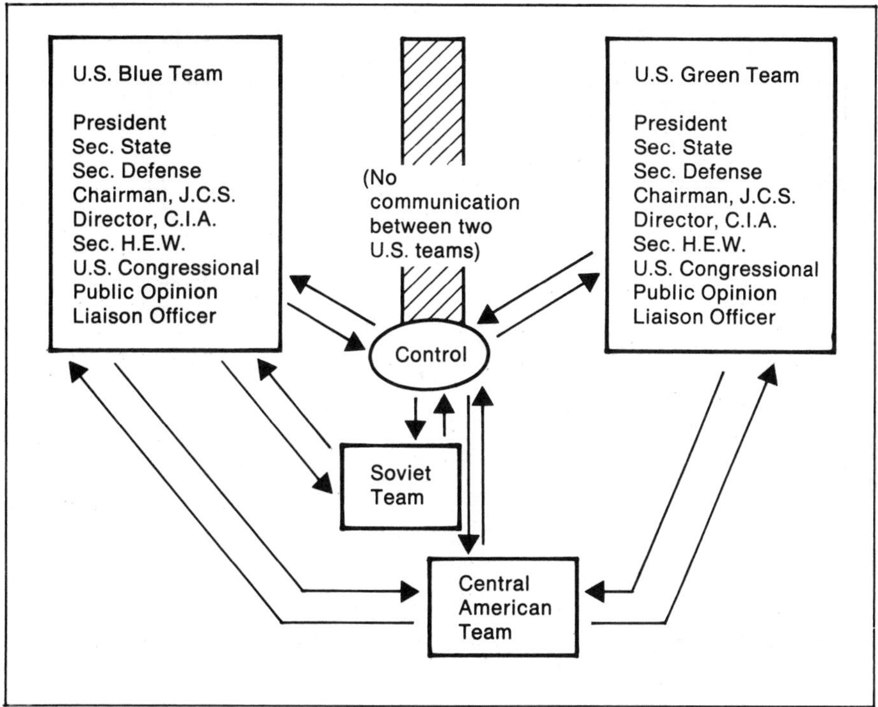

FIGURE A.6

chosen. Such a diagram can vividly demonstrate the effect of sequential interactions over time. It is interesting for the game designers to make up their own private version *before* the game, so they can compare it with what actually happens. A sample branch-point decision tree might look like this:

To sum up

A good POLEX is the product of (a) a good *game design;* (b) interested players who have done sufficient *homework,* and are intellectually committed to the game experience; *and* (c) clear, simple, effective *administration procedures and direction.*

EXAMPLES

There follows a sample organization plan for a classroom (or other) POLEX that gives the players a sense of the basic elements of the game. Next is a sample operations plan that provides specific instruc-

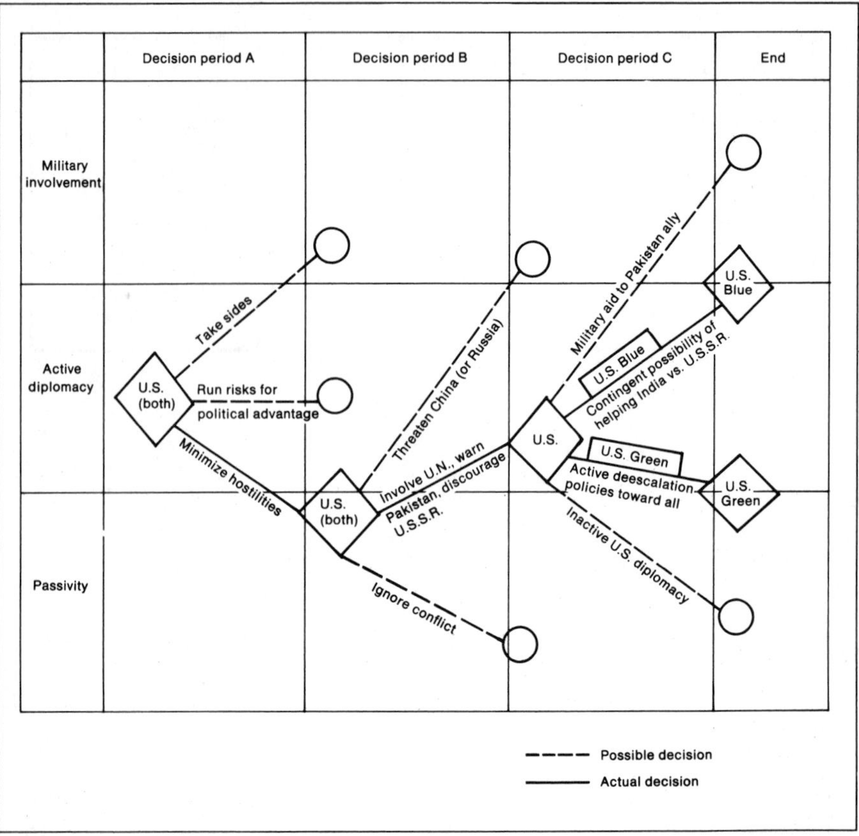

FIGURE A.7

tions and procedures for a game of virtually any size and duration, plus a game manager's administrative checklist.

Finally, you will find two sample scenario-problems. They can be varied in any way that suits the purposes of the particular game, and made as complicated and detailed as the game designers wish.

Sample Game Organization Plan

1. The POLEX simulates the *interaction of governments in a major crisis situation.* Participants are organized into teams, each of which represents a designated government that is deeply involved in the

crisis. The game consists of move periods during which teams decide their policies and actions, through discussion, argument, and agreement. A minimum of three move periods is normally needed to get the desirable sequential interaction between teams.

2. The game is directed by a Control Group. This group will give the teams an initial briefing about the game. Control will provide the players with a scenario-problem containing the hypothetical world situation which confronts the teams when the game starts. Control will also give teams the necessary background information before the game about the game "world," the "countries" involved, and the specific crisis situation being gamed out. Control will also give the teams information about game procedures, and will be the source of all decisions that need to be made about rules, and other questions. During the game Control may announce the outcome of game events, specify changes in game time, and so on. *Its word will be final. All team messages will go through Control.* Control will supply any additional information that may be needed, and may hand out scenario updates at the beginning of later move periods.

3. Each playing team will simulate the *decision-making process at the highest level of government in their country.* All decisions taken and messages to other governments must be in writing. The form for such messages will be provided by Control. Control will designate a member of each team as chairman; he or she will act as president or prime minister of that country. Other team members will act as a collective cabinet, National Security Council, Politburo, or whatever is appropriate for the body that makes the top-level decisions for team governments. Individual roles (for example, foreign minister, defense minister, press officer, congressional liaison, opposition party leader, and so forth) will be assigned to members of each team by mutual agreement within each team.

4. The policies of all other countries not represented by teams will be decided by the Control Group, to the extent that they are necessary for the exercise.

5. The game will involve the following teams _______________ _________________________. Control will issue a list of team assignments well in advance of the game so team members can study the policies pursued by their real-life counterpart governments, familiarize themselves with the geographic area, and get into their roles.

Sample Game Operations Plan

1. *Briefing.* The game starts with a briefing of all team members by the Control Group. Game rules will be explained and the scenario-problem will be handed out. The briefing will take place from ______ to ______ the day before the game. It will be in Room ______.

2. *Move Period A.* The game will start at ______ on ______. Teams will go directly to their assigned rooms, listed below. There they will find paper, pencils, and maps of the area of interest. There will also be a Game Calendar showing the move period (the first one is *A*) and "game time." (The game starts at "*S*," standing for scenario.)

3. The games will be divided into ______ move periods, each lasting approximately ______ hours. Between move periods, the Control Group will review the team moves, mesh them as necessary, distribute messages directed to the teams, and prepare new instructions to the teams for the beginning of the next move period.

4. In Move Period *A*, from ______ to ______, team members will carefully review the scenario-problem—including any last-minute additions handed out when the game starts—and discuss their country's reaction. To organize their thinking and provide a basis for their subsequent moves, they will develop a short Basic Strategy Paper (BSP) by the end of Move Period A.

5. *First Team Move (the BSP).* The BSP need not be long, but it should contain the team's preliminary agreed reactions and general thinking under the following headings:

a) *Problem:* Briefly, how does the team define the problem it faces?
b) *Basic Objective(s):* What are the main goals the team thinks it should try to achieve in dealing with the problem?
c) *Alternative Strategies:* What different general approaches are plausibly available to the team in coping with the problem?
d) *Chosen Strategy:* What is the main line of action among those alternatives which the team decides it will take?
e) *Initial Policy Moves:* What "tactical" actions does the team plan to make to carry out its chosen strategy? (These action moves should be briefly listed under headings as follows: diplomatic, economic, military, intelligence, domestic-political, and any others that are relevant.
f) (Optional) How are other governments likely to react to your moves?

6. At ______ the BSP should be ready in rough form. One team member should be assigned to write it up (preferably on a typewriter). The paper can be no longer than one page. It should be written up on a Standard Message Format (SMF), see Item 14. The team chairman should go to Control Headquarters at ______ when the move period is over to report to Control on the initial team strategy, so Control can begin its work without waiting for the paper to be typed and reproduced.

7. The first team message (the BSP), and all subsequent team messages, should follow the *standard message format* (see Item 14) and copied in ______ copies, all but one of which should be delivered to Control as soon as reproduced. Control will deliver messages to other teams as appropriate and keep a master file of all messages. (The teams should also keep a file.)

8. *Control Move.* Control will meet from ______ to ______. At ______ Move Period B will begin. The Game Calendar in each team room will be changed by Control to show the new move period (*B*), and the game time at which Control decides Move Period B starts. (See Item 15 for definition of game time.)

9. *Move Period B.* When Move Period B starts, each team will be given new documents by Control, including changes in the situation, messages sent to them by other teams, any necessary other information about the world, and any other information they may need.

10. Team messages (diplomatic notes, démarches, communiqués, and so on) can be addressed to other governments and should be delivered to Control as soon as drafted. Control will normally deliver messages immediately, but Control can also hold up a message for a realistic length of time or even leak information, if that is realistic in real-world terms. Move Period B ends at ______, at which time team chairmen go, one at a time, to brief Control on their moves decided upon.

11. *Control Move.* This period is shorter, ending at ______.

12. *Team Move Period C* begins at ______ with a new message from Control and a new game time. It runs to ______ at which time the team chairmen again brief Control. The game ends (even though teams—as in real life—will not have finished their work and will undoubtedly feel they ought to have more time!).

(A POLEX can be continued into the same evening, or into the next day, or resumed a week later, and so on, depending on the game purposes, time available, and so on.)

13. *Critique Session.* All participants will assemble at ______ to discuss and critique the game. They are no longer playing their game roles (although some feelings may well carry over into the session!).

14. *Standard Message Format.* All team (and Control) messages must be in writing. They should be brief but should follow a standard format for convenience of players (the form can be made up in advance or simply followed when messages are drafted):

TEAM ____________________	Consecutive Team Message Number ____________
MOVE PERIOD ____________	Urgent ( ) Unclassified ( ) Routine ( ) Secret ( )
TO ____________________	

MESSAGE ____

____

15. *Game Time.* The scenario will indicate the date and time (past, present, or future) of game events. Game time can be real time, or stretched, or shortened for game purposes. The Game Calendar in each team room will be kept up by Control. It will start with *S*. It will be changed with each move period (*S* Plus 2 hours or *S* Plus 2 days, *S* Plus 4 months, and so on).

16. *Direct Contacts.* The teams are assumed to be operating in their respective capital cities and thus are unable to have face-to-face summit meetings without special preparation. Urgent messages will be delivered by Control a short time after receiving them from the initiating team.

If it is necessary for a team to put a question directly to another team, or to otherwise have a face-to-face, *bilateral* (that is, two parties) meeting, Control should be notified. It will authorize and schedule such a meeting, with a representative of Control present, who will make a note of what happens for the use of Control. If the game requires a *multilateral* meeting (UN Security Council, NATO, Arab League, Warsaw Pact, OPEC, OECD, and so on), Control will arrange the time and place, and notify all teams.

17. *Information.* Game information is necessarily limited to that absolutely necessary for game decision making. If a team feels it needs "intelligence" information from its own sources, or reports from its diplomats abroad, or any other information, that should be requested

of Control. Teams may *not* themselves generate information as to what happens *elsewhere,* even in their own embassies abroad. Control may also issue news releases about happenings and events anywhere in the world. In some cases Control might release information that—as in the real world—is unverified, based on fragmentary news reports, or even deliberately inaccurate—"disinformation." Control may issue a periodic brief *World Newspaper* with key news items of relevance to the game. (This is good practice for would-be journalists.)

18. *Military.* If the game develops a military phase, Control will rule on the outcomes of military moves made by individual teams. It is not expected that teams will be expert in military matters, but they *can* make the kinds of decisions political leaders normally make about the production, development, and use of military forces under their command. (It should be remembered, however, that the chief purpose of diplomacy is to prevent wars from happening!)

19. *Room Assignments.*

Briefing Session ______________________
Control Group ______________________
Team ______________________
Team ______________________
Team ______________________
Team ______________________
Critique Session ______________________

20. *Recapitulation of Schedule (sample).*

Prior Day 1615–1800 Briefing Session.
0900–1100 Move Period A.
1100–1300 Control Move Period. Teams to lunch.
1300–1500 Move Period B.
1500–1600 Control Move Period. Teams break.
1600–1730 Move Period C. Game ends.
Following day 1000 Critique Session.

GAME MANAGER'S CHECKLIST

Game Design (designer's objectives, limits, framework)

Game Organization (available participants, kind of problem to be gamed, appropriate teams, governments to be covered by Control)

Operations Plan
Schedule (time available, length of move periods)
Rooms (one for each team, for Control, for meetings)
Meals
Refreshments
Washrooms
Supplies (paper, pencils, photocopying machine, maps)
Scenario-Problem
Team assignments: selection of chairmen
Game Calendars for Control and Team rooms
Briefing Session arrangements
Critique Session arrangements
Postgame Report(s) to be assigned

SAMPLE SCENARIO-PROBLEM 1 (PERSIAN/ARABIAN GULF)

Part one: general situation (given out one week ahead)

TIME: NOVEMBER 1, 198_

While there have been few specific drastic changes in the world situation, there has been a pronounced deterioration in the energy area, particularly with further shutbacks in oil production due to fighting and instability in the Middle Eastern oil fields. Oil prices have, as a consequence, shot up, with OPEC asking $60 a barrel and spot prices in Rotterdam hitting $70 a barrel.

The situation in ______ remains confused, with open warfare between the government, revolutionary forces, and local insurgent forces, along with growing armed bands styling themselves "Marxist-Leninist" and a disillusioned and frightened middle class. Clashes in the ______ area have spread to oil-producing areas, and ______ production is down to less than 1 mbd (million barrels per day). There are hourly broadcasts from the Soviet Union to ______ urging "liberation from the greedy imperialists," while reports increase of Soviet military buildups in the ______ area.

Meanwhile radical movements in the general Gulf area have strengthened, with open fighting between the armed forces of the two Yemens. The South Yemeni are armed by Moscow with Cuban advisers in the high hundreds, while U.S. aid to Sa'ana increases. The Dhofar rebellion has flared up again with major fighting, and Egyptian commando forces have stepped up their presence. Saudi Arabia has privately told the U.S. ambassador that the Saudi regime cannot ensure its own continued internal stability unless the U.S. moves decisively to defeat Soviet-backed insurgencies in the region, finds ways to get the Russians and Cubans out of Southern Yemen and the Eritrean shore of the Red Sea, and forces Israel to withdraw from the West Bank, Golan Heights, and East Jerusalem.

Soviet oil production is now acknowledged to be insufficient for domestic needs. Planned increases in production require large-scale credits and technology from the West, particularly the United States, which, however, remains disillusioned with Soviet adventurism. Moscow is counting on the Federal Republic of Germany to make possible a huge new gas pipeline to West Germany. Eastern European Communist states are turning to Middle East oil producers—as is Moscow. Rumors coming out of Moscow suggest a power struggle between hard-liners who favor new Soviet moves toward the Gulf to secure oil and deny Western influence, and moderates who argue for priority to getting SALT III discussions going to achieve a renewed détente with the West, including expanded trade and technology.

Some Americans are calling for a tougher policy including, if necessary, U.S. military intervention in the Gulf to secure unhampered access to Gulf crude at reasonable prices. An unusually cold winter is forecast in North America and Western Europe, while heating oil stocks are low again.

The Egyptian-Israeli Treaty is holding, and there are some signs that Egypt will benefit from increased U.S. aid and Israeli technology and trained advisers. However, the agreement is under serious strain as new settlements are demanded by Jewish settlers who claim a historical religious right to the areas they call "Judea" and "Samaria." The Arab "Steadfastness and Confrontation Front" is fracturing as Libya, Syria, Southern Yemen, and the Palestine Liberation Organization (PLO) demand a total embargo on U.S. activity in the region, against the wishes of Saudi Arabia, Jordan, Yemen, Algeria and Iraq (where the fighting goes on), Tunisia, and Kuwait, along with the

Gulf States. However, no Arab League member state other than Sudan and Oman has yet approved the treaty.

Part two:
(Given to teams as they begin game)

FLASH: NOVEMBER 2, 198_

According to wire service reports, power has been seized in ______ by a group calling itself the "People's Democratic Liberation Front—Marxist-Leninist." The present leadership is said to have fled by an Air France chartered jet to an undisclosed location. Broadcasts from Radio ______ are calling for massive aid from "our fraternal socialist brothers to the North." The radio also calls for a "total embargo of OPEC oil" to "any state that does not support the PLO and denounce the Zionists."

MOSCOW, NOVEMBER 3, 198_

Soviet regional broadcasts to the Middle East in local dialects are repeating hourly calls for "volunteers" to report to local party headquarters for immediate dispatch to "aid the brotherly socialist cause" in ______.

ISTANBUL, NOVEMBER 3, 198_

Observers note a sudden dramatic increase in the number and tonnage of Soviet warships pouring out of the Black Sea through the Bosporus toward the Mediterranean. Many overflights of large transport aircraft are also reported, though the latter cannot be confirmed.

WASHINGTON, NOVEMBER 3, 198_

A midnight emergency meeting of the National Security Council in the White House situation room resulted in a 3 A.M. order placing the 6th Fleet (Mediterranean) and the 7th Fleet (Asia and Indian Ocean) on "full alert." It is understood that in the course of the meeting a message was received from Crown Prince ______ asking for the immediate dispatch of a U.S. ground-sea-air combined force to his country. In a curious development, a subsequent message signed King ______ said the previous message should be ignored.

LONDON, NOVEMBER 3, 198_

The European Community has invited Japan to join them in an immediate emergency session to discuss possible reactions to the grave crisis unfolding in the Middle East. Ms. Thatcher was quoted as saying that "Europe must stand firm," but President Mitterand of France told a visitor from Algeria that "France will always sit down and reason with our African and Arab partners."

SAMPLE SCENARIO-PROBLEM 2 (CENTRAL AMERICA)

Part one: general situation (Given out one week ahead)

TIME: JANUARY 198_

As the situation in Cuba has deteriorated, Fidel Castro has stepped up his drive to spread his ideas and influence to the rest of the hemisphere. Dialect-speaking Cuban arms and guerilla trainers have reportedly landed in many parts of ______ and have worked to arouse the long-dormant majority Indian population to unprecedented levels of discontent.

The ______ government has ruthlessly repressed the growing dissident movement, slaughtering peasants and students in a series of violent incidents which the leftists claim were provoked by army units, and the government says were designed by the communists to create popular martyrs.

Washington has debated sending additional military equipment and personnel to help the ______ army, but Congress seems resistant after the El Salvador experience. Castro recently went to Moscow and made a fiery speech denouncing the U.S. as a "fatally wounded imperialist beast" which has already lost the struggle in Latin America. He said it is now time for the "Peoples' Revolutionary Forces" to make a decisive move.

Reports have come from various national intelligence sources of new facilities being constructed in Cuba for large-scale equipment of a completely new type, possibly cruise-missile launchers. Soviet submarines are calling in Cuban ports in unprecedented numbers, and three high-ranking Soviet generals have been reported seen at the Havana airport.

Beijing radio announces that it will henceforth support with massive military help plus badly needed grain any legitimate efforts by Vietnam to "cast off the yoke of hegemonic social imperialism"—meaning the Soviet Union. Hanoi is believed to be open to a renewed China connection in order to disengage from the intrusive Soviet presence, which it believes has frustrated its efforts to normalize relations with the U.S. and acquire economic assistance. Meanwhile, Chinese soldiers have fired at Soviet troops along the Ussuri River (where fighting took place in 1969). A TASS dispatch says that Moscow "will know how to administer a decisive rebuff to America's secret running dogs however large their population."

Part two:
(Given to teams as they begin game)

FLASH: JANUARY 2, 198_

The American embassy was stormed by a mob in the streets of ______. Simultaneously the radio station and airports were taken over by unidentified guerilla units, while fighter-bombers with no markings bombed and strafed the barracks where units of the regular army were garrisoned, producing many casualties. Washington is trying through every channel to find out what has actually happened, but cannot reach any responsible officials either at the Foreign Ministry or the U.S. embassy. There is unanimous agreement that some of the militants were Cubans in civilian clothes, and suspicion exists that Castro has in fact launched a major, if unacknowledged, offensive in

WASHINGTON, JANUARY 3, 198_

A midnight meeting at the White House brought a decision to issue a 24-hour ultimatum to the embassy occupants to release their captives, plus a 48-hour ultimatum to Cuba to withdraw all its military elements from ______ or face unspecified retribution from the United States. Elements of both U.S. airborne divisions were put on high alert, as was the Atlantic Fleet and U.S. Southern Command. There still does not seem to be any governmental authority in ______ with whom to deal on the embassy capture.

BRUSSELS, JANUARY 3

An emergency meeting of the European Community's Council of Ministers produced an appeal to all parties to keep cool while negotiations were attempted, and called for an immediate emergency meeting of the UN Security Council.

HAVANA, JANUARY 3

U.S. satellite imagery shows that cruise missile launching sites in seven different areas have now been completed. Large covered loads have been spotted at the ports and on the roads heading for these sites. Eight large Soviet cargo vessels have been counted in the harbor.

BEIJING, JANUARY 3

China launched what appears to be a series of limited military probes along the Sino-Soviet border. A transport plane arrived from Hanoi carrying what Western reports say is a high-level delegation representing the Vietnamese Politburo. Hanoi denies the story.

UNITED NATIONS, NEW YORK, JANUARY 3

This month's Security Council President (India) called a meeting of the council for tomorrow at 10 A.M. to discuss the question of restoring international peace and securitv in ______.

SUGGESTED READINGS

INTERDEPENDENCE

Bergsten, C. Fred, ed., *The Future of the International Economic Order.* Lexington, Mass.: Heath, 1973.

Bloomfield, L. P., and I. C. Bloomfield, "The U.S. Interdependence and World Order," *Headline Series,* no. 228 (December 1975). New York: Foreign Policy Assoc.

Camps, Miriam, *The Management of Interdependence.* New York: Council on Foreign Relations, 1974.

Cleveland, Harlan, *The Third Try at World Order.* Aspen, Colo.: Aspen Institute, 1976.

Manning, Bayless, *Conduct of U.S. Foreign Policy in the Third Century.* Claremont, Calif.: Claremont University, 1975.

Wesson, Robert G., *Foreign Policy for a New Age.* Boston: Houghton-Mifflin, 1977.

POLITICAL–SECURITY DECISION MAKING

Acheson, Dean, *Present at the Creation: My Years at the State Department.* New York: W. W. Norton, & Co., Inc., 1969.

Allison, Graham, and Peter Szanton, *Remaking Foreign Policy: The Organizational Connection.* New York: Basic Books, 1976.

Campbell, John F., *The Foreign Affairs Fudge Factory.* New York: Basic Books, 1971.

Cohen, Stephen D., *The Making of United States International Economic Policy.* New York: Praeger, 1977.

Cohen, Warren I., *Dean Rusk,* Totowa, N.J.: Cooper Square, 1980.

Commission of the Organization of the Government for the Conduct of Foreign Policy, *Report* (June 1975). Washington, D.C.: Government Printing Office, 1975.

Destler, I. M., *Making Foreign Economic Policy.* Washington, D.C.: Brookings Institution, 1980.

Estes, Thomas S., and E. Allan Lightner, Jr., *The Department of State.* New York: Praeger, 1976.

Gelb, Leslie H., and Richard K. Betts, *The Irony of Vietnam: The System Worked.* Washington, D.C.: Brookings Institution, 1979.

Halberstam, David, *The Best and the Brightest.* New York: Random House, 1972.

Hoopes, Townsend, *The Devil and John Foster Dulles.* Boston: Little, Brown, 1973.

Jackson, Henry M., ed., *The National Security Council.* New York: Praeger, 1965.

Kalb, Marvin and Bernard Kalb, *Kissinger.* Boston: Little, Brown, 1974.

Kissinger, Henry A., *White House Years.* Boston: Little, Brown, 1979.

Morris, Roger, *Uncertain Greatness: Kissinger and American Foreign Policy.* New York: Harper and Row, 1977.

THE PRESIDENCY

Barber, James D., *The Presidential Character* (2nd ed.), Englewood Cliffs, N.J.: Prentice-Hall, 1977.

Dallek, Robert, *Franklin D. Roosevelt and American Foreign Policy 1936-1945.* New York: Oxford University, 1979.

Divine, Robert A., *Eisenhower and the Cold War.* Oxford: Oxford University, 1981.

Donovan, Robert J., *Conflict and Crisis: The Presidency of Harry S. Truman 1945–1948.* New York: W. W. Norton & Co., Inc., 1977.

Eisenhower, Dwight D., *The White House Years: Mandate for Change 1953–1956.* Garden City, N.Y.: Doubleday, 1963.

George, Alexander L., *Presidential Decision-Making in Foreign Policy: The Effective Use of Information and Advice.* Boulder, Colo.: Westview, 1980.

Hess, Stephen, *Organizing the Presidency.* Washington, D.C.: Brookings Institution, 1976.

Johnson, Richard T., *Managing the White House.* New York: Harper and Row, 1979.

Kissinger, Henry A., *White House Years.* Boston: Little, Brown, 1979.

Neustadt, Richard E., *Presidential Power: The Politics of Leadership, with Reflections from F.D.R. to Carter.* New York: John Wiley, 1980.

Reedy, George E., *Twilight of the Presidency.* New York: The New American Library, 1971.

Rostow, Walt W., *The United States in the World Arena.* New York: Harper and Row, 1960.

Safire, William, *Before the Fall: An Insider's View of the Pre-Watergate White House.* Garden City, N.Y.: Doubleday, 1975.

Schlesinger, Arthur M., Jr., *A Thousand Days: John F. Kennedy in the White House.* Boston: Houghton-Mifflin, 1975.

Sherwood, Robert E., *Roosevelt and Hopkins: An Intimate History.* New York: Simon & Schuster, 1948.

Sorensen, Theodore C., *Kennedy.* New York: Harper and Row, 1965.

Spanier, John, and Eric Uslander, *How American Foreign Policy Is Made.* (2nd ed.), New York: Praeger, 1978.

Szulc, Tad, *The Illusion of Peace: Foreign Policy in the Nixon Years.* New York: Viking, 1978.

Truman, Harry S., *Memoirs, Two Vol.* Garden City, N.Y.: Doubleday, 1955.

Woodward, Bob, and Carl Bernstein, *The Final Days.* New York: Simon and Schuster, 1976.

CONGRESS AND FOREIGN POLICY

Cheever, Daniel S., and H. Field Haviland, Jr., *American Foreign Policy and The Separation of Powers.* Cambridge: Harvard University, 1952.

Franck, Thomas M., and Edward Weisband, *Foreign Policy By Congress.* New York: Oxford University, 1979.

Frye, Alton, *A Responsible Congress: The Politics of National Security.* New York: McGraw-Hill, 1975.

Pastor, Robert A., *Congress and the Politics of U.S. Foreign Economic Policy, 1929–1976.* Berkeley: University of California, 1980.

Ripley, Randall B., and Grace A. Franklin, *Congress, the Bureaucracy, and Public Policy.* Homewood, Ill.: Dorsey, 1976.

Spanier, John, and Joseph L. Nogee, *Congress, The Presidency and American Foreign Policy.* Elmsford, N.Y.: Pergamon, 1981.

Wilcox, Francis O., *Congress, the Executive and Foreign Policy.* New York: Harper and Row, 1971.

Wilcox, Francis O., and Richard A. Frank, eds., *The Constitution and the Conduct of Foreign Policy.* New York: Praeger, 1976.

PUBLIC OPINION AND FOREIGN POLICY

Almond, Gabriel A., *The American People and Foreign Policy.* New York: Praeger, 1950.

Bloomfield, Lincoln P., *In Search of American Foreign Policy: The Humane Use of Power,* New York: Oxford University, 1974.

Cohen, Bernard C., *The Public's Impact on Foreign Policy.* Boston: Little, Brown, 1973.

Hughes, Barry B., *The Domestic Context of American Foreign Policy.* San Francisco: W. H. Freeman, 1978.

Rosenau, James N., ed., *Domestic Sources of Foreign Policy.* New York: Free Press, 1967.

Verba, Sidney, and Norman H. Nie, *Participation in America: Political Democracy and Social Equality.* New York: Harper and Row, 1972.

DIPLOMACY

Bohlen, Charles E., *Witness to History, 1929–1969.* New York: W. W. Norton & Co., Inc., 1973.

Macomber, William, *The Angels' Game: A Handbook of Modern Diplomacy.* New York: Stein and Day, 1975.

Nicolson, Harold, *Diplomacy,* (2nd ed.), London: Oxford University, 1963.

Nicolson, Harold, *The Congress of Vienna.* New York: Harcourt, Brace, 1946.

Weil, Martin, *A Pretty Good Club.* New York: W. W. Norton and Co., Inc., 1978.

MODELS AND THEORIES

Allison, Graham T., *Essence of Decision.* Boston: Little, Brown, 1971.

Bacchus, William, *Foreign Policy and the Bureaucratic Process.* Princeton: Princeton University, 1974.

Destler, I. M., *Presidents, Bureaucrats, and Foreign Policy.* Princeton: Princeton University, 1972.

Downs, Anthony, *Inside Bureaucracy.* Boston: Little, Brown, 1967.

Halperin, Morton H., P. Clapp and A. Kanter, *Bureaucratic Politics and Foreign Policy.* Washington, D.C.: Brookings Institution, 1974.

Halperin, Morton, and Arnold Kanter, *Readings in American Foreign Policy: A Bureaucratic Perspective.* Boston: Little, Brown, 1973.

Modelski, George, *A Theory of Foreign Policy.* New York: Praeger, 1962.

Rosenau, James N., *The Scientific Study of Foreign Policy.* New York: Free Press, 1977.

Steinbruner, John D., *The Cybernetic Theory of Decision.* Princeton: Princeton University, 1974.

Warwick, Donald P., *A Theory of Public Bureaucracy: Politics, Personality, and Organization in the State Department.* Cambridge: Harvard University, 1975.

PLANNING

Bowie, Robert R., *Shaping the Future.* New York: Columbia University, 1964.

Destler, I. M., *Presidents, Bureaucrats and Foreign Policy: The Politics of Organizational Reform.* Princeton: Princeton University, 1972.

Kennan, George F., *Memoirs 1925–1950.* Boston: Little, Brown, 1967.

Rothstein, Robert L., *Planning, Prediction and Policymaking in Foreign Affairs.* Boston: Little, Brown, 1972.

POLITICAL GAMING

Bloomfield, Lincoln P., C. J. Gearin, and J. L. Foster, *Anticipating Conflict-Control Policies: The CONEX Games as a Planning Tool.* Cambridge: M.I.T. Center for International Studies, 1970.

Guetzkow, Harold, et al., *Simulation in International Relations.* Englewood Cliffs: Prentice-Hall, 1963.

Raser, John R., *Simulation and Society.* Boston: Allyn and Bacon, 1969.

INDEX

H

I

J

K

L

M

W

Y

Z

The author gratefully acknowledges permission to adapt some material originally presented in *The Foreign Policy Process: Making Theory Relevant,* SAGE PROFESSIONAL PAPERS IN INTERNATIONAL STUDIES Vol. 3, Series 02-028, copyright, 1974, courtesy of the Publisher, Sage Publications, Inc. (Beverly Hills/London). Also permission to use in Chapter II some material adapted from *The U.S., Interdependence and World Order,* HEADLINE SERIES, Foreign Policy Association, Inc., New York, 1975, co-authored with Irirangi C. Bloomfield, and in the Appendix material adapted from "Political Games: Experiments in Foreign Policy Research," which appeared in *Technology Review,* October/November 1974, pp. 50-59, co-authored with Cornelius J. Gearin, copyright Alumni Association of Massachusetts Institute of Technology. Finally, to reprint almost in its entirety in Chapter IX "Planning Foreign Policy: Can It Be Done?" which originally appeared in the *Political Science Quarterly* 93 (Fall 1978): 369–91. All the above are by the present author.